Word Warrior

THE NEW BLACK STUDIES SERIES

Edited by Darlene Clark Hine
and Dwight A. McBride

*A list of books in the series appears
at the end of this book.*

Word Warrior

Richard Durham, Radio, and Freedom

SONJA D. WILLIAMS

UNIVERSITY OF ILLINOIS PRESS

Urbana, Chicago, and Springfield

1 2 3 4 5 C P 5 4 3 2 1
♾ This book is printed on acid-free paper.

Library of Congress Cataloging-in-Publication Data
Williams, Sonja D., 1952–
Word warrior : Richard Durham, radio, and freedom /
Sonja D. Williams.
pages cm. — (The new black studies series)
Includes bibliographical references and index.
ISBN 978-0-252-03987-4 (cloth : alk paper)
ISBN 978-0-252-08139-2 (pkb : alk paper)
ISBN 978-0-252-09798-0 (e-book)
1. Durham, Richard, 1917–1984.
2. African American authors—20th century—Biography.
3. African American journalists—Biography.
4. African American political activists—Biography.
I. Title.
PS3507.U855Z55   2015
818'.5409—dc23   2015003805

For
Clarice Davis Durham
and
Mildred Sonia and Clarence Banks Williams

radioed with a grant from
Figure Foundation
speak, word syllable word

Somewhere in this ocean of Negro life, with its crosscurrents and undercurrents, lies the very soul of America.

It lies there regardless of the camouflage of crackpots and hypocrites—false liberals and false leaders—of radio's Beulahs and Amos and Andys and Hollywood's Stepin Fetchits and its masturbation with self-flattering dramas of "passing for white" such as *Pinky* and *Imitation of Life*.

It lies there because the real-life story of a single Negro in Alabama walking into a voting booth across a Ku Klux Klan line has more drama and world implications than all the stereotypes Hollywood or radio can turn out in a thousand years.

—Richard Durham, 1949

Contents

Acknowledgments

This book would not have been completed without the loving support of family members, friends, and professional associates. Certainly my parents, Mildred and Clarence Williams, primed me for this journey. For as long as I can remember, they encouraged my love of literature and the arts. Dedicated readers themselves, they did not think it strange that my face always seemed to be in a book throughout my childhood.

Additional encouragement came from my godparents Joan Jones and James Thomas, second Mom Dorothy Israel, brother Craig, sister-in-law Maria, nieces Symone and Tiffany, aunt Bernita Babb, cousins Cleo Alexander, Melanie and Pamela Babb, Florence and Joe Bennett, Doris and Leatrice Brown, Shannon Donley Levan, Charles and Linda Jones, Luther Jones, Susan McLean, Clara and Blaine Richardson, and Leica and Sean Williams.

Cherished longtime friends Debra Floyd and Stacie Brown have also been there from the book's conception and first words, pushing me to write, revise, and revise yet again. Other friends sustained me by offering places to stay, meals, critical analysis, or just plain encouragement. They included Barbara Allen, Chris Arrasmith, Joanna Banks, Emmitt Bowes, K. Brisbane, Carlotta Campbell, Elissa, Shanta, Rebe, and Yohance de la Paz, Mimi Duncan, Frank Edwards, Candice Francis, Linda Davis-Fructoso, Marcia James, Dottie Green, Dinah Griggsby, Maisha Hazzard, Willard and Susan Jenkins, Kipp Kahlia, Michelle Lawrence, Rodger McCoy, Joan Merrill, Isheri Milan, Peggy Miller, Richard Newell, Rochelle Fortier-Nwadibia, Heather Parish, LaTonya Peoples, Sandra Rattley, Lloyd Redwing, Clerene Romeo-Jackson, Dianna Tazolli, Karolyn van Putten, my breast-cancer-fighting walking buddies and fellow DC Water Wizards swim team members.

Writer-friends Michele Bertrand, A'Lelia Bundles, Stephanie Deutch, Marcia V. Ellis, Sharon Ford, Amina Hasaan, Oya Johnson, Raki Jones, Elaine Lee, Matthew Nicther, Andrew Marble, E. Ethelbert Miller, and Ronald Williams were working on their own projects but still found time to offer advice. Additional feedback came from some wonderful writers I met while taking classes at The Writer's Center (TWC) in Bethesda, Maryland. Thanks to Stephanie Boddie, Nancy Derr, Michael Kirkland, Paul Langosch, Cheryl LaRoche, Bonny Miller, Diana Parsell, and Michael Scadron for their insightful critiques and monthly camaraderie. TWC workshop leaders, including Ken Ackerman, Shannon O'Neill, and David Stewart, along with publishing consultant Krishan Trotman, helped me fine-tune everything from my book proposal to chapter drafts. And I truly appreciated the analysis and inspiration provided by Zora Neale Hurston/Richard Wright Writers' Workshop leaders Wil Haygood and Jabari Asim, as well as fellow "Haygood Literary Lionesses" and other Hurston/Wright workshop participants.

Also, I want to send thank you hugs to my Howard University colleagues who read and commented on various chapter drafts. Those scholars include Professors S. Torriano Berry, Lamont Gonzalez, Yanick Rice Lamb, Judi Moore Latta, Candace Shannon Lewis, Abbas Malek, Reginald Miles, Kay Payne, and Ted Roberts; Chairs Gregory Carr, Phillip Dixon, Bishetta Merritt, James Rada, and Dana Williams; and Deans Gracie Lawson-Borders, Chukwuka Onwumechili, Jannette Dates, and Rochelle Ford.

Howard University alums Keith Alexander, Daudi Gardner, Larry Shields, Dackeyia Simmons Sterling, TaJuan Mercer, and Stephanie Vann regularly checked in to spur me on, while graduate students Janelle Bowe and Fredric Kendrick graciously assisted with the research and organization of manuscript notes and citations. Naming my students, past and present, who have inspired and humbled me could easily fill several pages. Suffice to say that these young people represent the best of their generation.

Fellow academicians Kelly Cole, Richard Courage, Brian Dolinar, Michelle Gordon, Aisha Hardison, Michael Keith, Jason Loviglio, Daniel Marcus, Imani Perry, Alexander Russo, Christopher Sterling, and Susan Sumylan provided thoughtful critiques. Retired Northeastern Illinois University professor and author J. Fred MacDonald has cheered me on from the beginning, generously providing access to relevant audio/visual materials and scripts from his resource-rich media archives, now housed in the Library of Congress.

I would also like to thank Chicago history scholar Timuel D. Black Jr., along with Susan Motley and Stephanie Dortch of the Vivian G. Harsh Society, who supported me with a research fellowship in Professor Black's name. Fellow recipient Sherry Williams (no relation) and I spent many days and long hours in the Harsh Research Collection's reading room. Retired senior archivist Michael Flug, curator Robert Miller, librarians Beverly Cook, Denise English, and Cynthia Fife-Townsel, and clerks Lucinda Samuel and Page Nadia Thomas made our work in the collection a joy.

Richard Durham's surviving relatives, including siblings Caldwell, Clotilde, Earl, and Winifred, and nieces Barbara J. Durham Smith and Bernice Durham, along with his wife, Clarice, and adult son Mark were very supportive. I am especially grateful to Mrs. Durham for her patience, quiet dignity, and gentle pressure. She graciously answered my endless stream of questions. Additionally, she put me in touch with several of her husband's colleagues and friends, and she provided access to materials not contained in the documents she donated to the Harsh Collection. She inspired me to stay on the path and get the book done.

Research for this book took me to the special collections or manuscript divisions of the libraries of Columbia, Emory, Howard, Northwestern, Syracuse, and Yale Universities, the University of Maryland, Abraham Lincoln Presidential Library, Library of Congress, and the public libraries of Chicago and New York. In addition, I utilized the archives of the Catholic Archdiocese of Chicago, Illinois Labor History Society, Chicago History Museum, Wisconsin State Historical Society, Ford Foundation, Rockefeller Archives Center, and the John Hay Whitney Foundation. The University of Illinois Press's senior acquisitions editor Larin McLaughlin answered my many manuscript editing and book production questions—often with a smile. Larin's successor, Dawn Durante, has been equally as supportive, knowledgeable, and warm.

Finally, I'd like to thank everyone who allowed me into their living rooms, offices, or studios to interview them about their association with or knowledge of Richard Durham and his times.

Prologue

I couldn't move from my chair. I wanted more.

Flipping the cassette tape to side B, I pressed the machine's play button and sat back. *Amazing!* I thought when the second show finished. Those episodes from a radio series called *Destination Freedom* were captivating and surprisingly fresh, even though they had been produced nearly fifty years earlier.[1] I soon discovered that these and other *Destination Freedom* episodes proved that, however limited, black Americans produced or starred in some fascinating, or as in Durham's case, downright revolutionary radio broadcasts during the racially segregated and blatantly discriminatory America of the late 1940s and early 1950s.

In fall 1994 I had just started working as a writer/producer for the Smithsonian Institution's *Black Radio: Telling It Like It Was* project—a thirteen-part series exploring the legacy of African Americans in radio.[2] The Smithsonian's National Museum of American History in Washington, D.C., housed a unit that produced award-winning radio and television documentaries about the American experience. *Black Radio*'s production team, headed by series creator Jacquie Gales Webb, hoped to continue the Smithsonian's record of broadcast excellence. Starting in January 1996, our weekly half-hour *Black Radio* programs aired on more than two hundred noncommercial radio stations nationwide. Later, XM Satellite Radio carried the series.

Of the five shows on my producing plate, I felt the most trepidation about the one exploring African American contributions during radio's "theater of the mind" heyday of the 1930s and 1940s. Blacks were rarely featured in local or national dramatic broadcasts then. So the more information I unearthed about *Destination Freedom*, the more I was struck by this series' lyricism, dramatic flair, and fiery rhetoric. African American writer Richard Durham created this series in 1948 and served as its sole scriptwriter. A master storyteller, Durham seductively conjured aural magic, inventively dramatizing the lives of black history makers.

And Durham used his desire for universal freedom, justice, and equality to inform his storytelling choices.

But just who was Richard Durham? Durham had died in 1984, so my interviews with his wife, Clarice, actor/singer Oscar Brown Jr., and writer Louis "Studs" Terkel provided salient insights. Durham appeared to have been an astute, Chicago-based writer who employed poetic, hard-hitting prose to entertain, educate, and promote positive social change. He stood behind his convictions, even when the consequences of his actions caused him emotional pain, financial hardship—or both.

Durham's life was drama itself, full of unexpected twists and turns, of creative invention and reinvention. A few historians, such as J. Fred MacDonald and Barbara Savage, had explored the significance of Durham's *Destination Freedom* dramas. Yet I wondered why no one had written a book-length account about the totality of Durham's contributions and advocacy.

Dare I write such a book?

Durham's story certainly fascinated me. His accomplishments reinforced my own belief that the media, in all its incarnations, should serve a higher purpose than just mindless diversion. So after the *Black Radio* series ended, I planned to work on Durham's biography. Unfortunately, other documentary projects monopolized my time. I also continued teaching in my academic home, the Howard University Department of Radio, Television, and Film. Appointment to an administrative position in my department eventually forced me to sandwich research for this book into spring or summer breaks and other far-too-fleeting time frames.

Still, a Howard University–sponsored research grant in 2002 enabled me to start immersing myself in Durham's world. Later, a 2009 Timuel D. Black Jr. Short-Term Fellowship in African American Studies sponsored by the Vivian G. Harsh Society enabled me to spend a summer in Chicago.[3] I practically moved into the Woodson Regional Library, home base of the Harsh Research Collection of Afro-American History and Literature, where Richard Durham's papers reside.[4] Finally, a sabbatical from my university during the 2010–11 academic year allowed me to make significant progress toward the completion of this book.

I have strived to represent Durham's writing and his life faithfully, and I hope that you will be equally as inspired by his compelling story and activism.

CHAPTER 1

Remembering

A. A. Rayner and Sons Funeral Home
Chicago, Illinois—South Side
Wednesday, May 2, 1984

The sanctuary buzzed with energy.

People staked out all available spaces, sitting or standing shoulder to shoulder in the funeral home's cream-walled, brightly lit, three-hundred-seat chapel. Ushers had to direct the rising tide of attendees into an adjacent chapel—a mirror image of the main sanctuary. When that room reached capacity, people claimed whatever space they could in the hallway between the two chapels.[1]

Everyone was there to honor Richard "Dick" Durham.

Some of the attendees came straight from work in their best business attire. Others dressed more casually, wearing light sweaters, jackets, and shawls in Chicago's mild, near-sixty-degree weather.[2]

A few motorists parked in the funeral home's small lot. Other drivers pulled into whatever spots they could find in front of the middle- and working-class black neighborhood's modest single-family brick bungalows and smattering of apartment buildings. Still other attendees let city buses chauffeur them down either Seventy-First Street, Dr. Martin Luther King Jr. Drive, or State Street on their way to Rayner's two-story, red-brick building at 318 East Seventy-First.[3]

Many African American Chicagoans turned to this black-owned business to handle funeral arrangements for their loved ones. Nearly thirty years earlier, Rayner and Sons Funeral Home helped to galvanize the national civil rights struggle when a heartsick, defiant young mother asked owner Ahmed A. Rayner Jr. to prepare her murdered son's body for an open-casket funeral.[4] Thousands of mourners walked past the horror of fourteen-year-old Emmett Till's bloated remains. Millions more were shocked by photos in the black press of the teenager's mutilated body. Till had been tortured, killed, and dumped in a river for allegedly whistling at a white woman while on summer vacation in the hamlet of Money, Mississippi.

Through his writing and advocacy, Richard Durham sought to eliminate this kind of injustice. And as the director of the antidiscrimination unit of the United Packinghouse Workers of America (UPWA)—one of the most progressive labor unions in the country—Durham helped the union organize around the Till case.

Tonight however, Dick Durham would take *his* place in the spotlight.

In Rayner's main chapel, a huge bouquet of pastel carnations, green ferns, and multihued gladiolas released their sweet scents. This regal display sat in the center of the chapel's front alcove. A casket was conspicuously absent. The family had been clear; they had not wanted Dick's memorial service to be a solemn affair. And since he had not been a religious man, Clarice Durham did not ask a preacher to officiate. Instead, she recruited family members and friends to share their recollections about her husband.[5]

At about 7 P.M., ushers led Durham's family members to the main chapel's reserved front row. Durham's thirty-four-year-old son, Mark, then stepped in front of the crowd. He brought a gold-colored mouthpiece to his lips and coaxed a melody from his tenor sax. Accompanied by organist Ron Scott and drummer Billy Leathers, Mark's interpretation of jazz pianist Horace Silver's *Song for my Father* elicited smiles.[6] The song was an apt salute from a son who adored his father.

Mark fluidly improvised on Silver's simple yet elegant melody. Dick had loved his son's playing, and he was a big jazz fan. In some ways, Durham's life and career echoed the music and musicians he cherished. Like the unpredictable, innovative jazz trumpeter/composer Miles Davis, Durham was daringly outspoken in his storytelling and bravely improvisational in his approach to life and creative expression. Durham also may have channeled jazz composer, pianist, and bandleader Edward "Duke" Ellington in his ability to fashion broadcast and print masterpieces that inspired fellow artists, colleagues, and even audience members who might not have known his name.

Dick Durham had been a soft-spoken man. Brown-skinned and heavyset, Dick had a receding hairline that left a pool of exposed skin on the top of his head. He stood just shy of 5'9". Yet Durham's influence had been long-limbed—reaching into many aspects of life in Chicago. A virtual Who's Who of Chicago's political and cultural worlds populated Rayner's sanctuaries.[7] City officials and congressmen, educators and social workers, labor leaders and artists, journalists and other writers were just a few of the hundreds who came to remember—and to say goodbye.

At age ten months, Maya Durham, one of Dick Durham's two granddaughters, may have been the youngest attendee.[8] Other attendees had lived a lot longer than Richard Durham's sixty-six years. Whatever their ages, the crowd represented the diversity Durham championed throughout his life. There were blacks and whites; the wealthy and the struggling; the religious and the secular.

Most people were still in shock. Durham had died unexpectedly of a heart attack five days earlier, April 27, 1984, during a business trip in New York City.[9]

As the last note of Mark Durham's poignant salute hung in the air, one of Mark's uncles, his mother's oldest brother, walked to the front of the room. Robert Davis moved slowly. He had not felt well as he traveled with Dick's younger brother Caldwell from Los Angeles, where they both lived.[10] Davis stiffly stepped up to the chapel's oak podium and leaned toward the attached microphone. He started talking about how he and Durham met and became friends more than forty years earlier.

Robert Davis and Richard Durham had much in common. They were born the same year, 1917, almost exactly six months apart, Robert on March 7, Richard on September 6. Both had trekked to Chicago with their families. Davis came by way of Mobile, Alabama, and Chattanooga, Tennessee. Durham was from rural Raymond, Mississippi. Both had literary dreams.[11] Davis and Durham met as members of a writing group where they waxed poetic about "Bronzeville," their overcrowded, all-black South Side neighborhood.

Beginning in the late 1930s, these twenty-one-year-olds documented life in a cash-strapped, Depression-era Chicago while working as writers for the federally funded Illinois Writers' Project (IWP).[12] Robert Davis smiled as he told the attentive crowd that he developed some level of trust and respect for Durham early on—since he introduced Dick to Clarice, his baby sister. Ever the protective big brother, Davis said that he approved when Dick and Clarice started dating in 1941. He also approved of their wedding a year later. For the next forty-two years Davis kept tabs on Clarice and her husband, his friend. Davis told the crowd he still couldn't believe that Dick was gone.[13] He would sorely miss him.

Pulitzer Prize–winning author Louis "Studs" Terkel echoed Robert Davis's sentiments. Terkel reminisced in his deep, slightly nasal voice that listeners could readily identify because of his many years as a Chicago radio talk show host. The short, stout Terkel said that his friendship with Dick Durham also dated back to the Depression years. Terkel and Durham met while working as scriptwriters in the radio division of the IWP.[14]

In Terkel's eyes, his friend was one of those writers who had "a certain clarity of vision as well as clarity of style." The best example of that, in Terkel's opinion, was Dick's *Destination Freedom* radio series. "There was nothing quite like it ever on radio," Terkel asserted. "It was a story of African Americans, but they were little-known stories, you know, of unsung heroes."[15] For two years starting in 1948, Durham penned lilting, opinionated scripts that profiled Negro leadership and courage while railing against injustice each week on Chicago station WMAQ.

A talented ensemble of local performers, including Studs Terkel and singer/actor Oscar Brown Jr., brought Durham's scripts to life. Terkel acknowledged that his friend was not as well known as black writers like Richard Wright, Ralph Ellison, or Toni Morrison. Yet Terkel noted: "Dick Durham was a very important figure in African American literature. . . . He took the medium of radio and used it for a series that was serious about life and history. For that alone," Terkel concluded, "he should be honored."[16]

Nods and applause followed Terkel as he returned to his seat. A short, petite black woman then rose and placed three pages of typed comments on the podium. Her name was Margaret Burroughs, the talented visual artist, writer, and co-founder of the South Side's Du Sable Museum of African American History.

Burroughs said that she first became aware of Richard Durham when his "beautiful and sensitive" poetry appeared in the *Chicago Defender* newspaper. Burroughs and Durham soon became friends, and she found out that her fellow artist's birth name actually was Isadore. Some family members and friends never stopped calling Durham by his childhood nickname, Izzy. Later, he sometimes used the name Vern Durham, Burroughs said, as "his poetic *nom-de-plume*." Durham eventually crowned himself Richard. Burroughs said that the fighting spirit and courageous exploits of England's Richard I, the twelfth-century king known as Richard the Lionheart, inspired Durham.[17]

What better name for a young man who saw himself as an increasingly muscular, creative force?

Long before the advent of the "Black is Beautiful" identity movements of the 1960s and 1970s, Burroughs indicated that Durham broke through "a thoroughly racist-ridden electronic media of radio and TV." His dramatic creations, including *Here Comes Tomorrow, Destination Freedom,* and *Bird of the Iron Feather,* "were like an oasis in the desert or like a Balm in Gilead which strengthened and encouraged our sin-sick souls," Burroughs said. "I can still remember how eagerly we looked forward to these programs which gave us something positive that we could identify with about ourselves."[18] She also praised Durham's work as a probing journalist, labor union organizer, and author of *The Greatest: My Own Story,* boxing champion Muhammad Ali's autobiography.

Durham was, in Burroughs's estimation, "a people's artist," a man who "carved out his monument by the works and the legacy that he left to us." She hoped that

FIGURE 1. Pictured from left to right, Ron Scott and Richard Durham's son Mark. Courtesy of Mark Durham.

his life and writing would serve as "a role model for other young warriors who are surely coming on to follow the path that he cleared to carry on his message and his work." "Truly," she concluded, "Richard the Lionheart would be quite pleased."[19]

To appreciative applause, Margaret Burroughs stepped aside as another artist took her place. This woman, singularly calling herself Chavunduka, faced the audience and let her voice soar between the high and low notes of the bittersweet ballad "Everything Must Change."[20] The tune's lyrics spoke about life's contradictions and transformations, of life's grounded yet ethereal nature.

For a moment, Rayner's funeral home became church. Its congregants clapped and nodded and Amen-ed in encouragement. Tears left watery tracks on some people's faces. Others swayed to the gentle rhythms of the ballad and the beauty of Chavunduka's rendering. When the song ended, Chavunduka and her accompanists, Ron Scott on piano and Mark Durham on sax, humbly acknowledged the memorial crowd's enthusiastic praise.[21]

Once Rayner's sanctuaries settled back down, journalist Vernon Jarrett and activists Ishmael Flory and Edward "Buzz" Palmer testified about Durham's voracious reading habits, his sharp analytical mind, and his generous nature.[22] Another beneficiary of Durham's mentoring spirit was a compactly built bundle of energy—the singer, actor, and activist Oscar Brown Jr. "Dick was a pal to me, you know?" Brown said in his distinct, raspy voice. "He was someone who advised and taught and helped a young person do his passage into adulthood."[23] Brown was eighteen years old when he met Durham in 1945.

"I remember through the years, conversations with Dick Durham were always informative," Brown recalled. He revealed that Durham had been a leftist, a Communist, who explained the intricacies of Marxism and Leninism to him. "But he was a champion of Negro people like you never saw before," Brown asserted, remembering that Durham believed that Communist philosophy was more in line with the liberation of Negroes and other oppressed people than capitalism.

"Dick was a character," Brown laughingly recounted. "You know at one point, I don't know what was going on, but I didn't want to talk to Dick, so I told my wife to tell him I'm not home. She'd hung up, and the phone [rang] immediately. . . . Dick had just called and he'd double back on you and catch you in that lie. He was really super slick. When you have a friend like that, you gotta be on your P's and Q's." Brown concluded, stating: "I hope the world gets to know what a towering genius this dude was, and what a brave man he was, and what a Negro he was and what a fighter for our people he was."[24]

Then the entertainer Oscar Brown Jr. belted out a few verses from the *Battle Hymn of the Republic*, one of Durham's favorite songs,[25] identifying as he did with the song's crusading spirit and its clarion call for truth and freedom. People clapped in rhythm, and some sang along as Brown vamped on the song's chorus: *Glory, Glory Hallelujah, Glory, Glory Hallelujah, Glory, Glory Hallelujah, His truth is marching on.*[26]

More speakers subsequently paid tribute to Durham—the most prominent was Harold Washington.[27] A year earlier, Washington had become Chicago's first black mayor.

Mayor Washington recalled how he had met Durham.[28] As a Roosevelt University undergraduate student during the 1940s, Washington frequented the university's cafeteria—the watering hole and informal meeting place in downtown Chicago for politically active students and nonstudents alike. Dick Durham, his brother Earl, and some of their friends participated in a few of the cafeteria's spirited debates.[29] Harold and Dick became friends as a result. Fast forwarding to more recent times, Mayor Washington talked about Durham's constant presence in his life once he jumped into the Democratic mayoral primary race in 1982.[30] Durham joined the Washington campaign's press department; he had a desk in the campaign's main headquarters at 53 West Jackson Boulevard.[31] But if you wanted to catch up with Durham, you had to find Washington.

And both men were fast-moving targets.

Most mornings, Harold Washington and his driver picked up Dick Durham from his home at Twenty-Sixth Street and South Michigan Avenue.[32] Dick and Harold would then glide through the city in Washington's black Oldsmobile. Durham whispered advice to this would-be king as they headed to various campaign stops.

Durham also wrote or fine-tuned several of the candidate's speeches, bringing a unique spin and powerful analysis to the process. Mayor Washington said that Durham planned on writing a book about his mayoral campaign.[33] Given his friend's keen observational and literary talents, Washington said that he was sure that Durham would have written a masterful account.

As the mayor stepped away from the podium, he embraced Earl Durham, the memorial service's final speaker. Earl looked around Rayner's still-packed funeral home and asked soberly, "How do you say goodbye to a brother who has meant so much to you?"[34]

Earl was the baby of the Durham family, the youngest of eight children—seven of whom survived to adulthood. Earl said that his own life's journey led him to teach at the university level. But he doubted that he would have taken this path if Dick, six years his senior, hadn't snatched him by his collar and made him become somebody. Once Dick got turned on to African American history, "he started proselytizing to me and the others about how they needed to get back to their heritage," Earl said. "He beat me over the head with all that stuff! I was the youngest and I guess that he figured he had more of a chance with me."[35]

As he matured, Dick became, in Earl's view, "advocacy-oriented." Dick always tried to bring people together, firmly believing that "if you want to fight injustice . . . you have to organize people to do it," Earl said. Dick instilled this philosophy in his youngest brother, and because of Dick's skills as an organizer, "he became sort of a mentor to all kinds of operations going on in the city," Earl said. "He had a way of analyzing whatever situation they were in, talking about it and working something out to move things [along]."[36]

Earl acknowledged that his brother's strategies didn't always work. Dick lost his job as a star reporter for the *Chicago Defender*, and he was fired from a leadership position in a local union when his organizing efforts angered administrators.

Despite those and other setbacks, all types of people "hung around him because he seemed to be full of creativity and ideas," Earl said. "He was a success in the cultural field when few blacks had made a dent, without giving up their principles."[37]

After Earl Durham ended his remarks, tears and hugs, laughter and animated conversation danced in the funeral home air. People slowly moved outside into the spring night, continuing to reminisce about a man they would not soon forget: the complicated family man, friend, and mentor—as well as the writer and dedicated freedom fighter alternatively known as Isadore, Izzy, Vern, Dick, or Richard Durham.

CHAPTER 2

Rural Wanderings

Cotton Croppers

A citron sun, a ghost of gold,
Pours thick heat down on the field.
Heat burst the bolls and floods the air
Where ragged croppers, like patches in a cotton cloud,
Dot the billowy acres,
Bag the bolls, swell the sacks.
Plod the rows; pick the cotton.

Wading through the turbid waves unable to feel
The glory of day for the hell of heat!
And to a winding road snaking besides the field
They have but to lift their eyes to see,
Unworried over the sun, the cotton,
The plight of the pickers,
Comfortable cars rolling by the road,
Touring through the heat
Plowing through the air.[1]

—Isadore Richard Durham, undated

"Izzy!"

Silence.

"Izzy, where are you!?"[2]

Only the whisper of the wind moving through magnolia leaves disturbed the quiet.

Izzy Durham was nowhere to be found. Again. The energetic toddler was exploring as much of the land around his family's house as his young legs could travel. But one of his older sisters was not amused. She could never find her brother when she needed to, like when their parents expected them back in the house.

"All I remember is looking for him all the time," Clotilde Durham Smith explained. "Being a boy, I guess he would wander around. . . . He started that early in his life."[3] Although Clotilde was only two years older than the sibling whom she and other family members called Izzy, Clotilde saw herself as his protector—the big sister who needed to make sure that her younger brother was OK.

Izzy was just fine. In his wanderings, this inquisitive child who entered the world on September 6, 1917, as Isadore Durham—this mischievous young boy who would become the probing journalist, innovative dramatist, and astute political analyst known as Richard Durham—was soaking up his environment, learning how to observe and dissect the world around him.

During the early 1920s Isadore's world was ripe for exploration. The Durham home sat on eighty acres of verdant farmland just outside the town of Raymond in Hinds County, Mississippi. Fruit from the farm's sticky-sweet peach, pear, and fig trees provided fodder for the canning jars of Chanie Tillman Durham, Isadore and Clotilde's mother.[4] The children's father, Curtis George Durham, cultivated the farm's cotton crops and cornfields. "Both Mr. Durham and I worked diligently to support our home and children. This was not always easy," Chanie told her oldest daughter, Claudia Marie, years later. "Many times crops were lean due to natural disasters. At such times we had to dip into our meager savings to tide us over until the next harvest."[5]

To supplement their income, Curtis worked several odd jobs. According to Chanie, her husband cut hay, mended fences, and made molasses.[6] Curtis also raised livestock in order to sell meat, and every Saturday he saddled his horse and rode five miles into the town of Bolton to work as a clerk in the general store.

Yet even as Isadore's father attacked life's daily challenges, he had a slight advantage. Curtis George Durham owned his own land, earning him membership in a small universe of Negro landowners in Mississippi during the late nineteenth and early twentieth centuries. According to U.S. Census figures, Negroes owned only about ten thousand of a little more than eighty-seven thousand black-occupied farms in 1890. Those numbers increased slightly by 1910. After that year, black landownership in Mississippi declined.[7]

On his land Curtis Durham parceled out small plots to two tenant farmers.[8] Records no longer exist detailing the type of rental agreement Isadore's father had with his tenants. Whatever the specifics, Curtis's tenants brought in some of the additional resources he needed to support his family. Chanie contributed to the family coffers by working as a teacher in Hinds County's Negro schoolhouse.[9] But given rural Mississippi's brief school year—a four- or five-month period between November and April[10]—Chanie had to find other ways to supplement the family income. For a while she made and sold soap. Most of Chanie's customers lived in Jackson, the state capital, located roughly fifteen miles northeast of Raymond. However, making the roundtrip journey to Jackson by horse and buggy yielded Chanie little profit.[11]

So Izzy's industrious mother searched for and found a lucrative trade. She enrolled in the Walker Beauty School in Jackson, part of a successful national chain of hair care and cosmetic training schools established by the pioneering Negro businesswoman who called herself Madam C. J. Walker.[12] Born Sarah Breedlove in Louisiana two years after the end of slavery, Madam Walker tirelessly promoted her patented hair growth and beauty products to Negro women. One advertisement for Walker's beauty schools claimed that women who learned "Walker's Scientific Scalp Treatment" procedures could earn between fifteen dollars and forty dollars a week working in their own homes or salons.[13] "With this new trade I did very well because the country folks as well as those in the towns went for the new process of 'straightening hair,'" Izzy's mother explained.

Contrary to popular belief, Madam C. J. Walker did not invent the "hot comb," the utensil that allowed black women to straighten and style their hair in ways unimaginable prior to its creation. But Walker's innovative marketing schemes, training programs, and distribution strategies made her rich. Chanie Durham was just one of the many Negro women who helped Walker build her empire—worth about $600,000 when the Madam died in 1919.[14]

In addition to styling hair and teaching, Chanie helped her husband cultivate their farmland. Raymond, situated in the west-central part of Mississippi, was blessed with nutrient-rich soil.[15] Since the early 1800s, Raymond (and Hinds County in general) had supported plantations that thrived on the cash crops of cotton and corn. And as cotton production exploded throughout the Natchez and Yazoo Basin/Mississippi Delta regions, Mississippi's economy soared.[16] To handle the massive production needs of their cotton- and corn-fueled economy, plantation owners imported scores of slaves from other southern states. "The cotton-slavery boom reached a climax in the 1830s when cotton output quadrupled and the slave population increased by nearly 200 percent to constitute, for the first time, a majority of the state's total population," Mississippi historian William Scarborough determined.[17]

Isadore's parents could easily trace their roots back to Mississippi's ubiquitous slave culture and agricultural life. Chanie recalled that when she first met the man who became her husband, she described Curtis Durham as "the son of a more prosperous farmer who was buying his own farm." She was referring to Curtis's father, Napoleon Durham, a "mulatto" or mixed-race former slave born in 1855. Napoleon's white father, Robert Bonner, had been his owner. Napoleon's mother was a fifteen-year-old slave named Clareta.[18]

Most slaves had one name. If they were given a last name, it matched their owners."[19] With his biological and legal ties to Robert Bonner, it is not clear how Napoleon's last name became Durham. After slavery's demise Isadore's paternal grandfather may have chosen, for reasons unknown, the Durham surname. Or the name might have held some significance for Clareta, Napoleon's mother. Whatever the origin of their surname, Napoleon Durham and his mother continued to live and work on the Bonner farm once slavery ended. In 1874 Napoleon married fellow Raymond resident Sarah Laws. Shortly thereafter, a real estate broker sold Izzy's paternal grandparents eighty acres of nearby land.[20]

Many white landowners *had* to sell portions of their land to survive after the Civil War ended. In *Black Reconstruction in America (1860–1880)*, scholar W. E. B. Du Bois provided a detailed analysis of conditions in the postslavery Reconstruction era. As an adult, Isadore Durham would often turn to Du Bois's writings, intrigued by the distinguished scholar's insights. *Black Reconstruction* became one of Durham's favorite books.[21] In it, Du Bois estimated that pre–Civil War property land values in Mississippi stood at about $291 million. After the war, Southern landowners lost one of their biggest assets—the free labor of slaves. Therefore, property values in Mississippi tumbled to approximately $177 million. "The whole industrial system was upset," Du Bois wrote, and the cotton crop, which weighed in at about 12 million bales in 1860, generated less that half that amount in 1870.[22] Historian James Revels reported that as large plantations disintegrated, the average size of Mississippi farms fell from 370 acres in 1860 to 83 acres by 1900.[23]

The farmland that Napoleon Durham and his wife bought fell within that average. But Isadore's grandparents worked for years to pay off their farm's $1,000 price tag. "They had trouble keeping up so they wound up having to take second loans and things like that to get it together," Isadore's younger brother Caldwell explained."[24]

Still, Napoleon and Sarah Durham persevered, raising ten children on land they eventually owned. Isadore's grandfather later deeded the property to his oldest son, Curtis George, born in 1880.[25] For more than one hundred years, the Durhams remained Mississippi landowners. But Napoleon Durham's descendants sold the property in 2005. By then it was clear that no one in the family intended to return to Raymond.[26]

Yet back in the early 1900s the Durham family's landholding status not only impressed Chanie Tillman, she became smitten with Curtis himself. "Being a very handsome young man, with copper skin and a head of black, curly hair, and being permitted to drive the family's horse-drawn buggy, he was sought after by many a 'well-to-do' [woman]," Chanie recalled. "Compared with many of his girlfriends, I was the poorest and probably the least sophisticated of the lot. I had been bred, born, and raised in the country."[27]

Chanie and Curtis must have met as they traveled around Raymond and Hinds County. Curtis might have been attracted to the short, pretty Chanie because of her spunky personality and fierce determination. And Chanie knew how to pique Curtis's interest. "Even though I fell in love with Mr. Durham and liked his attention," Chanie told her daughter Claudia Marie, "I never felt that I could win his true affections by chasing him. If there was any chasing to be done, I felt that it was the male's prerogative and not that of the female. I believe this lack of outward show on my part added to my charm as far as Mr. Durham was concerned."[28] Chanie also possessed a confidence and maturity that belied her humble background. Born in 1879, Chanie came from a large, hardscrabble family of sharecroppers.

For Chanie, life with her sixteen siblings and sharecropping parents meant "a succession of moving from one farm to another. The house was always a two-room cabin joined by a large hallway in which we piled the cotton during cotton-picking time," Chanie recalled.[29] Her mother, Celia Tillman, cooked family meals in a big black skillet that sat in an open fireplace outside the house. Chanie's father, William Tillman, built most of the family's furniture. Celia fashioned work clothes for her children from the same scratchy cloth used to make sacks for picking cotton.[30]

Sharecropping demanded that laborers maintain an intimate relationship with the land while harboring a constant fear of failure. A poor harvest or disappointing crop sales meant that "croppers" like Celia and William Tillman would be unable to pay back the credit extended to them by the landowners for whom they worked. That credit allowed croppers to buy necessities like seeds, food, and essential farming or household supplies.[31] But for many sharecroppers, getting out of debt was a bit like trying to stay in the same spot in an ocean while its undercurrents swirl: basically impossible—especially if landowners employed questionable accounting methods. Consequently, sharecroppers could remain tied to a particular landowner indefinitely. Or they might be asked to leave, forcing them to negotiate new sharecropping arrangements with another landowner.[32]

Finding themselves in the latter category, the Tillmans moved often, spending a year here, two or three years there. One time the family landed on a Mississippi farm owned by the Wells family. "My father didn't do well there at all," Chanie remembered. "He came out behind, [and] when you don't pay your debts . . . they take all you have."[33] The family was forced to move yet again.

Because of this nomadic existence, Isadore's mother was introduced to something that became her lifelong passion. At age eight, Chanie learned the alphabet from a young boy she took care of. "I was curious about books," she recalled. "I listened to him read with fascination."[34] And so began Chanie Tillman's love affair with knowledge and education—a love she later passed on to Isadore and all of her children.

But just as she was nurturing this new love, tragedy struck. Chanie's father— Isadore's grandfather—died, leaving the family emotionally and financially adrift. The Tillmans had to move to yet another farm. "I thought that my formal education had come to an end," Chanie said. Celia Tillman desperately needed help working the land, so her children pitched in. Chanie learned how to plow as well as any man. Yet she kept pestering her mother. Chanie wanted to continue her education.

Chanie's persistence eventually paid off. Celia let her daughter enroll in a school five miles away. Each weekday morning just before dawn, Chanie worked in the fields as long as she could before walking to a schoolhouse in Bolton. There, Chanie marveled at her instructor's ability to teach students how to solve math problems, diagram sentences, and discuss history. "I thought that there was nothing in this world that she did not know," Chanie said. "I decided then and there that I wanted to be a teacher."[35] Chanie's teacher rewarded her interest and academic promise by giving her extra books to study during the long school breaks.

When Chanie turned 18 in 1897, another teacher, Mr. Grandberry, asked her to become his assistant. Chanie would teach first grade through third, while Grandberry taught students in the fourth through sixth grades. "I guess I was the happiest young woman in the whole wide world," Chanie said. "As I walked home that evening, I saw nothing, I felt nothing. It was like floating on clouds. I kept saying over and over to myself, me, a teacher!"[36]

Chanie's teaching career was well underway when she met Curtis. Undoubtedly, she was delighted to learn that this good-looking man loved to read. In the late 1890s Curtis Durham had been a student at Alcorn University. When he arrived on Alcorn's campus, Curtis saw other "colored" Mississippians who were just like him—descendants of slaves or former slaves long denied education. They flocked to Alcorn, the oldest public land-grant institution of higher education for blacks in America.[37]

Throughout the country, education-starved black Americans eagerly enrolled in schools established by the federal government's Freedmen's Bureau, religious and philanthropic organizations, and by state or federal land grant decrees. Many of these modest institutions became the historically black colleges and universi-

FIGURE 2. The only surviving photograph, circa the early 1940s, of Chanie and Curtis George Durham together. Courtesy of Caldwell Durham.

ties (HBCUs) of today.[38] Alcorn University started welcoming students in 1871. Located on 225 acres in southwestern Mississippi, the school offered a two-year preparatory program for students with limited formal education, along with three- and four-year courses of advanced study in English, Latin, mathematics, and industrial education.[39]

Isadore's father completed two years at Alcorn before running out of money. To secure tuition funds, Curtis worked numerous odd jobs. "But pressures were great on him at the time, both from within his farming family and from without socially," Chanie explained.[40] Curtis returned to farming and never completed his formal education. However, his love of knowledge and the printed word stayed with him. This passion he shared with Chanie may have cemented their relationship. Curtis Durham and Chanie Tillman married in 1905.[41] She was twenty-six; he, a year younger.

Chanie continued teaching and styling hair as she embraced motherhood. A child entered the couple's life every two years, beginning in 1909 with Curtis George Jr., then Claudia Marie (1911), Winifred (1913), Clotilde (1915), Isadore (1917), Maudeline (1919), and Caldwell (1921). Since the services of the county hospital were reserved for whites, black midwives guided the births of the children.[42] And with her expanding family and her teaching responsibilities, there was little time or opportunity for Chanie to pursue her own educational dreams.

So for the Durham children, education became a mantra. "Educating their children was important to both our parents, and it was probably one of the main reasons why they eventually left Raymond," Isadore's younger brother Caldwell explained.[43] Facilities in Mississippi, as throughout the South, were strictly segregated, and the inequity of racial discrimination was always evident. Each weekday, a bus filled with white children passed the Durham home on its way to and from the better-equipped, whites-only school. Clotilde remembered seeing the school bus and wondered why she and her siblings had to trudge through winter cold or spring warmth to get to their weathered, one-room schoolhouse.[44]

As Isadore's oldest brother and sister, Curtis George Jr. (nicknamed CG) and Claudia Marie (the family simply called her Marie), finished the one school open to colored students in Raymond, the children had no choice but to leave town to advance their studies. By the mid-1920s, only three public high schools served black students in the entire state.[45] "No state spent less on black education," historian Neil McMillen ascertained. Although Negroes constituted 60 percent of Mississippi's school-age children during the early 1900s, they benefited disproportionately from a smaller amount of designated funds.[46] For example, during the 1921–22 academic year—just a year before four-year-old Isadore entered the public school system—Mississippi allocated eighteen dollars to schools for each white student. Merely four dollars were reserved for each black student during the same period.[47]

Isadore's parents enrolled CG and Marie in the Southern Christian Institute (SCI), a boarding school for colored students roughly fifteen miles away in Edwards, Mississippi.[48] Established about ten years after slavery's demise, the SCI initially accepted students free of charge. That practice proved unsustainable, so the institute started charging tuition in the mid-1880s.[49] The couple's fluctuating income meant that Chanie and Curtis struggled to pay their oldest children's school fees.[50] And Isadore's parents knew that their younger children would soon follow along. There had to be a better path to education.

Chanie and Curtis looked north.[51] North to the promise. North to the realistic possibility of greater economic and educational opportunities.

Isadore's parents kept abreast of life outside their rural confines by subscribing to the *Globe Democrat*—a popular St. Louis newspaper.[52] Founded in 1852, this paper's originators had been staunch advocates of antislavery sentiments and freedom in Missouri.[53] Papers like the *Globe Democrat* and the black-owned, advocacy-oriented *Chicago Defender* trumpeted tales of better economic and educational opportunities in northern cities. Inspired by such tales, in 1921 Curtis Durham visited cousins already living in Chicago. There he found blue-collar jobs plentiful and schools in session from September to June.[54] In the Windy City, Curtis, his wife, and all of their children could be together under one roof. Just as important, the Durham kids could receive a better education—hopefully leading to a better life.

Again, education—the mantra. Education—the journey. Education—the opportunity.

Curtis and Chanie yielded to the pull. They resolved to relocate to Chicago during spring 1923. Yet as they prepared for this major move, the Durhams suffered a devastating loss.

One day, Chanie was teaching while one of her sisters watched Maudeline, the baby who followed Isadore. Barely three years old at the time, Maudeline somehow fell into the open fireplace in the Durham's cooking area. "My Aunt couldn't get her out soon enough," Isadore's sister Clotilde said. "I remember someone coming to school and telling my mother that, and of course we all went home."[55] Curtis jumped onto his horse and rode as fast as he could to fetch a doctor in the next town. Bolton's white physician returned with Curtis and prescribed a treatment for the badly burned child.

According to Clotilde, "at that time the treatment for burns was to put you in a wax cast, which is the wrong thing, because you have got these blisters [that] formed." The family held vigil, caring for the child in their home. Maudeline survived the night. But she died the next day.[56] Maudeline's death was a painful testament to the frailty of life, aching proof that life could change in an instant. Given the extent of her burns, Maudeline Durham might not have survived even if she had been treated in a hospital. But the ugly truth of life in the segregated South meant that even in an emergency, its Negro citizens could not use or depend on existing health care facilities.

After the heartbreak of Maudeline's death and the constant struggle to survive in their home state, Curtis and Chanie believed that life up north, in Chicago, offered the change they needed.[57] The North represented freedom—the freedom to learn and grow and develop in ways that were only dreamed about in the South of the 1920s. With great hope, Isadore along with his five surviving siblings, his father, and his pregnant mother would join the great exodus of black Americans who decisively left the bubbling heat and stifling racial straightjacket of the Jim Crow South for the promise of Northern opportunity and freedom.

CHAPTER 3

Chicago

City

A baked brick desert
With oases of parks,
A necklace of streets,
Electric pearls . . .
Rain and a sun
Wash and dry the necklace,
Brown bricks and winds
Make the sounds of a song[1]

—Richard I. Durham, undated

Five-year-old Isadore Durham and his siblings got ready to leave the only home they'd known for a place they'd never seen.

Some place called Chicago.

This somewhere place had already captured their mother. Four months earlier, Chanie had moved to Chicago to find their new home.[2] She sent for her children once she found a suitable place.

So on a warm day in late August 1923, Isadore, Clotilde, baby Caldwell, Winifred, and Marie loaded their bags full of clothes and toys onto their father's horse and buggy.[3] Curtis carried his children to Jackson where they would catch the Illinois Central (IC) Railroad's Chicago-bound train.

Once aboard, Isadore's oldest sister led the charge. Although she was only twelve years old at the time, Marie had become a surrogate mother to her younger siblings. The only child not in Marie's care during that August train ride was fourteen-year-old Curtis Jr. C.G. had stayed in Raymond to help their father sell their last set of crops, livestock, and household furniture.[4]

For the ride north, "we had our shoebox filled with fried chicken and other food," Isadore's sister Clotilde remembered.[5] The children blended in easily with their fellow Negro travelers who also carried fried chicken, hard-boiled eggs, and biscuits—staples of black Southern cuisine. People sometimes called the trains shepherding African American migrants north the Chicken Bone Special.[6]

Migration chronicler James Grossman noted that the segregated so-called "Negro car" was attached to the coal tender or baggage car. Exhaust fumes and dirt inevitably wafted into this segregated car as the train chugged through Mississippi, Tennessee, and Kentucky.[7] Once the train entered Illinois, the first Northern state on that IC route, its Negro passengers could make a liberating move. "We could have changed to an integrated car," Clotilde recalled, "but we stayed in our section until we got to Chicago."[8] After spending hours in a place where the familiar lilt of black Southern voices mixed with recognizable food aromas, that dirty, overcrowded car might have felt a bit safe to the Durham children.

When the train finally lurched to a stop in Chicago, Chanie scooped up her children—likely wide-eyed with excitement. The children probably pelted her with questions as they took in one unfamiliar sight after another. Undoubtedly, Isadore eyed Chicago's gigantic brick, concrete, and iron structures, taller than any tree on his family's farm and grander than any building he'd ever seen.[9] All around him, a hurricane of humanity whizzed past, more people than he ever knew existed. He saw a body of water—Lake Michigan—so blue and expansive that it seemed to touch the sky. And on the paved streets of this strange place, clanging buses—his mother called them "streetcars"—screeched by like roving beasts, swallowing up people and flying down roads busier and wider than any he'd ever walked.

What a thrilling, intimidating new world!

In short order, Isadore and his siblings stood in front of what they must have perceived to be a towering structure. Built during the 1890s, this three-story, light-gray limestone and brick building, attached on both sides to two identical structures, sat on an unpaved street eight miles south of downtown.[10] Chanie guided her children up seven stone steps that led to a small stone porch. She opened a heavy front door and led her kids into a tiled vestibule.

They were home.

To the left of the vestibule and in front of them was a moderate-sized living room. Bright, natural light filtered through the center bay and two smaller side windows on the living room's front wall. A wood-burning fireplace took up the

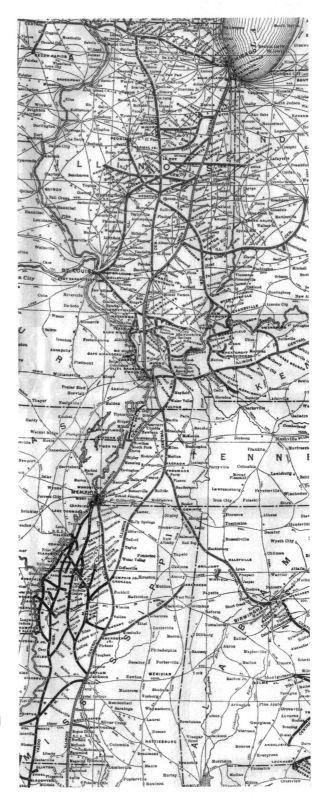

FIGURE 3. This map displays the various routes of the Illinois Central (IC) Railroad as they existed by December 31, 1922, a few months before Chanie Durham and her children boarded IC trains in Jackson, Mississippi, heading to Chicago, Illinois. Courtesy of the Illinois Central Railroad Historical Society.

center portion of the wall on their right. Adjacent to this room were separate sitting and dining rooms, each about the same size as the living room. All of these rooms' hardwood floors were a rich, dark brown.

The dining room led into a kitchen that took up the rear of the house. On the kitchen's left wall sat a gas stove, sink, and icebox—the refrigerator of that time. People filled these containers with large blocks of ice to keep food and drinks cold. Near the rear of the kitchen's right wall, a set of stairs led to the basement and to the house's second floor bedrooms and third floor kitchenette.

Isadore and his siblings likely ran through the kitchen's back door and bounced down the steps into a fenced-in, grass-filled yard. The kids must have wondered why their yard looked like a pebble, a tiny afterthought compared to the sprawling acres on their Raymond farm. Yet this bite-sized plot of city land, and the house that sat on it, suited Isadore's mother and father just fine. "Mr. Durham had insisted that he wanted his children to have access to the whole house, the basement and the yard," Chanie recalled. "His previous experience in Chicago had taught him that landlords [were] not always anxious to have children play in the backyard, even though they pay rent to live in the building."[11]

Once they re-entered the house, Chanie guided her children up to the second floor. She told them that for a short time they could use only two of that floor's four bedrooms. The home's white owner still lived there with her daughter, although they were preparing to leave.[12] Many whites reacted to the waves of black migrants flowing into Chicago with a definitive action. They moved—distancing themselves as much as possible from the perceived threat of these new residents.

Sociologists St. Clair Drake and Horace R. Cayton reported in *Black Metropolis*, their classic study of Negro life in Chicago, that unscrupulous realtors sometimes artificially created panic among whites with the rallying cry, "The Negroes are coming." Headlines in local newspapers further inspired white flight by blaring:

Half a Million Darkies from Dixie Swam to the North to Better Themselves; or *2,000 Southern Negroes Arrive in Last Two Days (Stockyards Demand for Labor Cause of Influx)*[13]

Once white Chicagoans moved, realtors increased rents, even for deteriorating buildings.

In contrast, Chanie watched her children explore their sturdy, well-maintained home. Now in the last trimester of another pregnancy, Chanie was happy but exhausted. She had been in Chicago since mid-April 1923, staying with her husband's relatives while she learned how to navigate the city.[14] At Cook County Hospital, Chanie secured prenatal care for the baby boy who would be born in November. And every day that she could, she searched for just the right home and schools for her children.

In her search, Chanie joined thousands of Southern-born black Americans who sought housing in or near the South Side area that would alternatively become known as Chicago's Black Metropolis, Black Belt, or Bronzeville. Reportedly, Negro journalist James Gentry coined the Bronzeville name to describe the area where the vast majority of black Chicagoans lived.[15] Gentry believed that bronze best described the skin color of Negro residents. The Bronzeville term gained traction when the *Chicago Defender* sponsored a "Mayor of Bronzeville" campaign, honoring prominent Negro residents during the early 1930s.[16]

By the time Isadore and his family settled into their new hometown, a little more than 109,000 blacks lived in Chicago—a 148 percent increase from the previous decade, when only 44,000 Negroes called themselves Chicagoans.[17] However, even in the North, Jim Crow segregation relegated black Americans to prescribed sections of town—areas that generally had lost the luster or prestige of a prior era. Although Chicago's meatpacking houses, railroad yards, nearby steel mills, and other industries provided jobs with comparatively high wages for blacks, affordable and adequate housing was hard to find. New construction had essentially ceased during the World War I years, spawning the large number of run-down tenements and haphazardly partitioned apartment buildings that defined Chicago's black neighborhoods.[18]

One of the famous black writers whose work an older Isadore Durham would study and learn from was fellow Mississippian Richard Wright.[19] Wright had moved to Chicago during the late 1920s, and through the biting prose of his book, *12 Million Black Voices*, Wright described the deplorable living conditions Negroes endured. He particularly decried Chicago's kitchenettes. Profit-hungry landlords, or the "Bosses of the Buildings," as Wright crowned them, might take a seven-room apartment and cut it up into seven small, one-room kitchenettes.[20] Each of these tiny units contained a small gas stove and sink. "Hence," Wright wrote,

> the same apartment, for which white people—who can get jobs anywhere and who receive higher wages than we—pay $50 a month, is rented to us for $42 a week! And because there are not enough houses for us to live in, because we have been used to sleeping several in a room on the plantations in the South, we rent these kitchenettes and are glad to get them.[21]

But Isadore's parents were more fortunate than fellow black Southerners who arrived in Chicago with their few prized possessions and little money. Curtis and Chanie used most of their life savings, about $1,200, as a down payment toward the purchase of their South Side home at 419 East Forty-Eighth Place.[22] They negotiated a contract with the owner to lease the house with an option to buy, an unusual arrangement during the 1920s. Slowly, Curtis and Chanie chipped away at their contract until the house—with its ten rooms, useable basement, and backyard—became theirs during the mid-1940s.[23]

Isadore's new home stood near a wide thoroughfare, a tree-lined, six-lane road called Grand Boulevard—known today as Dr. Martin Luther King Jr. Drive. Wealthy, middle-class, and working-class whites of Irish, Scottish, English, and German descent populated the Grand Boulevard neighborhood's elegant mansions and stately apartment buildings. Also, black Americans accounted for about one-third of the neighborhood's seventy-six thousand residents.[24]

Isadore's block—a short street that dead-ended into Vincennes Avenue from Grand Boulevard—was an eclectic mix of freestanding and attached single-family houses and apartment buildings. Just about every day, Isadore and his family watched as street venders on horse-drawn wagons hawked their goods.[25] A milkman delivered bottles of nonhomogenized milk each morning while a hodgepodge of other venders sold bread, fifty-pound blocks of ice for iceboxes, as well as fruits and vegetables. "Meat, chicken, eggs, and other produce could be purchased at the corner store," Isadore's brother Caldwell recalled. "Chickens were chosen alive and beheaded on the spot. You did the plucking at home." Before dusk, a city employee lit the gas lamps that illuminated each street at night.[26]

Chanie and Curtis knew that they would never be able to afford their ninety-dollar monthly rent without help. So like thousands of other transplanted Southerners, they took in boarders. The Durham family lived on the first floor, renting the second-floor bedrooms and attic kitchenette to a variety of short- and long-term tenants.[27]

• • •

Turning right from their front door on East Forty-Eighth Place, Isadore, Clotilde, Winifred, and later younger brothers Caldwell and Earl could easily walk the three blocks to the Frances E. Willard Elementary School.[28] The school had a predominately white student body when Isadore and his older siblings first walked under the school's transom.[29] Yet as tens of thousands of Negro Southerners poured into Chicago, Bronzeville's boundaries slowly pushed farther south and east.[30] Therefore, by the time Isadore graduated from Willard in 1931, the school and his neighborhood essentially had become all-black.[31]

Bronzeville's expansion could be contentious. A few homes and churches were fire bombed or vandalized as blacks moved into previously all-white neighborhoods. Some property owners and real estate developers employed restrictive covenant practices—agreements designed to prevent Negroes from renting or owning units in certain areas of the city.[32]

Upon their arrival in Chicago, Isadore's sister Marie was old enough to enroll in the overwhelmingly white and highly regarded Hyde Park High. The school sat three miles and two bus rides southeast of the Durham home. In light of the Chicago Board of Education's districting rules, Marie should have attended Wendell Phillips High—the one public high school then open to Negroes on the

South Side. However, education scholar Michael W. Homel determined that years earlier, white Grand Boulevard residents complained about having to send their children to the increasingly black Phillips. The city's school board responded by making Willard Elementary a feeder school to Hyde Park High.[33]

Willard continued sending its graduates to Hyde Park High even after the neighborhood surrounding Willard became black. Isadore and his sisters all attended Hyde Park High as a result. But in 1935, the board of education assigned Willard graduates to a newly built school, christened the Jean Baptiste Point Du Sable High School—named in honor of the black man who settled Chicago.[34] Caldwell would be the only one of Isadore's siblings to attend this all-black school.

C.G., Isadore's oldest brother, planned on joining Marie at Hyde Park High. C.G. and his father had arrived in Chicago in mid-November 1923, just in time to celebrate the birth of the family's newest member, Earl. But since the academic year had already begun, the only school that accepted C.G. was the increasingly overcrowded, all-black Wendell Phillips High.[35]

Isadore's father found work as a laborer in a large printing plant. But Curtis often juggled his daytime job with a second one at night to support his family. "His influence was quite a bit in terms of the demonstration of discipline and consistency and doing the right thing," Isadore's youngest brother Earl explained. Their father didn't smoke or drink, and while Curtis was not a particularly talkative or demonstrative man, Clotilde and her brothers agreed that he provided the stability the family needed. When he carved out free time, Curtis took his children to play in the lush Washington Park nearby. He also handed out gold coins to each of his children on their birthdays.[36]

Given Chicago's high cost of living, money was tight in the Durham household even before the Great Depression era. Without the formal training the Chicago Board of Education required, Chanie could not work as a teacher in her new city. Instead, she stayed home, raising her children and managing their boarders. To help their parents, Isadore and his siblings found after-school jobs. Isadore had a paper route.[37] He delivered copies of the *Pittsburgh Courier*, a black weekly that appealed to readers throughout the country. As he moved through the black world around him, Isadore earned money and witnessed the growth and the decay of this bustling city within a city.

Isadore often frequented Bronzeville's main street. Like One Hundred Twenty-Fifth Street in New York's Harlem or U Street in Washington, D.C., Forty-Seventh Street was black Chicago's business and cultural hub. By the late 1920s the majestic, newly built Regal Theater and the popular Savoy Ballroom held court near the corner of Forty-Seventh Street and South Parkway—the new name for Grand Boulevard. Black South Siders could catch the latest movies and be entertained by legendary Negro performers on the Regal stage. Or they could dance the night away at the Savoy.[38] Popular lore held that if a person stood on the corner of Forty-Seventh and South Parkway long enough, he or she could see everyone who was anyone in the black community while catching up with friends and family.[39] Forty-Seventh Street was a magnet for activity, and Isadore got caught up in the street's kinetic energy.

At home, Isadore proved to be as mischievous as ever. Each of the Durham children had regular household chores, and Isadore always found ways to shirk his. "Izzy was supposed to wash dishes one night and I would wash the next night," Clotilde remembered. "He would soak the dishes and put them in the oven or anyplace he could find to hide them. Mother would find them, blame me and because I was the oldest, she'd make me wash them."[40] Isadore and Clotilde fought over his actions—a sibling rivalry that lasted for years.

As Isadore approached his teen years, his left leg started bothering him. His family initially chalked up his discomfort to growing pains.[41] When the pain intensified, Chanie took her son to a doctor. The physician's treatment, however, didn't help. Older sister Marie, then studying to be a nurse, stepped in and took Isadore to an orthopedic specialist. Finally, his condition was properly diagnosed as osteomyelitis, a chronic infection that can affect the bones in children's legs or arms. The doctor put Isadore's leg in a cast and told him that it might have to stay put for months or years.[42]

Isadore was crestfallen—although his condition paved the way for his future writing career. Exiled to nonphysical, homebound activities, he turned to the radio. By the end of the 1920s, radio was fast becoming the most popular mass medium in the country. Just as later generations treated television, families gathered around their radio sets to enjoy their favorite shows. Since radio programs were free—after you purchased the receiver—it was "enough to create a tremendous nationwide boom," broadcast historians Christopher Sterling and John Kittross observed.[43]

Isadore and thousands of other Chicagoans tuned to local stations like WMAQ, WGN, and WLS. But Negro listeners realized that radio's music, variety, and talk shows largely ignored them. "For African Americans, radio followed the well-trodden course established by mainstream theaters and motion pictures," author Mel Watkins asserted. "There was almost no acknowledgement of the ferment in urban centers, of the Harlem Renaissance, of blacks' struggle for equality or the repressive measures amassed against that struggle."[44] Still, Isadore was thrilled when he heard the latest arrangements of the Fletcher Henderson and Duke Ellington big bands or other broadcasts that occasionally featured Negro musicians.

Comedy eventually became "the most consistently popular form of programming in radio," historian J. Fred MacDonald noted.[45] Isadore was ten years old when the show that evolved into the most popular, and controversial, comedy in the history of radio made its debut on WMAQ in early 1928.[46] *Amos 'n' Andy* was such a hit in Chicago that the NBC network broadcast it nationwide the following year. *Amos 'n' Andy* "was, in effect," author Mel Watkins wrote, " a comic, black-voice soap opera that, like minstrelsy, allowed America obliquely to scrutinize and laugh at its own problems."[47] The comedy's main characters, Amos Jones and Andrew H. Brown, were Southern-born blacks who had migrated north. Two white vaudevillians, Charles J. Correll and Freeman F. Gosden, created and voiced Amos, Andy, and their motley crew of supporting characters.

Amos 'n' Andy contained the usual minstrel stereotypes. Its Negro characters were ignorant, naïve, ne'er-do-wells who regularly butchered the English language. Still, the show apparently resonated with white *and* black listeners because it "humorously mirrored the plight of the nation's common man, caught in the transformation from an agrarian society to a complex urban one," Mel Watkins noted.[48] So many listeners tuned into *Amos 'n' Andy's* fifteen-minute broadcasts each weekday evening that movie theaters interrupted their screenings to play the show.[49] The comedy inspired a national listening frenzy that would not be replicated until *The Bill Cosby Show* sitcom similarly captivated TV audiences—particularly black viewers—during the mid-1980s.

Sitting at home, Isadore had plenty of opportunity to hear *Amos 'n' Andy* broadcasts. This show and others with stereotypical Negro characters inspired Isadore in later years to create more realistic, nuanced black characters who spoke out against injustice and inequality.

Because of his limited mobility, Isadore also read constantly—and he didn't discriminate.[50] Encyclopedias, newspapers, magazines, and, of course, books were all nutrients in Isadore's literary diet. He loved the characters that inhabited Lillian Hellman's *The Little Foxes* and all of Charles Dickens's novels.[51] Isadore's literary excursions also led him to the story of Richard I, England's twelfth-century warrior king often referred to as Richard the Lionheart [*Coeur de Lion*] or Richard the Lionhearted. King Richard I was a brilliant military strategist, best known for his exploits during the so-called "Third Crusade"—the battle to recapture the city of Jerusalem from Muslim control during the late 1100s.[52]

During his teens, Isadore started sporadically calling himself Richard.[53] His siblings speculated that he must have been thinking about Richard the Lionheart when he picked that name. "But of course to the family he was always just Izzy," Clotilde said. Isadore once told his sister that he didn't really like his birth name. Clotilde was not sure if kids teased him about his real name, and she wondered if his adoption of the Richard moniker was in part a response to such ribbing.[54]

• • •

Like millions of other Americans, the Durham family eventually found themselves struggling in a harsh new economic reality when the relative prosperity of the early to mid-1920s disappeared by the end of the decade. Former U.S. Treasury Secretary David Kennedy once told writer Studs Terkel that throughout the 1920s "about 600 banks a year" closed, and that between 1929 and 1930 bank closings "got into the thousands."[55] A February 1929 *Pittsburgh Courier* editorial suggested that with America's deteriorating economic conditions, "a snug little bank account . . . preferably in a Negro bank" would be a "real life-saver" before winter and growing unemployment "arrive simultaneously."[56] However, the Binga State Bank, Chicago's once prosperous black-owned financial institution, also failed in 1930.[57]

The stock market crash of October 29, 1929, had caused a tsunami of economic destruction. Many Americans lost their jobs, life savings, and homes. Even their dreams seemed to evaporate as employment rates dropped to depths the country had never before seen. Economists estimated that the country's unemployment rate hovered around 25 percent. In Chicago's black neighborhoods, unemployment estimates ranged between 30 and 50 percent.[58]

"We were always poor in Chicago," Clotilde Durham Smith said. "The Depression was just another continuation as far as I know." For a time, Curtis Durham lost his main job. He eventually found other work,[59] yet fear and insecurity reigned. People didn't know whether they would be able to find work, how long any job might last, or if their wages would cover expenses. Fortunately, Isadore's mother was hired as a night-shift cook for the South Side's Jackson Park Hospital. The older Durham children pitched in as well. C.G. established a dry cleaning and tailor shop in the basement of the Durham home. Marie worked as a registered nurse at Provident Hospital, the facility founded by renowned Negro surgeon Dr. Daniel Hale Williams. Winifred and Clotilde took care of other people's children to earn money.[60]

When Isadore's cast finally came off, he could not wait to get active. He jumped into a sport that had long fascinated him, one that demanded physical strength, agility, and mental toughness: boxing. In 1931 Isadore joined the Savoy Athletic Club (SAC), located a few blocks from his home. He would later write in an unpublished essay that the SAC "furnished many of the headline prize fighters from Chicago" for the citywide and regional tournaments of the Golden Gloves, Catholic Youth Organization, and National Amateur Athletic Association.[61]

"My father [thought] he took up fighting so he could beat me!" Clotilde laughingly recalled.[62] More likely, the sport fueled Isadore's desires for fame and fortune. "I used to run around the park with him in the morning when he was in training. He was going to be the world champion," younger brother Earl said.[63]

Amateur boxers could not earn money from their fights. Yet these young contenders did receive "expense" money. "Oft times this 'expense money' constitutes a large sum," Durham wrote, "but usually it varies from only two to six dollars for a fight. To boys from the slums, this seems like adequate compensation for nine minutes of fighting."[64] One of the SAC's best boxers was a Negro lad named Vern Patterson. Perhaps inspired by this young fighter's "clever and classy style," Isadore briefly adopted Patterson's first name as his own a few years later,[65] introducing himself to new friends as Vern Durham and using the name in bylines on some of his early poems.[66]

Durham trained hard in the Savoy Athletic Club's gym at Forty-Ninth Street and South Indiana Avenue. Fighting as Richard Durham, he won his first fights. "He thought it was kind of easy," Earl Durham remembered. By early 1934, sixteen-year-old Isadore/Richard had developed into a fine, 135-pound welterweight contender and qualified for the Golden Gloves tournament annually sponsored by the *Chicago Tribune*. On February 25, 1934, the *Tribune* reported that 312 boxers from 39 teams would fight the next evening. Twenty thousand screaming fans usually jammed into the Chicago Stadium Arena for Golden Gloves matches.[67] Durham planned on standing in front of the cheering throngs as one of the tournament's victors.

However, Durham's opponent, Bob Johnson from the Vincennes Club, had other ideas. "The guy beat the hell out of him," Earl Durham recalled, smiling. "He came home that night and said there must be a better way. He lost a tooth and everything."[68] That fight was probably Durham's last. No records document subsequent bouts, and both Earl and Caldwell said that their brother's boxing career was short lived. But Durham's love for boxing and respect for the men who practiced the sport endured—eventually playing a major role in the writing life Durham would pursue.

Just about the time Isadore had started training at the Savoy Athletic Club, he entered Hyde Park High. The school sat on the edge of the tony Hyde Park neighborhood. From the school's location on Stony Island Avenue and Sixty-Second Street, students could walk just a few blocks to the shores of Lake Michigan or to the campus of the prestigious University of Chicago. Isadore, his three older sisters, and just a few other Negro students, including a girl named Gwendolyn Brooks, attended Hyde Park High. Brooks would go on to become the first black awarded a Pulitzer Prize, earning the honor in 1950 for her poetry collection, *Annie Allen*.[69] But during the early 1930s, Brooks and other Negro students at Hyde Park High received an icy reception from their white counterparts. "I realized that they were a society apart, and they really made you feel it," Gwendolyn Brooks reflected. "None of them would have anything to do with you."[70]

Isadore rebelled. "In high school he was kinda incorrigible," Earl Durham said. "As a matter of fact, now you would call him a delinquent." Isadore started skipping classes. In the evening, he stayed out later than he should have and offered entertaining if implausible explanations about how he acquired items he brought home that his parents hadn't purchased.[71] He was a wonderful storyteller—although his family had to wonder just how many of those stories were true.

One day, Isadore's questionable extracurricular activities caught up with him. School authorities caught him stealing from a classmate's locker. No one in the family knew exactly what Chanie said to her wayward son in a long, private conversation they had once they returned home. She may have appealed to Isadore's sense of reason and high intellect. Perhaps she cajoled and threatened him. Whatever transpired between mother and son, Clotilde and Earl said that their brother did a 180-degree about-turn after that discussion. Earl speculated that Isadore might have wanted to get caught so that he could get away from whomever he was running with at the time. When his siblings asked their mother how she got Isadore to straighten up, Chanie simply attributed his turnaround to God.[72]

Chanie and her husband were religious, spiritually curious souls. Like most black Southerners, these Christian parents brought their religious beliefs with them to the North. Chanie and Curtis joined well-established though separate Baptist churches. They were probably drawn to churches that suited their personalities.[73] Chanie preferred Pilgrim Baptist Church where Thomas A. Dorsey—the pianist/composer recognized as the father of gospel music—organized and led the large congregation's first gospel chorus.[74] Curtis preferred Ebenezer Baptist Church, Dorsey's first religious home in Chicago.[75] Historian Michael Harris found that many black migrants flocked to Pilgrim, Ebenezer, and other huge "old line" black churches "because these institutions had social programs that included aid for settling in Chicago and for finding employment."[76]

Isadore's parents often took their children with them to their preferred churches. Later, Curtis and Chanie's spiritual quest led them to other worship homes. Curtis started attending the Eighth Church of Christ Science-Colored, an all-black Christian Science congregation.[77] During the mid-1930s Chanie was drawn into the cult-like web of the charismatic religious leader who called himself Father Divine. Born George Baker Jr. in 1876, Father Divine and his Peace Mission Movement developed a massive national following during the 1930s and 1940s. Devotees loved Father Divine's message that salvation was possible through hard work, positive thought, and integration. Father Divine also proclaimed *himself* to be God.[78]

Although Chanie and Curtis exposed their children to their evolving beliefs, they were never dogmatic about religion. According to Clotilde, her parents believed "that you tried to do unto people as you wished them (to do unto you). That was the tenet." Chanie and Curtis wanted their children to make their own informed decisions—religious or otherwise—based on exposure and education.[79]

Isadore never told his siblings whether he, like his mother, believed that a higher being informed his transformation. He did tell Clotilde that "there was so much he had to do and so little time to do it."[80] The energy he had plowed into truancy and thievery was now directed back into education. One of his regular haunts became the George Cleveland Hall Branch Library, located at Forty-Eighth Street and South Michigan Avenue, about five blocks from his home.

Nearly twelve hundred people jammed into Bronzeville's first public library on its January 18, 1932, opening day.[81] Chicagoan Vivian Gordon Harsh headed the branch. Harsh had made history eight years earlier when she became the first Negro librarian in the Chicago Public Library (CPL) system. She soon established a "Special Negro Collection" with books and other items documenting Negro history.[82] Now called the Vivian G. Harsh Research Collection, it is the largest archive of African American history and literature in the Midwest.[83]

Basically, the Hall Branch Library became Isadore's personal resource bank. "A section of the building was dedicated to fiction, and Isadore read everything in that section," Caldwell Durham remembered.[84] Actually, Isadore read as much as he could throughout the four dedicated reading rooms in the library named for prominent Negro physician Dr. George Cleveland Hall.[85] Eventually, three writers—Charles Dickens, Langston Hughes, and William Edward Burghardt Du Bois—emerged as Isadore's favorites. These men were prolific scribes who provided a powerful voice for the voiceless, the oppressed, the poor. Durham once told radio historian John Dunning that Dickens was "one of the greatest writers who ever lived" and that he "spent a lot of time studying Dickens" before getting into writing.[86] Dickens's ability to capture readers' attention quickly and draw them into his characters' world fascinated Durham; he believed that Dickens's novels were "almost like a piece of music" because they set "a tone . . . a mood for you" through recognizable characters like Oliver Twist, Ebenezer Scrooge, and Tiny Tim.[87]

In addition, Durham loved the humor and social commentary in Langston Hughes's poetry and short stories. "The writer is like the chemist," Durham told Dunning. "He has certain things that he puts in to make a thing taste sweet, bitter, sour or whatever. Consequently, he is in control of the characters."[88] Through the sometimes acidic, funny, or insightful observations of the characters he created, Langston Hughes, Durham believed, was a literary chemist of the highest order.

Finally, Durham was thoroughly taken with W. E. B. Du Bois's eloquent analysis. The young Durham and one of his best friends, Andrew Paschal, spent hours dissecting the noted black scholar's writings. "Just about everything [Du Bois] ever printed was part of the ideological base for much of Dick's stuff—and he passed that on to me," Earl Durham noted.[89] "If you want to know why we are having so much trouble [in America] now, read Du Bois," Earl said about the man who famously wrote in 1903, "The strange meaning of being black here at the dawning of the Twentieth Century . . . is not without interest to you, Gentle Reader: for the problem of the Twentieth Century is the problem of the color-line."[90]

· · ·

As Durham absorbed the insights of his favorite authors along with many other writers, he began expressing his thoughts on the printed page. His parents and siblings found out about his literary musings only after his first poems were published.[91] Durham once told an interviewer: "If I had to put my finger on the single most influential piece of writing in my career, it would be the children's parable I read when I was 14 years old." He was referring to Hans Christian Anderson's celebrated fairy tale and morality lesson, *The Emperor's New Clothes*. "It's the story of a little girl who, when everyone else was praising the emperor's new clothes, spotted the fact that he was naked," Durham explained. "That's what the writer's got to do. I've got to be like that little girl—see people naked, as they really are. And be willing to be naked myself."[92]

Here lies an interesting dichotomy in Durham's nature. On one hand, he could be very secretive. Several of his friends and colleagues thought he relished working and wielding power behind the scenes, in the shadows.[93] On the other hand, Durham could be extremely open and giving, allowing himself to be "naked," so to speak. He willingly offered astute advice while pursing his passions, and he encouraged others to do the same.[94] And as his desire to write increased, Durham searched for like-minded artists. A few writing groups and workshops existed on the South Side during this period, and although he never became a member, the philosophical approach of the South Side Writers Group clearly influenced him.

Novelist Richard Wright established this group of about twenty young writers in spring 1936. With Wright as the South Side Writers Group's fiery focal point, apprentice and published black writers gathered on a biweekly basis to read and critique each other's work. Regular members included playwright/sculptor Marion Perkins, poet Margaret Walker, and Durham's future brother-in-law, Robert Davis. Published authors Arna Bontemps, Frank Marshall Davis, and Fenton Johnson also attended.[95] Wright challenged group members to write about the "Negro masses" from a consciousness "informed by Marxism," Wright's biographer Hazel Rowley revealed.[96]

At the time, Wright was an active Communist Party member. As such, he embraced Marxism—the historical, economic, and social revolution theories developed during the 1800s by German philosopher Karl Marx. According to philosophy scholar Stanley Hook, Marx's doctrines did not "merely describe the phenomena of class society and class struggle." Instead, Hook noted, Marx's theories were "guides to a mode of action which he believed would forever eliminate class struggles from social life."[97]

Yet Richard Wright insisted that Marxism should only be a starting point. He wanted black writers to embrace the entirety of their literary heritage, including European, white American, and Negro influences. Wright presented those views to a broader audience in his article "Blueprint for Negro Writing," published in *New Challenge*, a 1937 journal Durham likely read.[98]

Scholar Robert Bone believed that the South Side Writers Group served as the creative nexus for what is now called the Black Chicago Renaissance. Between 1935 and 1950, black writers in the Windy City generated substantial literary output. Their creativity, some say, rivaled that of the Harlem Renaissance writers of the 1920s. Chicago black writers' attention to urban life, as seen through the prism of the Great Depression and Marxism, contrasted with the Southern folklore-centered writing of their Harlem Renaissance predecessors.[99]

Several of Durham's published poems reflected Richard Wright's suggested aesthetic. Durham examined the plight of the Negro "proletarian"—the Marxist term for a member of the working class—in his *Hell's Kitchen* and *Death in a Kitchenette* poems, published in the April 1938 editions of *New Masses* magazine and the *Chicago Defender*.[100] Seeking feedback about his writing, Durham audaciously sent several of his poems to Langston Hughes, even though he had never met the internationally recognized poet. Despite his hectic travel schedule, Hughes actually read Durham's work. In a belated September 1939 reply, Hughes wrote:

> This letter went to Paris with me, then to Hollywood, back to New York, and now to California again along with half a suitcase of unanswered mail that never seems to get any less. . . . I trust that you will forgive me for being so long in answering and returning your poetry. My comments are written on the margins. Some of the poems I liked. Certainly I think they show talent, and I hope that you will continue to write.[101]

In his sprawling, looping handwriting, Hughes added, "What a swell subject for tremendous poetry the South Side is! I want to live there sometime." He particularly liked Durham's *Death in a Kitchenette*:

If death had been time itself—
If death had been the landlord—
If death had known the way blindfolded
Upstairs to Joe Johnson's Kitchenette,
When the rent fell due
He could never have been more punctual;
But prayers and tears were the landlord's rent
When he met Mrs. Johnson and the six little Johnsons
"We were only here by the grace of God—
And the government," she moaned.
"Mostly the government," he mumbles,
And crawls to the next kitchenette
Like a vexed but well-fed roach.
Somebody is giving a riot of a party
In the house, in this room.
He knocks and thinks of Joe:
Joe ought to be glad
Even to go to hell:

He had it hard enough here.
Life had become a liability
And death was his greatest asset.
Still . . .
Pneumonia and death had cheated him
Out of two weeks' rent . . . [102]

"This [poem] is *good*," Hughes wrote. He encouraged Durham to "write a whole series of South Side poems." Hughes also liked *Hell's Kitchen*, Durham's broader take on ghetto life, although he told Durham to "tighten it up a bit—cut extra words."[103] Hughes showed Durham exactly what he meant in the following excerpt from *Hell's Kitchen:*

Durham's Version	Hughes' Edits

Some come and stare as if seeing
    an odd painting
	Some stare as if seeing
	    an odd painting

Done by a proletarian artist and
    call it a masterpiece:
	Done by a proletarian artist,
	    a masterpiece:

Noting the dark and dirty shading
    of rottening wood:
	Noting the dark, dirty shading
	    of rotting wood:

The tone of oily greasy windows	The tone of greasy windows[104]

"I hope that I shall have the pleasure of meeting you the next time I come to Chicago," Hughes wrote. He suggested that Durham read the poets Emily Dickinson, Walt Whitman, and Fenton Johnson, as well as Edgar Lee Masters's *Spoon River Anthology* and the *Bible* to help him develop his own style.[105]

Durham welcomed Hughes's advice. Building on this initial correspondence, the two men established a friendship that would last more than two decades. "Langston was an unusual kind of person," Durham reflected years later. "Much as he had to do and famous as he was then, he would spend all kinds of time with you, share contacts that he had with absolutely no competitiveness. . . . He liked the way I wrote, and the way I organized writing particularly."[106]

Durham loved the freedom of expression that poetry provided. "I think it's the highest form of writing," he once told a reporter.[107] Some of his first poems were published under his given name. But with each new missive, Durham used a different pen name. He was I. Vern Durham on some work, Vern Durham on others.[108] He had sent his poems to Langston Hughes as Vern Durham. In his reply, Hughes politely asked, "Are you a boy or a girl? Pardon, but I can't make out from your name."[109]

Perhaps in an attempt to be more definitive about his name and his creative strength, Durham started using Richard as his pen name. By early 1938 the twenty-

FIGURE 4. Richard Durham in his early twenties, during either the late 1930s or early 1940s. Courtesy of Clarice Durham.

year-old published a few poems as Isadore Richard Durham.[110] His byline later morphed into Richard I. Durham. Finally, he simply signed his work Richard Durham. He adopted the Richard moniker in his personal life as well—although some family members and childhood friends continued to call him either Izzy or Vern.

Once Durham's relatives found out about his writing, they encouraged him. His oldest sister Marie became one of Richard's greatest cheerleaders. "She said he ought to write, and she manipulated the household so that he had a private room in the house," Earl Durham recalled.[111] That "private room" was one of their home's second-floor bedrooms. Marie bought her brother a shiny black Royal manual typewriter, and Richard taught himself to type. He improved his skills by challenging anyone "who could type faster than he," his sister Clotilde said. "He would always win. I think he always wanted to excel in whatever he did." Durham often stayed up late, writing well into the night. When he took breaks, he'd head down to the kitchen to eat snacks.[112] This habit added pounds to Durham's frame, weight he would have trouble keeping off throughout his life.

During the mid to late 1930s, Durham enrolled in a class or two at Northwestern University in Evanston, one of Chicago's leafy northern suburbs.[113] Money continued to be extremely tight in the Durham household, and he looked for work that would enable him to cover tuition. He eventually found a job at a cleaning plant where he stood on a floor that was often coated with some kind of chemical solution. Dick's left foot soon began throbbing with pain, and his leg was cast bound—again.[114]

Richard decided that there must be a better way to make a living. Luckily for him and millions of other Americans, the jobless despair caused by the Depression led the Franklin D. Roosevelt administration to create federal agencies with "relief" programs designed to revive America's economy and get people back to work. One of those federal agencies was called the Works Progress Administration (WPA).

Richard Durham decided to give it a try.

CHAPTER 4

Radio Beckons

Dawn Patrol

Night creeps over the city;
Streets spangle with kilowatt pearls,
Lights splatter over seas of shadows
Damning the flood of darkness.
Drunken night,
A hobo bowed over a bar of time,
Brooding over a black bottle of stars
Blinking like beer bubbles,
Soon comes the police patrol of dawn,
Night slowly staggers away
And then the day[1]

—Richard Durham, 1941

Richard had been warned.

He had heard reports about endless lines at the local relief station, and he was told to get there by 7:30 A.M.[2] Instead, he got up hours earlier on a late-December day in 1938 and hobbled to the station. Richard's left foot was still in a cast.

Durham arrived at the relief station at 6 A.M. What he saw and experienced so moved him that he recorded his impressions in an essay titled, "A Day At the Relief Station." "Every available space in front of the building was filled," Durham recalled.

Snow covered the heads of some of the waiting clients, and a frigid wind blew off Lake Michigan. "Most of the people had on light coats or no coats at all. I doubt if many of them had coats to put on," he wrote. Durham found himself squeezed between an old man and a woman he described as large and talkative. When the relief station opened at 8:30 A.M., the doorman blocked this woman's entry, and "she had a splendid curse vocabulary and used it on him freely," Durham reported.[3]

Three crowded lines snaked through the station. One contained people needing welfare services; another was for elderly pensioners. Durham took up residence near the end of the WPA line. Created by the federal government in 1935, the WPA funded construction and other public works projects, as well as programs for writers, musicians, and theater and visual artists.[4] From the start, the arts programs—officially called Federal One—almost drowned in controversy. Detractors believed that federal support of the arts wasted taxpayers' money. Supporters argued that Federal One projects were essential for the documentation and preservation of American culture during the Great Depression.[5]

Back in the relief station, Durham calculated that his line moved about one-and-a-half feet an hour.[6] He finally reached the relief clerk's desk around 4 P.M. and nervously began his job pitch. Suddenly, he said, "[the clerk] stopped me and pointed to my crutches and cast-bound foot," Durham said. "God! I had forgotten all about that." He explained that he could do all kinds of work even though he could not walk. The clerk was not convinced. Durham begged and pleaded, and "lied," he said, "to the best of my ability that my crippled foot would be only a short temporary matter, and that soon after I had a job it would probably be well anyway."[7]

"Very, very sorry," the clerk said in effect, "but er . . . perhaps there could be the possibility of an interview tomorrow."[8] The clerk handed Durham an appointment card and he slowly limped out of the building. "For the first time in my 21 years, I felt beaten," Durham wrote. Despite his despair, Durham returned to the relief station, intent on securing employment with the WPA-funded Illinois Writers' Project (IWP). He filled out the form requiring proof that applicants could write and were qualified to receive relief. Durham knew he would make the grade on both accounts.

By the time Durham applied to the WPA, several of his poems had been published in the *Chicago Defender* newspaper, as well as in *Youth* and *New Masses* magazines.[9] The *Pittsburgh Courier* had published one of his essays, and his book review of Dale Carnegie's bestseller *How to Win Friends and Influence People* appeared in the September 1938 issue of a periodical called *Northwestern Review*.[10]

Durham's book review provides a glimpse of his wry sense of humor and developing analytical skills. He commented on the "fertility" of a book market that found financial success with books written in the "how-to-be-a success-in—one-easy-lesson" vein. "If any of the patent panaceas printed have the desired psychological effect on even a small percentage of readers," Durham wrote, "the nation has nothing to worry about: soon we will be swamped with geniuses, creators, an abundance of pleasant people, and men who use every minute of their time effectively."[11]

During a time when many Americans desperately searched for work, got food from relief bread lines, and struggled to find places to live, Durham lamented that Carnegie's tome "outsold every book published within the current year. That points to a sad low for intellectual America."[12] Richard was not at all impressed with Carnegie's recommendations to avoid arguments, be a good listener, and remember names, concepts Durham believed any normal nine-year-old possessed.

Durham conceded that Carnegie's book contained "many points of common sense scattered throughout." But he added that America had not yet "reached that social acme where by reading some simple examples, no matter how salable they are, it is likely to be of any help in solving our social and business problems." A reader could almost see Durham winking as he concluded: "Now that reminds me. There is a fellow around the corner who has been owing me six dollars for some time. I'll go right over, slap his back, call his name and lo and behold! With a smile he will hand over my money, thanks to Dale Carnegie. Truly this is a wonderful age!"[13]

Armed with copies of his published work and proof that he could type—another WPA requirement—Durham submitted his application. As 1939 dawned, the WPA's Illinois Writers' Project hired him. In the IWP's downtown headquarters at 433 East Erie Street near Lake Michigan, Durham rubbed shoulders with published authors such as Arna Bontemps, Nelson Algren, and Jack Conroy. He also joined the ranks of up-and-coming writers like future Nobel Prize–winner Saul Bellow and future Pulitzer Prize honoree Louis "Studs" Terkel.[14]

IWP supervisor Arna Bontemps believed that "no other writers' project in the country produced comparable Negro talent during the Depression."[15] As proof, Bontemps pointed to novelists Willard Motley and Frank Yerby, poet Margaret Walker, and budding anthropologist/choreographer Katherine Dunham. Each of these artists created significant work after their IWP tenure. And Bontemps was thoroughly impressed with Richard Wright, the man he called "the most typical as well as the most famous example of the Depression-bred WPA writer."[16]

During his time with the IWP, Wright authored essays about life on Chicago's black South Side while also turning out "rugged, fighting poems and thudding, belly-punching stories between Project assignments," Bontemps said.[17] Years later, Richard Wright enjoyed international acclaim for his searing novel *Native Son* and his compelling autobiography, *Black Boy.* Yet when Durham began working on his IWP assignments, Wright had already transferred to the Federal Writers' Project in New York.

Wherever the WPA writers worked and whatever their race, their writing served a specific purpose. As conceived by federal officials, the fruits of the writers' projects work would be published in American Guidebooks—a series of volumes from each state "in which history and tradition are blended with present-day effort and achievement," IWP director John T. Frederick explained.[18] The WPA Guide to Illinois, published in 1939, was considered to be one of the best-written state guidebooks.[19]

Under Arna Bontemps's supervision, the IWP also undertook an ambitious The Negro In Illinois study, a comprehensive examination of black life throughout the state.[20] Richard Durham worked on a smaller, related study—The Negro Press in Chicago—designed to examine the city's past and present thirty-four black newspapers and eleven magazines.[21] Durham was assigned to author this study's "Don't Spend Your Money Where You Can't Work" chapter. This chapter borrowed its title from a similarly named antidiscrimination campaign waged by Chicago's Negro periodicals between 1929 and 1932.[22]

Durham had to be excited about focusing on the interconnectivity between race, economics, and media for his first IWP assignment. After abandoning his teenage delinquency phase, Durham studied under a high school teacher who introduced him to economic theories, sparking what would become a lifelong fascination with economics.[23]

On February 20, 1939, Durham limped to his first interview with Major Adam E. Patterson, editor-in-chief of the South Side Business and Professional Men's Review.[24] Durham interviewed other Negro publishers and/or editors and conducted additional research during the next few months.[25] By spring 1939—exact dates were not indicated in federal files—Durham had enough information to write his treatise. He began his twenty-nine-page "Don't Spend Your Money Where You Can't Work" chapter by declaring:

> The basic problem of life is living—finding ways and means of subsistence. The most telling and detrimental form of discrimination, consequently, is economic discrimination. . . . The issues raised by the Negro being the "last hired and the first fired" becomes crucial when one considers the movement of Negroes into direct competition with whites, the refusal of employers to pay Negroes the same wages for the same work, and the creation of artificial barriers to advancement.[26]

Durham determined that "editors of Bronzeville's journals have consistently urged its readers to patronize Negro enterprises, hoping to offset the growing unemployment by increasing Negro business." For example, in October 1920 the Chi-

cago Defender editorialized, "When you patronize your own merchants you are building a solid foundation for yourself and the future generation to stand on."[27] Durham detailed how earlier and later Negro newspapers echoed this sentiment.

Bronzeville's periodicals also praised federal entities like the WPA and civil service agencies along with private employers like the Walgreen Drug Company and F. W. Woolworth stores when they positively responded "to the demand for job representation by colored workers," Durham wrote. He noted, however, that the Negro press criticized discrimination in the city's labor unions: "Some of the strongest white labor leaders have failed to see that one group of workers forced to work for subsistence wages forces all laborers towards the same level."[28]

Although a few labor unions enjoyed the support of Chicago's Negro press, the same could not be said for Communist labor organizers. According to Durham, "The Communists, because of their preoccupation with the proletariat, have invariably attracted the attention of the press—although at first the reaction resulted in dislike and antagonism rather than any alliance."[29] Durham thought that the Negro press seemed to mimic the white press's anti-Communist attitudes. For instance, the outspoken *Chicago Whip* once editorialized:

> The Communists have framed a program of social remedies which can not fail to appeal to the hungering, jobless millions, who live in barren want, while everywhere about them is evidence of restricted plenty in the greedy hands of the few . . . Food, shelter and clothing, [and] adequate employment are the only answer to the challenge of Communism.[30]

However, Durham did not reveal in his chapter that the Communist Party's ongoing efforts to bring working-class people together to eliminate economic and social injustice actually spoke to him. Given his earlier exposure to Marxist thought, Durham joined the Communist Party during the late 1930s.[31] He likely found the party's aggressive attempts to stop housing evictions, organize workers, and integrate labor unions to be what historian Mary Helen Washington called "beacons of light" for Chicago's struggling black population.[32]

In "Don't Spend Your Money Where You Can't Work," Durham also noted that the Franklin Roosevelt administration and its New Deal initiatives presented black Americans with a dilemma. Historically, most Negroes aligned themselves with the party of Abraham Lincoln—the Republican Party. President Roosevelt was a Democrat. Negroes and their newspapers had to, in Durham's estimation, "either give up [Republican] party loyalty or continue the attack upon the Democratic Party by pointing out inadequacies existing within the New Deal agencies." Durham felt that the *Chicago Bee* expressed the prevailing attitude of the Bronzeville press toward Roosevelt's New Deal policies when it declared, "The New Deal Seems a New Day as Well as New Methods."[33]

Durham noted that some Americans worried about what might happen if the fascism practiced by Hitler's and Mussolini's governments ever reached American soil. "For Bronzeville inhabitants," Durham opined, "fascism is not 'coming,' it is already here and Negroes are looking for a time when it will 'leave.' The economic position into which [Negroes] are forced makes a mockery of American democracy." Durham concluded his chapter by pointing out that the Negro press was "the strongest advocate of economic rights" in America and that Bronzeville's periodicals were "the advance guard in the warfare against economic injustice."[34]

. . .

In addition to his *Negro Press in Chicago* assignment, Richard critiqued articles published in mainstream periodicals about wartime censorship and other civil-liberties issues.[35] While working on those critiques, Richard became intrigued by what he saw taking place in one section of the Illinois Writers' Project headquarters. Each week a group of men and women sat around a conference table, animatedly talking, laughing, and arguing. "We were critical of one another," writer Studs Terkel recalled, "but there was a comradeship there."[36]

This lively group was the IWP's radio division—a unit where writers created scripts for local radio dramas with titles like *Postal Oddities, Moments of Genius*, and *Legends of Illinois*. Radio division writers also adapted, for broadcast, classic tales by artists such as Anton Chekhov and Edgar Allan Poe. The IWP's radio unit operated "with an efficiency and zeal that was often lacking in other departments in the Project," claimed former WPA administrator Jesse Mangione.[37] From its birth in 1939 through its demise nearly four years later, about forty-seven writers contributed all types of dramatic scripts.[38] The project's radio unit "was about the only project at the time that had deadlines, direction, immediate production," scriptwriter Sam Ross explained. "We were linked to the community. I learned my dramatic craft there. So did the others."[39]

From his supervisory vantage point, Arna Bontemps took notice when two of the IWP's youngest Negro writers, Richard Durham and Robert Lucas, "began playing around with the radio unit and trying their hand at scripts." In Bontemps's opinion, "radio's appeal to the writer is evidently something like the theater's to the dramatist. Neither Lucas nor Durham ever recovered."[40] Nor would Durham have wanted to recover from his growing infatuation with radio scriptwriting or from his close friendships with fellow scriptwriters Bob Lucas, Studs Terkel, and David Peltz.

Durham wrote his first radio script, dated June 23, 1940, for WAAF's *Legends of Illinois* series.[41] Durham dramatized Mormon leader Joseph Smith's attempts to establish a settlement in an Illinois swampland during the early 1800s. This script demonstrated that Durham had much to learn about writing for the ear.

He created far too many characters to keep track of in a fifteen-minute production. His dialogue was wordy, and he presented background information in far too obvious a manner.

But Durham learned quickly. He benefited from the radio division's weekly critiquing sessions, and his scripts—about ten of them, based on evidence from WPA files—improved.[42] His dramas documented the contributions of men as varied as General Benedict Arnold, French sculptor Auguste Rodin, and painter Winslow Homer.[43]

One script Durham wrote in February 1941 for WGN's *Great Artists* series displayed flashes of the compelling style that eventually defined his writing. Produced in conjunction with curators from the Art Institute of Chicago, IWP writers, and actors from the Goodman Theater, WGN's series profiled famous artists or works of art exhibited at the institute. In "Goya: The Disasters of War," Durham cleverly reveals why Spanish painter Francisco Goya created his famous prints depicting the horrors of war. Durham's script starts in the middle of a crisis during the early 1800s:

> SOUND: (*Fade in insistent and frenzied rapping on door.*)
> ARMID: (*trying to control his voice*): Goya! Goya! (*Pause, knocking more insistent.*) Goya! Let me in. Let me in!
> SOUND: (*Troops running in the distance. Double-quick time.*)
> ARMID: (*Now knocking loudly and shouting*): Goya! It's Armid! Save me! Open the door! Open the door before they—(Breaks into groan as——)
> SOUND: (*Crack of gun from distance stops Armid's voice. Door opens quickly. Body slumps.*)[44]

Durham immediately establishes a sense of urgency and tension. Who is chasing Armid? How is he connected to Goya, and was Armid killed?

Soldiers from French Emperor Napoleon Bonaparte's army, then an invading force in Spain, quickly arrive at Goya's door. They insist on being let in to search for "an escaped prisoner"—Armid. Durham's Goya character humbly says that they'll find nothing in his studio except for a few pictures and paint. Just then, a soldier sees a puddle of blood on the floor. Goya responds:

> GOYA: (*Surprised.*) Blood? Where's any blood?
> CAPTAIN: Right there on the floor! (*Growls.*) Now don't try to hide anything or we'll take you to the hills with the rest of the prisoners.
> GOYA: That's not blood you see on the floor.
> CAPTAIN: (*Leering.*) Then what is it? Milk? What else makes red puddles in wartime but blood!
> GOYA: You men should know better: blood's your business. But I'm a painter—and I know paint when I see it. And that's red paint.[45]

Durham then pitches a curve ball, throwing in a detail that will take his soldier characters—and his radio audience—by surprise. Goya tells the soldiers to taste the "paint" on his floor:

> GOYA: If it's blood, it won't harm you. But red painter's coloring—I've known a man who died two minutes after it touched his lips. We'll find out in a minute what's on that floor.[46]

Goya's deception scares the soldiers. But their captain orders Goya to draw something with the red "paint." Goya obliges, although his depiction of Napoleon's troops as monsters enrages the captain. He makes Goya put the paintbrush in his mouth and laughs, telling Goya that he'll "never live to draw another picture like that again." The soldiers depart and Goya composes himself. He tells his friend that all is now safe. Armid contends that they are helpless in the face of the French invaders' power. However, Durham's Goya declares:

> GOYA: Look over there at that canvas. What do you see? A picture painted in your blood. I'm going to do what I've done all my life. . . . I want to paint the mobs trying to fight guns and cannons with sticks and clubs. . . . I want to paint the servants, the water-carriers, the wood cutters dying in the streets, slaughtered in the hill![47]

With this script, Durham was starting to find his dramatic voice—effectively using tension and release, plot twists and humor to capture listeners' attention. "Disasters of War" also highlighted a philosophy Durham would return to often in his work—that the socially conscious artist should provide a voice for the voiceless through his or her work.

• • •

When he wasn't working, Durham maintained an active social life. Many of his friends were culturally and politically active, including one of his buddies from an earlier poetry group, fellow IWP writer Robert Davis. Like Durham, Davis and his younger siblings Marguerite, Clarice, and Charles were transplanted Southerners. The Davis kids became Chicagoans after tuberculosis took the lives of their parents during the early 1930s. The children's maternal grandfather, Charles Robert Williams, brought his grandchildren to live with him in his Bronzeville home.[48] One of the children's aunts took care of their daily needs. But the siblings also looked up to and emulated their oldest brother, and Robert encouraged them to get involved in their Bronzeville community.

During summer 1941, Robert Davis's description of a progressive, Chicago-based organization called the National Negro Congress (NNC) sparked his sister Clarice's curiosity. Founded in 1936, the NNC committed itself, according to historian Mark Solomon, to mounting a "three-pronged" attack against injustice by creating an alliance between Negroes and the labor movement, bringing Negro and Communist groups together as a "broad front of struggle for civil rights," and fostering "international solidarity" against fascism.[49] The NNC boldly campaigned against lynching, voting restrictions, and employment inequalities.[50] The day Clarice visited the Congress's office, Richard Durham was there with her brother. Robert introduced Clarice to his friend.

Clarice thought that Richard, two years her senior, was "a nice, shy young man."[51] Durham was smitten. He asked the pretty, petite, honey-colored Clarice out on a date a few days later. The couple went to a beach party in nearby Indiana. But their first date on those sandy shores overlooking a sparkling Lake Michigan almost derailed their relationship before it could get started. "I think Dick felt that I invited him just to have an escort," Clarice recalled. "He didn't know anyone there and felt that I paid more attention to my friends than him. Of course I apologized to him. I was sorry that he felt slighted."[52] Fortunately, this first-date misstep didn't stop Clarice and Dick from wanting to see each other again.

They acted on that desire frequently.

"Our dates were dates where you didn't have to spend a lot of money," Clarice said. "We went rowing in Washington Park, we took long walks and we would go to the movies." Clarice and Dick joined the legions of other black Chicagoans who frequented the popular Regal Theater, one block from the Durham family home. Like the Apollo Theater in Harlem, the Howard Theater in Washington, D.C., and the Paramount Theater in Los Angeles, the Regal offered first-run movies and live stage shows to its Negro clientele.[53]

After about four or five months of dating, Clarice felt that their relationship was getting serious. "I was impressed with Dick's intelligence and the fact that he had a career going," Clarice said. "He was someone I wanted to be with and support, and we had common political and musical interests."[54] Clarice and Dick both loved jazz and shared a commitment to battling discrimination. So by winter 1942, Dick and Clarice knew they were in love. Dick asked Clarice to marry him that March. Clarice happily accepted. The couple applied for a marriage license and set an early May wedding date. "But Dick kind of got cold feet and keep putting the date off," Clarice said. "I was afraid that the marriage license would expire."[55]

Durham might have been concerned about his ability to support a wife. Based on reports about the relatively low pay scales in the Illinois Writers' and the Illinois Art Projects, Durham likely made between eighty-five and ninety-five dollars per month.[56] Yet conservative anti–New Dealers continued pushing for the elimination of the WPA arts programs—deemed to be, according to *Chicago Tribune* owner Robert McCormick, "full of boondoggling Communists."[57]

FIGURE 5. Enjoying a night out at the Club DeLisa in 1942 (from left to right): Phyllis Peltz, Earl Durham, Clarice Durham, David Peltz (Phyllis's husband and Richard's IWP co-worker), and Richard Durham. Courtesy of Clarice Durham.

As Richard Durham approached his twenty-fifth birthday, he may have wondered whether he was ready to start a family. But he pushed past his reservations. Clarice Davis and Isadore "Richard/Dick" Durham married on June 19, 1942.[58] The couple could not afford a big wedding, so they had an intimate ceremony in the minister's chambers of the Progressive Baptist Church on Forty-Eighth Street between South Michigan and South Wabash Avenues. "My brother Charles gave me away, and Dick's good friend Haywood Kirkpatrick was his best man," Clarice recalled.[59]

The newlyweds started their life together in a small, four-room apartment at 6204 South Parkway—the same apartment where Clarice had lived with her adult brothers and sister during the Depression. Clarice and Dick made sure they set aside time to socialize with their friends and some of Dick's WPA buddies in popular South Side nightclubs like the Rhumboogie and Club DeLisa.

Durham and his friends undoubtedly talked about and lamented the virulent political opposition and dwindling governmental funding that was decimating the WPA. Durham apparently left the Illinois Writers' Project a few months before it officially closed. Shortly after his departure, he sent a long, candid letter to his sister Clotilde, telling her that he had been struggling mightily. "For two solid months I was writing stuff and sending it out," Durham wrote. "Everything was going out and nothing [was] coming in."[60]

By the time this undated letter was written, probably during fall 1942, America was fully engaged in World War II. Thousands of men Durham's age and younger voluntarily joined or were drafted into the armed forces. Like his brother Caldwell, Richard was drafted into the army. But Durham's foot condition earned him a deferment, and he never served.[61]

In light of America's wartime hiring frenzy, "I could have gotten a job, a defense job or any kind of job, easily," Dick told Clotilde. But such work would have kept him from further honing his craft. "Come home tired, you flop down and go to bed and you don't write," Durham wrote. "Soon you've forgotten all about writing. The little you've learned slips away from you."[62] Dick told his sister that the day before he wrote to her, he had almost given up trying to find work as a writer. Clarice's salary from her full-time job with the State of Illinois Unemployment Compensation Office covered most household expenses. But Dick needed money to pay other bills, and reluctantly he borrowed fifteen dollars from his sister, Claudia Marie.

"Then it happened," he told Clotilde. "Just a couple of hours ago I got a notice from NBC saying that they bought one of my scripts. Wow! I said to myself I wouldn't write till I could have my head in the clear. It's [now] in the clear." Durham continued by encouraging Clotilde's desire to write. He believed that his sister, a chemist, had what it took to be a good writer:

> Good writing requires good thinking. . . . The attempt to define an incident, a mood, an atmosphere, a character, calls for as exacting a type of thinking as it is to work on a chemical problem. . . . And above all there's the matter of point. The point you try to make or to prove will determine what details you select. If your perspective is wrong, there'll certainly be certain details missing.[63]

Near the end of this letter, Durham confided that although he had been depressed, he was now eager to start writing for Chicago's NBC affiliate, WMAQ. The station produced a weekly program called *Art for Our Sake*, and during late fall 1942 Durham wrote scripts for this series that also profiled artists featured in Chicago's Art Institute.[64]

Art for Our Sake was renamed *At the Foot of Adams Street* in February 1943. It is unclear what prompted the name change, except that in downtown Chicago, Adams Street dead-ends into the Art Institute's gothic structure. Three of the four surviving scripts Durham wrote for this series reflected patriotic themes evident in many radio programs broadcast during the World War II years.[65] WMAQ staffer Homer Heck directed this series, and Heck would play a major role in Durham's life five years later.

Before then, however, Durham would face new literary challenges in his advocacy of freedom, justice, and equality for all.

CHAPTER 5

Scripts and Scoops

Democracy U.S.A.—"Dr. Dailey
and the Living Human Heart"

NARRATOR: First—a definition: "The Heart"; A hollow,
muscular organ, which, by contracting
rhythmically, keeps up the circulation of
the blood. (*Pause.*) But, when the heart is
punctured (a beat) . . . What then?

MUSIC: (*Tense—throbs with heartbeat.*)[1]

—Richard Durham, October 13, 1946

Richard Durham was more than a bit anxious.

As he moved through the early 1940s, he had yet to snag a full-time writing job. He became a typical freelancer—constantly on the prowl for that next writing opportunity, painfully aware that getting paid on a script-by-script basis could be a frustrating way to make a living.

With his decision to apply for one particular scriptwriting possibility, Durham's relatives and friends thought he was chasing folly. Everyone told him he didn't have "a chance in a million" to write for a show that had firmly lodged itself in American hearts, galloping into millions of households three nights a week on the NBC network. The show was *The Lone Ranger.*[2]

Beginning its radio run in 1933, *The Lone Ranger* followed the fictitious exploits of a former Texas Ranger who protected his countrymen in the untamed West of the late nineteenth century. Riding on his majestic white horse, Silver, this Ranger traversed the western plains, upholding the principles of freedom and justice for hard working, law-abiding citizens.[3] Yet in an America sharply divided by race, the prospect of a black man getting paid to write about a crusading, justice-seeking white man seemed far-fetched.

But Durham had logged long hours as a teenager sitting in front of the family radio, soaking up its dramatic and musical offerings.[4] And as a young adult scriptwriter, he had studied a wide range of radio programs. Durham probably viewed *The Lone Ranger* through pragmatic eyes, seeing it as a viable opportunity to earn a living with his craft.

Surely, the show's storytelling possibilities intrigued him. While he protected others, the Ranger character wore a facial mask to conceal his identity. It wouldn't have been lost on Durham that Negroes and other oppressed people often had to figuratively wear a mask—as Paul Laurence Dunbar's 1896 poem "We Wear the Mask" so famously posited—in order to hide their pain and anger about societal indignities.[5] And Durham probably appreciated the fact that the Ranger was assisted by a man of color, a knowledgeable American Indian named Tonto. Once the pair successfully neutralized the bad guys and saved the day, the Ranger belted out a hearty, "Hi-Yo, Silver! Away!" He and Tonto then rode off into the sunset amid a cloud of dust.[6]

Durham had to be pleased when he was hired, probably in July 1943, as a freelance writer for *The Lone Ranger.*[7] Years later, Durham told historian J. Fred MacDonald that he had "been coached in writing along the theory that writing is mainly a thing of exposing injustices. I don't care whether it's the *Bible* . . . Charles Dickens's work . . . or what." For Durham, a writer needed to have a clear sense of right and wrong "because that is what gets the passion out of the audience." Durham embraced "the old axiom: the closer you come to the truth, the more explosive the drama."[8]

Yet while Durham freelanced for *The Lone Ranger*, full-time employment remained elusive. His insecurity about his fluctuating income created what Clarice described as an "unsettled quality" in their relationship. Durham's ego may have been bruised because his wife's income sustained them. The reliability of Clarice's one-hundred-dollar monthly salary from her work with Illinois' Unemployment Compensation Office, compared with the amorphous nature of his own earnings, weighed heavily on Durham. So several times during the first years of their marriage, he left his wife. Telling Clarice that he "needed time to get himself together," Durham went to stay with friends.[9] He once was gone for six months.

One of Clarice's aunts moved in with her during this separation, providing the emotional and financial support she needed. Clarice even laughingly recalled that her aunt, assuming that Dick had left permanently, was upset when he returned home. During the couple's separations, however, Clarice worked hard "to keep the lines of communications open" with Dick because she didn't want their marriage to fail.[10]

In better times, Clarice loved Dick's attention to detail and gestures of kindness. "He would sometimes buy clothes for me that were colorful and a bit more daring than my often conservative taste would dictate," Clarice recalled. To her surprise, Clarice liked his choices. She also appreciated Dick's eye for decoration. "Once I selected some rather plain upholstery material for chairs in our kitchen," Clarice said. "Dick picked out more bold colors, a pretty red and blue fabric that turned out to be perfect for the space."[11]

One thing Dick and Clarice consistently shared during this period of marital adjustment and sporadic discord was their commitment to education. Clarice had never wavered in her determination to be a teacher, and she started taking evening classes in early childhood education at Chicago's Pestalozzi Froebel Teachers College.[12] Dick Durham always regretted the fact that lack of resources prevented him from completing his studies at Northwestern University. So in the summer of 1943, he applied to the extremely competitive Summer Radio Institute jointly sponsored by Northwestern University and the NBC network.

The institute's primary goal, co-director Albert Crews explained, was to train people to "meet the tremendous man-power shortage in the Industry"—a shortage brought on because thousands of American men served in the armed forces during World War II. Of the more than 500 applicants to this six-week-long institute, Durham was one of only 22 men and 109 women accepted. Attendees could study various aspects of the radio industry: Durham chose the institute's program planning course.[13]

This may also have been the first time Durham interacted with the program's other co-director, Judith Cary Waller. Sometimes called the "First Lady of Radio," Waller, historians say, was likely the first woman in the country to serve as a radio station manager.[14] Because of her prior work experience in a New York advertising agency, personal friend and *Chicago Daily News* business manager Walter Strong asked Waller if she might consider running the station that the newspaper had just purchased. "I don't know what a radio station is," Waller said. "We really don't know what it is either," Strong replied. He convinced Waller to manage the station that became known as WMAQ. It made its on-air debut on April 13, 1922.[15] Waller's vision for this new medium included a strong mix of educational and entertainment programs. WMAQ joined the NBC network in 1931, and Waller headed the station's public service and educational programming division.[16]

Durham remembered Waller fondly and believed she had been "a positive influence" in the radio industry; she would also play a significant role in Durham's life several years later.[17] More immediately, however, Durham's graduation from NBC and Northwestern's 1943 radio institute opened new doors for him.

He landed writing assignments with a few of the top network radio shows of the day, including the tantalizing CBS dramatic mystery series *Suspense* and NBC's *Ma Perkins*, the ten-year-old daytime soap opera that originated at WMAQ.[18]

While his professional life expanded, Durham kept track of developments in the war-torn world around him. He'd then write vivid literary snapshots of events at home for his younger brothers and friends stationed in army and naval bases overseas or throughout America.[19] In late June 1943, Durham wrote to tell his buddy Andrew Paschal, "It's been one bloody, bitching week." He was referring to the race riots that engulfed Detroit starting on the evening of June 20. "Hell is not just in the streets of Detroit but everywhere in the atmosphere, in the air," Durham penned. "It'll burn the piss out of you if you take a deep breath."[20]

While summer heat, hot tempers, and vicious rumors ignited the Detroit riots, this deadly disturbance had been fueled by long-simmering tensions. White workers resented the overwhelming number of Negro workers who had migrated to Detroit from the South. Blacks hated the overcrowded, substandard housing they had to endure, along with the racially charged atmosphere that divided Negro and white laborers. Detroit's riots claimed thirty-four lives, including twenty-five blacks and nine whites. Hundreds more were injured, and property worth as much as $2 million lay in shambles before federal troops restored order.[21]

Dick Durham told Andrew Paschal,

> [Negroes are] at a fighting peak I never expected to see them reach in my lifetime. God! If only Du Bois had had this to work with during his prime! . . . The little guys are awakening. For once they've got something on the ball. It's up to some intelligent organization to grab the ball and run for a touchdown.[22]

Durham thought that the numerous social, political, and religious organizations in the Negro community "somehow must be brought into a central organization." In his view, organizations like the NAACP, National Negro Congress, church associations, and education and labor groups should operate within a type of federation governed by an elected body. Member groups could pool their finances to tackle issues like housing or employment discrimination, "throwing the bulk of their combined powers behind each punch," Durham said. "Perhaps some idea like this has been attempted before," he conceded.[23]

Durham no doubt knew that, dating back to 1936, the National Negro Congress had tried to "direct the efforts of many and diverse organizations interested in the problems of the Negro," as NNC supporter and Howard University professor Ralph Bunche explained.[24] But Durham thought his idea could work "if each group is allowed to rule its individual unit within the boundary of that central organization." He proposed that the organization's charter be modeled after the United States Constitution, allowing each group, like every state in America, to have certain self-rule privileges.[25]

With Durham's propensity for diligent if not stubborn dedication to causes dear to his heart, he would have shared his thoughts with like-minded colleagues. Yet there is no evidence that Durham acted on his suggestions. What is certain is that he did not like the way the Communist Party responded to some Negro concerns. He claimed that in the face of "a [race] riot, a lynching, an anti-Negro strike," party members tended to blame the violence on the fascism practiced by the "Axis" nations of Germany, Italy, and Japan. Communist Party loyalists acted, Durham told Paschal, "as if they don't know that if the Axis went out of business tonight, we'd still have riots, lynching, murders, anti-Negro white masses. And we'll have this as long as we have Jim Crow."[26]

"The [Communist Party] boys still follow the plan and pattern laid down by Moscow," he concluded. "Win [World War II] first. Fight for home freedom second." This approach rivaled sentiments expressed in the popular "Double V" campaign that the *Pittsburgh Courier* and other black periodicals promoted in Negro communities nationwide. It called for the simultaneous fight for victory against fascism abroad with the fight for victory against discrimination at home.[27] In Durham's opinion, Communist Party members seemed not to realize that while the United States and its allies had a good chance of winning WWII, there was "no guarantee of winning anything else" on America's racial home front. Durham said that his Communist Party comrades nearly "lynched" him when he presented those views.[28]

• • •

On July 24, 1943, a little more than a month after the Detroit riots, CBS aired its *Open Letter on Race Hatred.*[29] Directed by writer/producer William Robson, this hard-hitting, half-hour radio show exposed the rumors as well as the economic and racial tensions that led to the riots. One of the show's narrators noted that "from bloody dawn to bloody dawn" the riots wasted "one million man-hours," time that should have been devoted to the war effort. "How many of your sons will die for lack of the tanks and planes and guns which Detroit did not make that day?" Robson's narrator pointedly asked.[30] By the show's conclusion, the narrator implored listeners to "never allow intolerance or prejudice of any kind to make you forget that you are first of all an American with sacred obligations to every one of your fellow citizens."[31]

"I heard it and I was impressed by some of the elements in it," Durham said about the show. "At the time I was an admirer of Robson, this producer, [who] used to produce some of the experimental stuff for *The Columbia Workshop,* and he was considered very good." Durham admired Robson's radio dramas so much that he went to meet with the seasoned producer in his California home. "The trip didn't work out so well 'cause he was drunk most of the time I was there and we never got into a long conversation," Durham smiled, remembering. "But he had a very progressive outlook . . . and he was very kind to beginners."[32] Robson and Durham remained friendly for years.

Yet even with the professional inroads Durham made after his Summer Radio Institute experience, he kept searching. Applying. Struggling to find stable media employment.

Finally, in winter 1944, a full-time job offer provided him with a springboard onto a new writing path; the *Chicago Defender* hired Durham as a reporter. Founded in 1905, this black-owned, nationally recognized newspaper boldly asserted racial pride and advocacy journalism. The *Defender's* national editor, Ben Burns, extended the job offer to Durham.[33] Historian Bill Mullen described Burns as "the best kept and strangest secret in the history of interracial American radicalism."[34] Burns certainly seemed like an unlikely *Defender* employee. He was a white, former Communist Party member who had worked as a journalist for three different Communist newspapers during the 1930s. Despite what he called his "Red" background, Burns revealed in his autobiography that his *Defender* supervisor was "concerned solely about how I could help him shape a better newspaper."[35]

During the World War II years the *Chicago Defender* transformed itself, pursuing new objectives under new leadership. John Sengstacke, the nephew of *Defender* founder Robert Abbott, took over after Abbott's death in January 1940. According to Bill Mullen, Sengstacke sought "to hire national figures in black and white politics and culture who could recast the newspaper as allied with the most progressive forces in the country," thereby constituting a "modern black protest voice in the mass media." In this vein, some of the writers who contributed to the *Defender* included scholar W. E. B. Du Bois, visual artist Margaret Burroughs, and the man with whom Durham had by then established a close friendship, Langston Hughes.[36]

Durham was not shy about praising his friend's *Defender* columns. He loved the humorous musings of the character Langston created to represent himself and the black everyman. Hughes first called this character his Simple-Minded Friend; Langston eventually named him Jesse B. Simple.[37] "You and your Simple-Minded Friend have became the best columnists in the press, Lang," Durham wrote in his December 2, 1944, letter to Hughes. "Every time you converse with Simple, I go into spasms."[38] Durham then teased Hughes about his popularity among all types of readers. A young, shapely, white woman Durham had recently met told him that "her main object in life was to somehow meet Langston Hughes and marry him." With tongue firmly planted in cheek, Durham signed off, stating, "When the wedding comes off, invite."[39]

It is unclear exactly how Ben Burns came to hire Durham, although it's reasonable to assume that Burns must have known Durham because of their Communist Party affiliation. Years later, Durham told an interviewer that Burns enticed him into accepting the *Defender* reporting job by convincing him that the paper, with its regular weekly salary, could serve as a base for Durham's freelance script and poetry writing.[40]

Ben Burns claimed that the *Defender's* "ragtag reportorial staff," with its ongoing "parade of new faces," was "poorly paid with irregular hours, overtime pay unheard of and expense accounts minimal. Most memorable for me," Burns added, "was a small clique of no more than a half-dozen people who worked closely with me."[41] Durham and his former IWP colleague Robert Lucas were part of that clique. "The most important thing was that Ben gave me a freedom I'd never known before except in poetry," Durham said. "We did things on the *Defender* that no one had ever tried before."[42]

For Durham's first major assignment, Burns sent him back to the segregated South. In Memphis, Tennessee, Durham pulled off a journalistic coup. He interviewed a man who had never before granted access to a Negro reporter, nor had this man spoken with an out-of-town newsman in two years. The interviewee was Memphis's one-term mayor (but longtime Democratic powerbroker) Edward R. Crump.[43]

In a letter to Army Private Hayward Kirkpatrick, Durham told his friend that Crump received him in a "swanky" third-floor office in the heart of Memphis. Durham had been sent to interview "this Southern dictator" about a range of topics, including Crump's views on civil rights for Memphis's Negro citizens and the poll tax. Eight Southern states, including Tennessee, required residents to pay an annual tax in order to register to vote. The poll tax effectively restricted the voting rights of black and poor residents who could ill afford to pay the fee.[44]

But as hard as Durham pushed Crump to answer his questions, the Dixiecrat "was too slick to let me catch him in any definite attitude towards anything," Durham told Kirkpatrick. "The cutest trick of all," Durham wrote, was how Crump had tried to bar A. Philip Randolph, the respected head of the Brotherhood of Sleeping Car Porters, from speaking about union issues in one of Memphis's black churches.[45]

The lengthy article Durham wrote as a result of his Memphis visit landed on the *Defender's* April 8, 1944, front page. Durham's "Crump Thinks Negroes Given Fair Treatment," provocatively began:

> "Memphis is Murder." If Detroit was once "dynamite" with its festering race riots and labor clashes, then Memphis—which had all these factors and more— is "murder."[46]

How did Durham justify this statement?

> Look at it. There are 150,000 Negroes restricted and Jim Crowed in a city in which they form at least 40 percent of the population. Many are Negroes

recently immigrated from the Delta of Mississippi and Alabama who have stopped in Memphis on their way North looking for better jobs, better housing and equal opportunities. All are slowly recovering from one hundred years of "Jim Crow Shock" and are beginning to fight against the old Southern custom and pastime of "Keeping the Nigger in his Place."[47]

Durham reported that A. Phillip Randolph's appearance in the city "was not simply to uphold the principle of free speech, or to defy Ed Crump, but to counteract the anti-Negro expressions emanating from the local Memphis, AF of L [American Federation of Labor] unions . . . which has caused the AF of L to lose thousands of Negro workers to the more liberal CIO unions." Durham quoted Crump, who threatened: "If the Negroes of this community or any whites insist on [bringing in] these imported rabble rousers [like Randolph], creating hatred, they might as well make up their minds to abide by the consequences and the town will be better off without that type of citizen."[48]

As a rookie reporter, Dick knew that he needed help honing his journalistic skills. He soon came under the guidance of a physically slight man perceived to be a journalistic giant—Metz Tulus Paul Lochard, the *Defender*'s editor-in-chief.[49] Affectionately called "Doc," the Haitian-born editor had earned a doctorate from the University of Paris-Sorbonne, chaired Howard University's Romance Languages and Literature Department, and taught at other historically black institutions. *Defender* publisher Robert Abbott lured Lochard to his paper in 1932. During his fifty years with the *Defender,* Lochard was the "in-house intellectual, to whom all difficult questions were directed," reporter Enoch Waters said.[50] Like a benevolent godfather, Lochard mentored generations of black journalists.

Lochard and Ben Burns quickly recognized Durham's strong storytelling abilities. Burns called Durham "a fast learner," who was also "slow and sometimes careless in his copy."[51] He didn't explain how Durham's carelessness manifested itself, but Burns and Lochard realized that their twenty-six-year-old reporter's strengths lay in writing long-form feature articles. Thus, Durham became the paper's top investigative reporter,[52] and many of his articles landed on the *Defender*'s front page.

During the 1944 presidential election year, New York Governor Thomas E. Dewey became the Republican contender. Democratic president Franklin Roosevelt ran for an unprecedented fourth term; Roosevelt had already broken presidential election protocol in 1940 when he won a third elected term. Durham reported in his July 8, 1944, article, that GOP strategists admitted: "Without the support of the Negro voter, who holds the balance of power in 17 central states, their chances of defeating Roosevelt are less than in 1940."[53] A couple of weeks later, Durham determined that although the Republican platform "boldly

FIGURE 6. Durham's mentor and *Chicago Defender* Editor-in-Chief Metz T. P. Lochard. Moorland-Spingarn Research Center, Howard University.

denounced racial discrimination and advocated a permanent Fair Employment Practice Committee, Negro leaders wary of political promises have failed to give the party the enthusiastic endorsement GOP officials expected." Durham attributed Negro wariness to the Republican candidate himself, reporting that Governor Dewey "evaded and sidestepped" questions regarding Negro concerns during his first press conference as the GOP presidential candidate.[54]

By late July, Durham reported that "compared to the tricky, weasel-worded Republican pledge on the race issue, the Democratic plank was an ineffectual and vague affair." Durham noted that Negro leaders warned both parties "that their records on the Negro issue would be the sole determining factor on how the Negro casts his ballot in November."[55] Durham's articles reflected the fact that the *Chicago Defender*'s news coverage under John Sengstacke's stewardship often rejected the mainstream media's strict definition of objectivity—of middle-of-the-road, non-opinionated reporting. Scholar Bill Mullen noted that facts sometimes comingled with opinion in the *Defender*, blurring traditional divisions between journalism and other genres like poetry and fiction.[56]

In August 1944 one of Durham's features earned him a bit of national notoriety. He had traveled to the small town of Owosso, Michigan, a place he said had two claims to fame, "pro-Deweyism and anti-Negroism."[57] Owosso was the Republican presidential candidate's childhood home. With his gift for dramatic scene setting, Durham's *Defender* article carried his readers along with him as he arrived in Governor Dewey's "lily-white" hometown.

> "Staying here long son?" a grizzled policeman, tossing peanuts into his mouth, said as he eyed my suitcase and questioned me when I moved from the station toward the heart of town. "Just overnight," I answered. "Folks 'round here," he tossed up more peanuts, "don't usually [allow] colored folks in town after dark. Who'd you come to see?" he asked.[58]

Durham answered the officer's question and then walked down a well-maintained residential street toward the home of Mrs. M. George Dewey, mother of the Republican presidential candidate and daughter of an Owosso settler. Mrs. Dewey told Durham that there was no law against colored people staying in her town. In fact, she remembered that a Negro family once lived in Owosso.

The story's real revelation came when Mrs. Dewey made some anti-Semitic statements. She was concerned about what she called the Jewish "lust for power," and the fact that Jews were "so greedy and egotistical. . . . They've got so much money, why, they can just come in and buy up everything."[59] About a week after this article appeared, the *Defender* reported that Durham's feature caused "such a furor" in the Empire State's political circles that the *New York Post* decided to check the story's veracity. Mrs. Dewey said she was misquoted. Durham stood by his story, which he ended with Mrs. Dewey expressing concern that Negroes might endorse President Roosevelt for a fourth term—support she couldn't understand.[60]

President Roosevelt did win the election, but his victory was short lived. Roosevelt died from a massive cerebral hemorrhage on April 12, 1945, barely three months after his fourth inauguration.[61] Vice President Harry S. Truman completed the late president's term.

• • •

Durham settled into his journalism career as American families continued sending their loved ones off to war in armed forces that mirrored conditions at home: black men served in racially segregated units, and many Negro soldiers, sailors, and airmen suffered humiliation, injury, or death because of their race. One particularly egregious case became known as the Port Chicago Mutiny.

With its strategic location just a few miles from California's San Francisco Bay and its proximity to the Pacific war zone, the Port Chicago Naval base and ammunition depot serviced fleets heading into battle.[62] Negro sailors stationed at Port Chicago had to load, as quickly as possible, tons of live ammunition and bombs onto waiting ships. Shortly after 10 P.M. on a warm July night in 1944, a massive explosion rocked the base's docks, instantly killing 320 sailors; of these, 202 were black. Another 390 civilian and military personnel—including 233 black men—sustained injuries.[63]

Negro survivors claimed they had been poorly trained and worked under questionable safety conditions. Worried about persistent safety hazards and angry that the navy offered little to no counseling for Negro survivors, fifty black sailors refused to return to work. The navy charged them with mutiny. These Negro seamen were court martialed and sentenced to fifteen years' hard labor.[64] Months of national outcry and legal wrangling ensued. The navy finally set aside the sailors' convictions in 1946.[65]

The Port Chicago Mutiny saga deeply touched Durham. He could not get it out of his head. Maybe it was because his brother Earl, then serving in the navy, might well have been one of the hundreds of Negro men killed, maimed, or court martialed, had he been stationed there. Or the story may have spoken to Durham because of the role that race and injustice played in the incident. Whatever the reasons, he referred to the case often, telling others that he hoped to write about its dramatic and social justice implications in a novel at some point.[66]

And Durham continued to be drawn to stories about wartime injustice and triumph. He reported about how some Negro Women's Auxiliary Corps members handled the discrimination they faced while taking care of wounded soldiers.[67] At another California naval base—Port Hueneme in the southern part of the state—Durham investigated the brutal beating of four Negro sailors by a commander Durham nicknamed "a 20th Century Captain Bligh." The four men were savagely flogged for allegedly leading a two-day hunger strike to protest the "systematic race persecution" and Jim Crow discrimination at the base.[68] Durham reported that, after an investigation, the navy relieved the offending commander of his duties.

Defender editor Ben Burns believed that Durham was "highly creative in his feature interviews with big names" and "persistent and penetrating in his exposé stories."[69] Durham seemed to have a knack for getting interviewees to speak their minds, even if their opinions were totally counter to his. In a February 1945 article, for example, fifty-eight-year-old millionaire businessman Newton Camp Farr told Durham that the Oakland-Kenwood Association he headed had "recently hired a battery of highly paid lawyers to streamline their anti-Negro covenants in order to create a new type of agreement able to withstand court challenges." Farr was referring to restrictive covenant agreements designed to keep Negroes and poor

Jews out of white neighborhoods. Negroes "enjoy sex too much, [were] mostly uneducated . . . poor—ragged—dirty . . . underfed" and therefore "undesirable neighbors," Farr said.[70] Some Negro neighborhoods had a density of ninety thousand people per square mile—nearly twice the population rate in Chicago's most congested white communities. Yet Farr insisted that his push to have more houses built in Negro communities—while restricting blacks from other areas—would actually relieve the Negro housing strain.[71]

A plum assignment in spring 1945 allowed Durham to indulge his love of travel and satisfy his growing appetite for international affairs. Headlines in the *Defender*'s April 28 edition announced the paper's "All-Star Coverage," by reporters Richard Durham and John Robert Badger, editor-in-chief Metz Lochard, and columnists Walter White and W. E. B. Du Bois, of the "All-Nations Conference in San Francisco."[72] This historic gathering served as the launching pad for a new organization called the United Nations (U.N.), an entity slated to play a major role in international peacekeeping efforts.[73]

One of Durham's first stories from the San Francisco conference dealt with demands by tiny nations like Haiti and Liberia for the "equality for all races."[74] Durham subsequently interviewed Chinese, European, and American statesmen as they developed the U.N.'s charter. Sometimes weighing in with multiple stories for the same issue of the paper, Durham's articles reflected the political posturing, turmoil, and progress that eventually led to the U.N.'s birth.[75]

The compelling drama of the World War II fight against fascism abroad and the campaign for social and economic justice at home helped to make 1944 and 1945 boom readership years for the black press. "By the end of the war," Bill Mullen noted, "circulation for the *Defender* and other black weekly papers had risen 43 percent," topping out at slightly more than 1.8 million readers in 1945, as compared with 1.2 million readers in 1940.[76] Durham's articles contributed to the *Defender*'s circulation success, and during fall 1945 he was honored with a "Page One Award" by the local chapter of the American Newspaper Guild (ANG).[77] This New York–based union, established in the early 1930s, safeguarded the rights of newspaper writers throughout the country.[78]

"Nice going, eh?" Durham's brother-in-law Robert Davis asked mutual friend Langston Hughes about Durham's "Page One" recognition. From his Fort Huachuca, Arizona, army base, Davis told Hughes that their friend had been one of sixteen Chicago reporters honored by the ANG.[79]

In another 1945 letter to Hughes, Davis bragged about Durham's recent "sojourn" on the West Coast. The MGM Studio had offered Durham work "as a script analyst," Davis explained. But Durham turned the offer down because of a strike that unionized employees were waging against major Hollywood studios.[80] No matter how tempting the opportunity to get into the film industry may have been,

Durham would never cross a union picket line. Still, Davis acknowledged that an offer like this "wouldn't have happened four years ago" for his brother-in-law. "I'm proud of him!" Davis wrote.[81]

. . .

As 1946 approached, Durham continued covering stores for the *Defender* and free-lancing when he could. Hoping to extend its circulation boom, *Defender* reporter Enoch Waters said that Charles Browning, the paper's short, chubby, "energetic and imaginative" promotions director, came up with what he thought would be a great marketing tool.[82] Browning wanted the paper to sponsor a weekly, fifteen-minute drama series on a local radio station. The series, *Democracy USA*, would feature men and women who exemplified the principles of democracy and free-dom through their lives and accomplishments.[83]

Browning's interest in radio may have been inspired by a series that had flour-ished on WMCA in New York City since 1944. The show, *New World A-Coming*, took its title from a book of the same name by Negro journalist and native New Yorker Roi Ottley. Via dramatic vignettes, interviews, speeches, and commentar-ies, "this program was an extraordinary divergence from national radio's timid and cautious discussions about race inequality," historian Barbara Savage noted. "The series was laced with an unabashed political message," often featuring "a heavy dose of programming built around the war and the issues it raised for blacks."[84]

The *Defender*'s proposed radio series would be, according to reporter Enoch Waters, "the first of its kind offered on radio under the sponsorship of a black newspaper." Aware of their radio scriptwriting expertise, Browning asked Dick Durham and Bob Lucas to author the series.[85] Durham contacted William Rob-son, the CBS writer/producer he admired, to see if Robson could help the pro-posed series find a home on WBBM, Chicago's CBS affiliate. As a result, Charles Browning met with station head Ben Parks, and the men agreed to jointly spon-sor *Democracy USA*, evenly splitting the show's estimated $350 weekly produc-tion costs.[86]

Parks and Browning settled on an inaugural broadcast date of Sunday, May 4, 1946.[87] Richard Durham and Robert Lucas would share scriptwriting duties, and the first show was to be about *Chicago Defender* founder, Robert Abbott. But before the show made its debut, Durham was forced out of *Democracy USA*'s production loop.

The *Defender* fired him.

The paper sacked him, Durham claimed, "because I wrote a story in an area that the publisher, the owner [John Sengstacke], had put the 'forbidden' sign on and I didn't know it and the story was published." Sengstacke supported a particular political candidate, while Durham's feature "extolled the virtues" of a rival. The gaffe embarrassed Sengstacke, and he needed a scapegoat. According to Durham, he was it.[88]

Actually, Durham's firing had a lot more to do with his in-house activism than a publishing blunder. Durham had stubbornly lobbied for better working conditions and more equitable pay for the *Defender*'s writing staff through the American Newspaper Guild.[89] Durham's editor, Ben Burns, said that the *Defender* was not affiliated with the ANG when he joined the paper in 1942. Burns recruited "a handful of members into the union," even though he could not "function openly in the Guild" because of his management status.[90] Durham became an active ANG member and pushed the *Defender* to honor union policies and increase wages. Yet union negotiations with publisher John Sengstacke "went nowhere" for months, Burns explained in his autobiography. For his activism, the *Defender* fired Durham shortly after dismissing Ben Burns in late March 1946. Bob Lucas also left the *Defender*, telling his former IWP supervisor Arna Bontemps that he and Durham had landed "in the doghouse as a result of the Newspaper Guild fight we were making."[91]

Durham's firing meant that his nearly two-year, full-time employment safety net had disintegrated. At least in the short term, he needed to once again rely on freelance work. Although Clarice supported her husband's union activities, Dick's firing meant that the couple struggled to pay their expenses with Clarice's salary.[92]

However, Durham eventually landed a position as an associate editor and feature writer with a newly created progressive newspaper called the *Chicago Star*. In its July 6, 1946, debut edition, Durham wrote about one Negro woman's battle against restrictive covenant practices on the South Side,[93] and for the next four or five months, Durham contributed feature articles about housing and labor issues. Durham's Federal Bureau of Investigation (FBI) file indicated that he earned $65 a week at the *Star*. The Bureau's informants also claimed that the newspaper was "dominated and controlled" by the Communist Party.[94] The paper's board did include Communist Party or progressive writers such as Frank Marshall Davis, William Sennett, and Carl Hirsh.[95]

Meanwhile, the *Chicago Defender* must have realized the value of and need for Durham's and Lucas's scriptwriting skills. Whatever inspired the turnaround, Durham resumed his *Democracy USA* writing duties sometime during late summer 1946.[96] He and Lucas briefly shared script assignments, but of the two scribes Durham was "the much better writer," actor Oscar Brown Jr. said. "We all tended to gravitate toward his script[s] and toward him because of that."[97] A close examination of Durham's scripts demonstrates why. His writing was a tightly crafted mix of riveting conflict and dramatic resolutions. Durham's scriptwriting skills had clearly grown since his WPA days, and one script in particular demonstrated that growth. In the *Democracy USA* episode titled "Dr. Dailey and the Living Human Heart," Durham explored the life of distinguished Negro surgeon Ulysses Grant Dailey.[98]

Durham's script opens in Provident Hospital—the all-black medical facility on Chicago's South Side. Dr. Dailey is treating a patient named Jay, whose stab wound, in his heart, lands him in the hospital's emergency room. In the show, Jay's voice is treated with a filter, the radio production technique used to indicate that listeners are hearing a character's thoughts. As the attending nurse monitors Jay's vital signs, his heart rate, represented by rhythmic sound effects, slows down and almost stops. Dr. Dailey quickly injects adrenalin. Jay's heartbeat improves as Dailey commands his nurse:

> DAILEY: (Rapidly.) Call the emergency staff into the operating room; find his blood type; get the blood bank ready; the heart is split, leaking like a sieve. If we can sew it back—
> JAY: (Filter.) (Realizes.) Operate! Not on my heart!
> DAILEY: (Calm.) Don't let him move nurse. This man may live—
> JAY: (Filter.) (Fateful.) No, I'm going to die. I'll never see the sunshine again. You can't sew a heart together like a baseball.[99]

Durham then takes listeners back in time to Dr. Dailey's days as a student. Dailey's white professor, Dr. Stevens, respects the young Negro's intelligence and allows Dailey to grade the papers of his white medical students. Dailey tells Dr. Stevens that one student believes it is possible to suture the heart. Stevens dismisses that notion, lamenting that no doctor in the world has ever been able to repair a human heart and have the patient live.

Durham returns to the present as the adult Dailey operates on Jay's heart. After briefly concentrating on the slow, tense procedure, Durham offers another flashback—this time shepherding listeners into a Berlin banquet room during the early-1890s. A German doctor named Bommer is socializing with a group of jovial white American doctors, members of a surgical society. Bommer mentions that another American is studying there and asks if he can bring this student in to meet them. "The more the merrier," replies a doctor named Raymond, who adds, "Maybe we can get him to join our society." Yet in this German room, Durham lets Dailey walk straight into American racism:

> RAYMOND: Er—just a minute. I'm afraid your friend will not be welcome here.
> BOMMER: (Doesn't get it.) What do you mean?
> RAYMOND: This banquet is for doctors—
> BOMMER: (Begins before Raymond ends.) But Doctor Dailey just finished teaching at your Northwestern University - he came here to study—

RAYMOND: (*As if he hadn't heard.*) The society is for—white doctors—Herr
Bommer, we do not . . . well, admit (*Stops before finishing.*)

DAILEY: (*Quiet, firm.*) You mean you do not admit the truth of the science
you preach—or the oath you took. Blood, we learned, was a bond,
not a barrier—didn't we doctor?[100]

Dailey storms out of the room as Raymond admonishes Bommer, asking if he
noticed the color of Dailey's skin.

BOMMER: Yes, I did. He's the same color as the man I was going to tell you
about—in Chicago—You should remember the date—July 10,
1893—Dr. Dan Williams has just completed his first successful
[open] heart operation. And Herr Doctors, the patient lived!

Durham then brings Drs. Dailey and Daniel Hale Williams together. Dr. Williams describes the heart operation while his protégé performs the delicate procedure. Dailey gently lifts Jay's heart out of his body:

DAILEY: Now it's in my hand! Needle! Nurse, curved needle! Fine silk!

NURSE: (*Tense.*) Ready doctor——

DAILEY: (*Hushed as if to himself.*) If—the stitches will hold—three
stitches could stop the leak—one stitch—

MUSIC: (*Sharp simulation of a stitch.*)

DAILEY: Another——

MUSIC: (*Simulation of a stitch. Higher tone than preceding.*)

DAILEY: One more——

MUSIC: (*Higher tone. Quiver it. Then, ping, ping of a leak, stops completely.*)[101]

Success! The stitches appear to hold and Dr. Dailey tells the attending nurse to
start a blood transfusion. But in one last dramatic twist, Durham's nurse character can't find a vein. Jay's veins have collapsed. Without an infusion of blood, Jay
could die. Dailey makes a quick incision—and finally the blood flows. Jay survives.

Based on the strength of scripts like "Dr. Dailey and the Human Heart," the
Defender offered Durham a contract on Christmas Eve 1946, making him the
"exclusive" writer for *Democracy USA*. The *Defender* guaranteed Durham a minimum payment of $110 per script. WBBM and the *Defender* were entitled to the
show's "first broadcast rights." Durham retained all other rights.[102]

With a new year fast approaching, Durham found himself responsible for a
weekly drama series about accomplished Negroes.

He welcomed the ongoing challenge.

CHAPTER 6

Rare Broadcasts

**Democracy U.S.A.—"Colonel B. O. Davis,
Commander of the 332nd Fighter Squadron"**

NARRATOR: And so it came about that the men of the
332nd set out for the city of Berlin. And they
soared to 30,000 feet, their planes at right
angles with the rising sun. And as metal birds
in flight, they crossed the Adriatic Sea and the
Alps . . . [meeting] their bombers at 18 angels
high . . .

SOUND: (*Jet motor screaming by. General dogfight
mix-up. Machine gun chatter high. [Then] under——*)

DAVIS: (*Filter.*) Campbell! He's hit. He's spinning down!

COX: (*Filter.*) Shall I dive after him, sir! They're on his
tail!

DAVIS: (*Filter sharp.*) Stick with the bombers! They're
laying for 'em! Close formation! Tighten up!

SOUND: (*Full perspective of straining motors . . .
machine guns. Crisscrossing of planes. Establish
well; ease behind.*)

NARRATOR: And jet planes shot through the skies like
stars—and the flak was like bursting metallic
clouds—and planes plunged and burned down
over the city. And it came to pass that for thirty-
one minutes the pilots of the 332nd dipped,
dived and banked in the sun over Berlin until
the last bomber was empty of bombs and
wheeling for home.[1]

—Richard Durham, December 22, 1946

Richard Durham threw himself into his role as the primary writer of *Democracy USA* episodes.

As 1947 began, Durham banged away at his typewriter in the makeshift office he had fashioned in his apartment's small dining area. His scripts dramatized the triumphs and struggles of Negro leaders, although sometimes he found it "very difficult to do much in fifteen minutes."[2]

Durham soon started sharing *Democracy USA* scriptwriting duties with freelance writer Perry "Skee" Wolf.[3] The synergy between these writers and the hard work of the show's multiracial cast and production staff eventually paid off. By the series' first anniversary in May 1947, local and national accolades rolled into WBBM. The most prestigious award came from President Harry S. Truman, whose special certificate of merit to WBBM cited *Democracy USA* for its exploration of people "who by their living examples are seeking the answers to life's problems and inspiring our youth to follow their paths of achievement and citizenship." The *Chicago Defender* reported that this was the first time an American president had so honored a radio station.[4]

President Truman's citation also acknowledged the significant role the *Defender* and WBBM played in providing opportunities for Negro actors and scriptwriters who used radio "as a medium of education in race relations and the strengthening of the bonds of interracial harmony."[5] More praise for the series flowed from the Chicago Mayor's Commission on Human Relations, the local branch of the NAACP, the Chicago Council against Racial and Religious Discrimination, and the National Conference of Christians and Jews.[6] With or without these honors, Durham occupied rarefied space in radio, since only a tiny cadre of black Americans, including Robert Lucas, Roi Ottley, and occasionally Langston Hughes, wrote for the medium.

In fact, a comprehensive study of the media in 1947 by the National Negro Congress found that Richard Durham might have been the *only* Negro writer working full-time in radio.[7] The NNC's report was pretty damning. It called radio "one of the most powerful instruments" fostering American racial segregation and discrimination. Of radio's thirty thousand white-collar jobs—the medium's largest employment block—Negroes held no more than two hundred positions. The NNC claimed that most of radio's Negro workers "will probably have to remain porters, pages or manual laborers" since no blacks served as engineers or technical staff members. The congress identified only two Negroes, New Yorkers William Chase and Clifford Burdett, who worked as radio directors and producers.[8]

But Richard Durham did not chart his progressive scriptwriting course alone. Essentially, Durham and fellow scriptwriters like William Robson, Orson Welles, and Archibald Oboler, as well as radio's poet laureate, Norman Corwin, "sought to change their world, not just to speak to it," according to media historian Bruce

Lenthall. Those writers, Lenthall said, "belonged to a generation of artists—broadly defined—that believed in opening a cultural front onto the political battles of their day, all committed generally to ideals of social democracy, to anti-fascism, and to civil liberties." Through radio, Durham and other socially conscious writers could reach millions—even when they worked on what Lenthall called "less popular" sustained or sponsored programs in the *Democracy USA* vein.[9]

Durham basked in *Democracy USA*'s successes. Clarice noticed that as awards for the show poured in, her husband's confidence levels soared.[10] Dick no longer felt the need to leave their home to "get himself together," and Clarice supported her husband by proofreading and typing some of the mounting number of scripts he created.

However, Durham did feel hemmed in by the restrictions WBBM officials imposed. He was directed, for example, to "not bring in too many stories in which there was protest against the status quo."[11] For Durham, that was a bit like tying one of his hands behind his back and expecting him to recreate his teenaged Golden Gloves prowess. He wanted to throw two-fisted, smashing punches that KO'd injustice. Instead, "CBS wanted themes that had to eulogize America," and, Durham noted, "it was more difficult to circumvent restrictions."[12]

Still, Durham believed that his supervisors might "forgive and forget" their initial reservations about more hard-hitting scripts once they heard the story's "logic and quality."[13] So he pushed the limits when he could. For example, one *Democracy USA* episode explored the discrimination that businessman Albert W. Williams overcame to build the Philadelphia-based Unity Mutual Insurance Company into one of the country's most prosperous black-owned companies.[14]

Hoping to secure a financial cushion for his company as the Great Depression deepens, Durham's Williams character applies for a fifty-thousand-dollar loan based on the value of Unity Mutual's headquarters. After receiving the state commissioner's building assessment, Williams's face pales. Unity Mutual's building is valued at a mere $5,000, "and I think they calculated something else besides the property," Williams says. He confronts Commissioner Riley about the low appraisal, and Riley responds: "Well—you're an unusual risk—a Negro insurance company—a building in a Negro neighborhood—that's the way we've computed it . . . always been that way."[15] Williams counters: "I suggest we appraise property without considering the color of the owner's skin." The commissioner invites Williams back to his office, suggesting that he'll see what he can do.

Williams does return. But adding a twist, Durham reveals that Williams's return visit is ten years later. By then, Unity Mutual has thrived, insuring thousands of Negroes. Riley is amazed. "How on earth did you get through that Depression?" Riley asks. Williams replies as the show ends: "Well, I think it's because our kind of clients were good risks after all. And we have a feeling that all Americans of all colors are pretty good people to risk insurance on!"[16]

While Durham advocated for equality, however gingerly, in his *Democracy USA* scripts, he also searched for ways to fatten his income. One opportunity took him to the North Side home of Chicago native Irna Phillips, the woman who undisputedly reigned as the "Queen of the Soaps." Phillips created and wrote many of the popular serials known as soap operas—so named because companies that produced and marketed soap and other cleaning products sponsored the dramas.[17]

By 1943, Phillips had no fewer than five different soaps on the nation's radio airwaves.[18] The shows ran on different networks at the same time, enabling her to earn an annual salary of as much as $250,000—a staggering sum at that time. Phillips's dramas required her to write approximately two million words per year—the equivalent of several dozen novels. So Phillips hired writers who could help her meet concurrent production and broadcast schedules.[19]

Durham's association with Phillips began in the mid-1940s after he submitted a script for "What's New," a non-network show hosted by actor Don Ameche. Probably serving as the show's producer, Phillips told Durham that she "liked [his script] very much."[20] On the strength of that submission, Phillips invited Durham to her Astor Place home. Because of her reputation as a "quite mean" woman, "many people advised me to stay away from her," Durham recalled.[21] But he needed to make more money, so he took the chance. "She told me to come on up and be ready to stay," Durham said. "I didn't know what that meant until I got there. She worked in her apartment, which was a huge place in the area here that we call the Gold Coast because it is a very wealthy area near the Lake [Michigan]." Durham said that Phillips's philosophy was that a writer could work with her only if he or she could make her cry.[22] He planned to make sure that Phillips's tears flowed—and they must have. Durham became one of Phillips's support writers, so-called "dialoguers" who would flesh out the storylines Phillips developed. But few of these writers received on-air credit.[23]

Phillips was a tough taskmaster. "She always said that if she okayed a script, it was as good as her writing it herself," one of Phillips's actors explained.[24] Durham realized that Phillips, like Judith Waller, used radio to do more than entertain. Phillips believed that soap operas should educate listeners while fulfilling their commercial obligations to sell goods to the daytime dramas' predominately female audience.[25]

Many of Phillips's soaps became long-lasting hits. *The Guiding Light*, which she described as "close to my heart," aired on more than three hundred stations, reaching twelve million listeners by the early 1940s. *The Guiding Light* premiered on radio in 1937, moved to television in 1952, and survived on the CBS network until its demise in 2009.[26] In addition, Phillips's *As the World Turns, Days of Our Lives,* and *Another World* survived on television for decades.[27]

Durham had to have been impressed with the popularity of Irna Phillips's radio soap operas as well as her progressive streak. Phillips regularly incorporated social issues such as juvenile delinquency or child welfare into her stories. After World War II ended, Phillips's soaps reflected America's interest in postwar-related conditions like amnesia, alcoholism, or psychosomatic paralysis.[28] In later years, Durham used some of these dramatic devices in his own scripts.

Meanwhile, Durham's *Democracy USA* scripts continued to be brought to life by a talented group of Chicago-based black actors that included Oscar Brown Jr., Fred Pinkard, Weslyn Tilden, and Janice Kingslow. Durham said that those sophisticated, ambitious artists wanted more opportunities through which they could express their creativity.[29] This desire led to the formation of the Du Bois Theater Guild.

Durham told historian J. Fred MacDonald that the guild's name reflected the fact that W. E. B. Du Bois had made it possible for grants to come into the black community to support art and culture during the mid-1940s. When asked if the guild, like Du Bois himself, was Marxist-oriented, Durham disingenuously claimed, "We wouldn't have known [about] that at the time."[30] Dating back to his teenaged years, Durham had become well versed in all things Du Boisian—including the scholar's leftist views.[31] Durham certainly would have read the two masterful articles Du Bois published in the NAACP's *Crisis* magazine during the early 1930s. In these articles Du Bois defined Marxism and applied its main tenets to the plight of the Negro working class.[32]

Some of the Du Bois Theater Guild performances, like its interpretations of Clifford Odets's *Waiting for Lefty* and John Steinbeck's *Of Mice and Men,* fell into the so-called agit-prop category—productions that were agitation-oriented or propagandistic in their approach to social change issues.[33] Clarice Durham fondly remembered the guild's performance of *Lonesome Train,* a cantata about President Lincoln's assassination and the train that brought his body back to his Springfield, Illinois, birthplace. *Lonesome Train* was composed by Earl Robinson, whose *Ballad for Americans* cantata became a national sensation as performed by singer Paul Robeson.[34] Other Du Bois Theater Guild productions trumpeted black awareness themes. For instance, Oscar Brown Jr. said that the guild "feted Langston Hughes" with an original play about his Simple character. "That was the kind of creative activity we were involved in," he said. "It was a very exciting time."[35]

In his role as the guild's co-founder, Durham assessed the strengths and weaknesses of its members, demonstrating his ability to read people and to guide, if not manipulate, them. One example of Durham's influence involved a young Negro Tennessee migrant named Vernon Jarrett. Jarrett met Durham at a rally shortly after he arrived in the Windy City. The men became friends, and while serving as a cub reporter for the *Chicago Defender*, Jarrett got involved in many of the cultural and political activities percolating around him, including the Du Bois Theater Guild.[36]

"Oh, yeah, Vernon was there," Dick's brother Earl said. "He thought he was gonna be an actor." However, Jarrett "wasn't a very good actor," Earl Durham said, adding that Jarrett "kept fooling around with all these women." Durham figured that if he could get Jarrett to "settle down," he'd be a real asset to the group.[37]

So Durham hatched a plan: he convinced his brother to take out a woman whom Jarrett was particularly interested in. "I took her to a Communist Party rally," Earl said, "and we went and had a cup of coffee afterward and analyzed it." Richard Durham thought that this innocent date might get Jarrett's attention. It did. Earl Durham said that Vernon Jarrett thought that he was trying to move in on his girlfriend. Shortly thereafter, Jarrett asked the woman to marry him; Vernon and Frenetta Jarrett's marriage would last nearly fifty years.[38]

Durham's scheme had worked. Jarrett also became the guild's president.

"That was the way Dick was," Earl said. "He would find ways of transcending and working with individuals. He was a hell of a listener." As a result, Richard Durham knew that people often were full of contradictions; he told his brother that by concentrating on the positive aspects of a person's contradictions, he could find some "teachable moments"—times when he could get someone to start questioning or to consider changing their opinions. "Dick was extremely good at that," Earl said."[39] Richard Durham's ability to influence and even manipulate others into action would serve him well *and* cause him trouble throughout his life.

• • •

As a result of his experience writing for Irna Phillips, Durham figured that he could use the soap opera concept for his own purposes. "The principles for building a drama using white characters and one using black characters is really not much different," Durham told radio historian John Dunning. "It's like building a house. Who the characters are who live in the house . . . it really doesn't make a difference insofar as . . . you must have motivation, you must have conflict, you must have movement, you must have outlook, initiatives and so forth. So the ingredients are pretty much the same."[40]

Subsequently, Durham and his theatrical friends created a soap opera called *Here Comes Tomorrow*. Actor Janice Kingslow said that this series grew out of the need for Du Bois Theater Guild members to be proactive about employment. "A group of friends, equally jobless, were sitting in our living room one night when someone said, 'Well if there aren't any bookings for us, let's make up our own shows.' We all pitched in. No one person did it alone. But the result has been a series of radio shows to which huge audiences have listened," Kingslow said, referring to *Democracy USA, Here Comes Tomorrow,* and *Destination Freedom.*[41]

In the show's opening credits, Durham called *Here Comes Tomorrow* "the first authentic radio serial of an American Negro family," as told through "the unforgettable story of the Redmonds—of their search for happiness and a new world."[42] In Oscar Brown Jr.'s opinion, "There had been the promise during World War II that the post-war world was going to be different." Instead, Negro war veterans returned home to face the same oppressive conditions they had risked their lives fighting against in Europe. "What we needed was a whole approach to a class struggle, and a change of political philosophy, political direction in the country altogether," Brown asserted, "and we began to operate on that premise."[43] Through *Here Comes Tomorrow,* Durham could paint an aural portrait of a complex, nuclear Negro family of six—a family grappling with issues affecting most blacks in post–World War II America.

At the head of Durham's radio family stood Dr. Benjamin Redmond, a successful doctor and an uncompromising figure.[44] His more pliable wife, Becky, managed the home and took care of the couple's four children. The drama pivoted around Milton, the Redmond's oldest son. A war veteran, Milton returned home with amnesia. Sarah Redmond encouraged her brother to find himself by confronting his past. At the same time, Sarah and younger brother Rex began asserting themselves, pushing back against their father's stifling control. The youngest Redmond, preteen Chickie, provided comic relief and youthful perspectives.

Serving as the show's writer and producer, Durham secured a financial backer. Perhaps because of its prior experiences with radio, the Chicago Metropolitan Mutual Assurance Company, the largest Negro insurance company in Chicago, agreed to finance the show. Four years after its establishment in 1925, Chicago Metropolitan—then called the Metropolitan Funeral System Association—sponsored show-business veteran Jack Leroy Cooper's *The All Negro Hour* on Chicago station WSBC.[45] Cooper's variety show became so popular and financially successful that it marked the beginning of what has been called black appeal radio—the numerous stations throughout the country that specifically targeted black listeners.[46]

Chicago station WJJD started airing *Here Comes Tomorrow* on September 8, 1947, two days after Durham's thirtieth birthday.[47] Listeners could enter the Redmonds' world every Monday, Wednesday, and Friday at 10 A.M., and the series earned enthusiastic reviews.[48] Trade magazine *Billboard* claimed: "If all soap operas were as well written, produced and directed as this show, if they all had its intense dramatic content, its social significance and its potential as a weapon against intolerance, no one would ever again have to level an accusing finger at daytime dramatic serials."[49] Durham said that the show would always focus on social issues, and *Billboard* reported, "So far the sponsor has not objected to [the] habit of pulling no punches in placing blame for racial intolerance, and the station has received practically all complimentary responses from its listeners."[50]

A November 1947 review in the *Chicago Sun and Times* stated that not since NBC's *The Goldbergs*, a serial about a Jewish family in New York City, "has there been anything like *Here Comes Tomorrow*; nothing that [has] consistently—via dramatic presentation—done so much for an American minority." The paper concluded that *Here Comes Tomorrow* "might well be one of the best things that has come along to further understanding between the races."[51]

On a critical note, the trade periodical *Variety* reported that the show "bypasses the economic facts of Negro life through the simple device of dealing with a prosperous doctor's family."[52] A similar complaint would be levied against *The Cosby Show* nearly forty years later because an African American doctor and his lawyer wife headed the show's popular mid-1980s TV family. *Variety* further noted that although *Here Comes Tomorrow* scripts were "skillful . . . some scenes tend to develop too fast with the characters making split second shifts in emotions." The trade pointed out some technical difficulties in one episode, but overall, *Variety* conceded that *Here Comes Tomorrow* generated more sustained interest than "sister serials" on network radio.[53]

For a guided tour of a day in *Here Comes Tomorrow's* production life, readers could turn to the November 8, 1947, edition of the *Chicago Star*. Durham's tenure as associate editor and feature writer for the *Star* probably had ended by this time, since his hands were full writing scripts for both *Democracy USA* and *Here Comes Tomorrow*. Reporter Bill Alexander observed that on the morning he visited WJJD, its studio appeared to be "in a mild state of confusion" with the actors "milling" about, rehearsing their lines. In the adjoining control room, Durham checked his stopwatch and then commanded, "OK gang, let's take it down for a dress [rehearsal]." All eyes focused on Durham's raised arm. He gave the signal and the acting began. The *Chicago Star* reporter promptly fell in love.

"What comes through the loud speaker is as new and exciting as next week's headlines," Bill Alexander wrote. The "esprit de corps" and "sympathetic interpretation" of the cast impressed Alexander, and he admired Durham's ability to "drain the last drop of drama from the scripts he writes." For this reporter, *Here Comes Tomorrow* was an "outstanding serial show," with its "dignified portrayal of American Negroes devoid of stereotypes and 'Uncle Tomism.'"[54]

Durham juggled *Here Comes Tomorrow* and *Democracy USA* scriptwriting duties through the first two months of 1948. By the year's end, *Here Comes Tomorrow* won a second-place prize from *Billboard* magazine as one of the nation's top dramatic programs.[55] However, Chicago Metropolitan had stopped supporting the drama by then, and it was no longer on the air. "I don't know if the company felt that they could no longer afford it, or just what it was," Clarice Durham said.[56]

Meanwhile, personality clashes between WBBM producer Ben Parks and the *Defender's* Charles Browning had intensified. As a result, *Democracy USA* too left the air. Durham's last surviving *Democracy USA* script was dated February 15, 1948.[57]

In the meantime, Durham's friend Oscar Brown Jr. had brokered time on WJJD—the same station that aired *Here Comes Tomorrow*. Starting in early 1948, Brown produced a weekly morning program he called the *Negro News Front*. The show, in Brown's view, was "radical," presenting news with a leftist bent exclusively about black people around the world.[58] Brown served as the program's announcer, journalist Vernon Jarrett wrote the scripts, and Durham advised his friends.

"Dick was coaching us on giving some meaning to this 15 minutes that we were on the air," Vernon Jarrett said. "We were gonna change the world through our application of talents and awareness." And, Jarrett recalled, they started calling Durham "Buddha" behind his back. With his round, extended stomach on his stocky frame, Vernon joked that Dick would sit back "playing God," offering wisdom, pushing his friends to do their best and then urging them to try even harder.[59]

One of the stories that Brown's *Negro News Front* followed throughout 1948 concerned the presidential bid of Henry A. Wallace. A long time Democrat, Wallace had been President Roosevelt's vice president, and secretary of commerce under President Truman. Yet a few days after Christmas in 1947, Wallace announced his intention to run as an independent, Progressive Party presidential candidate. Wallace's platform in part called for enacting civil rights legislation and waging a victorious fight for freedom of speech and assembly throughout the world, ushering in "the century of the common man."[60] Durham supported the Progressive Party, keeping abreast of this fledgling third party movement through his wife's volunteering efforts, from Oscar Brown Jr.'s *Negro News Front* reporting, and via updates from his brother Earl, who headed a section of the party's youth division.[61]

Meanwhile, Durham was pulling together his next creative venture. Sometime in early 1948 he contacted an NBC official and the *Defender's* Charles Browning, hoping to convince the men to sponsor his proposed new radio series. He called it *Destination Freedom*. Durham said that he, along with friends Henry Jennings, Oscar Brown Jr., and Fred Pinkard "dreamed up" four possible show titles. The Negro spiritual "Oh, Freedom" inspired the *Destination Freedom* moniker, and the song would serve as the show's theme during its first months.[62]

Conceived as a series of half-hour dramas about the lives and contributions of prominent Negro history makers—freedom fighters all—*Destination Freedom* basically was a more hard-hitting version of *Democracy USA*. Remembering his earlier clashes with WBBM's Ben Parks, Charles Browning was not particularly enthusiastic about backing another radio program. But Durham worked his magic: he found a way to get Browning on board, although no surviving records document exactly how Durham did it.

Browning approached Irwin Showerman, vice president of NBC's Central [Midwest] Division, to discuss the possibility of airing Durham's proposed series on WMAQ.[63] Should the network affiliate agree to air *Destination Freedom*, Durham would once again work with NBC staff director Homer Heck, the man who directed Durham's *At the Foot of Adams Street* scripts five years earlier. Browning and Showerman soon reached an agreement, paving the way for this series' birth.

However, in what must have felt like a case of déjà vu for Durham, WMAQ and NBC officials imposed a strict set of restrictions on the series. NBC, for instance, did not want *Destination Freedom* to deal with segregation because they believed "that was a constitutional matter," and, Durham added, the network's restrictions "would have been murder on the series." Durham claimed, however, that he "wasn't particularly worried." He believed that the restrictions could be minimized, if not eliminated, once the strength of the storytelling became evident.[64]

WMAQ and NBC agreed to cover all internal costs, including studio fees and the services of director Homer Heck, the musicians, and audio technicians. The *Defender* would pay Durham and the show's actors.[65] As the series' sole writer, Durham initially asked for $175 per script. He settled for less; one account indicated that he received $125 a script; another claimed the figure was $150.[66]

Although Durham's income had increased from the $110 script fee he had earned writing for *Democracy USA*, he knew that his pay was not at the level it should have been. Years later he claimed that $200 was the standard pay for half-hour scripts. In addition, Durham said that other "biographical social drama" shows of that time had substantial writing and research staffs. CBS's *Calvacade of America*, for example, used more than fifteen writers a year. According to communications scholar Matthew Ehrlich, that long-running series "dramatized notable events from the nation's past"—although it virtually ignored Negro achievements.[67] Durham lamented that while other serials employed several writers, he did not even have money to pay a researcher.[68]

So channeling his favorite jazz musicians, Durham improvised.

He returned to one of his favorite childhood haunts, the Hall Branch Library, and enlisted the help of head librarian Vivian Harsh and her staff. Oscar Brown Jr. said that "Homer Heck and the powers that be down at NBC" reviewed "the political correctness" of the list of names Durham submitted for show topics. Durham then gave his approved list to Vivian Harsh. She and her librarians "would just plunge in there," Brown said, providing Durham "with that raw data which he, of course, would have to cull through and come up with a story."[69]

Richard Durham and his Du Bois Theater Guild colleagues brought a keen sense of purpose to the series. "At the time you were running with the wind in your face," Durham explained. "There was that thing of a crusad[ing] spirit . . . a drive to get the story over."[70] Durham's list of potential subjects included such strong, principled Negroes as abolitionists Frederick Douglass and Sojourner Truth, innovators Daniel Hale Williams and George Washington Carver, educators Mary McLeod Bethune and Carter G. Woodson, boxing greats Joe Louis and Sugar Ray Robinson, as well as musicians Hazel Scott and Fats Waller. Through such characters, Durham planned to "cut [through] the lies, the distortions, the falsehoods, the stereotypes and slanders that clutter up the field and hide the real nature of Negro characters." Reflecting what he saw as a universal human desire for freedom and equality, Durham said he sought to

> find the kernel of Negro life and to plant it in the sunshine of some artistic form which will reveal its inner beauty—its depth—its realistic emotions—its humanness—much as did Balzac with the Frenchmen of his day, Dickens for the poverty-stricken English, Gorki and Chekhov for the Russians.[71]

Nor was the irony lost on Durham that *Destination Freedom* would air on the same station where *Amos 'n' Andy* began its climb to national stardom. In fact, Judith Waller, WMAQ's educational and public affairs programming director, had shepherded *Amos 'n' Andy* to the NBC network in 1929.[72] Therefore, Durham thought that Waller "might be one of those who would be most reluctant to put on a story realistically depicting the plight of black people in America." Yet when the scripts reached her desk, Waller approved them, Durham said. "She was powerful enough," he added, that if "[she] says OK, then you had to think before you attacked Judith"—or questioned her judgment.[73]

WMAQ scheduled *Destination Freedom*'s debut for Sunday, June 20, 1948, at 10 A.M.[74] The first episode examined the life of Crispus Attucks, a former slave, dedicated rebel, and reportedly one of the first casualties of the American Revolutionary War. "What was remarkable about it was that [Durham] didn't just sort of document and narrate a story," Oscar Brown Jr. said. "He would come up with some kind of dramatic concept, so that when he read about Crispus Attucks . . . he'd give him a personality."[75] Durham used one of Attucks's distinguishing physical characteristics to humanize his protagonist and provide humor.

Durham's script reveals that Attucks was a "big fella," 6'2" tall, with deep scars on his back—the result of being whipped after his first unsuccessful attempt at escaping slavery. When asked to identify his master after his successful escape, Durham's Attucks replies, "I am my own master . . . I'll never go back to slavery alive."[76] Later in the script, Attucks applies for a job on a Boston-based whaling ship. The ship's skipper asks Attucks where his loyalty lies:

ATTUCKS: My loyalty?
SKIPPER: With the King [of England] or with the colonies?
ATTUCKS: (*Considers.*) It depends, sir.

SKIPPER: (*Suspicious.*) On what—

ATTUCKS: On what side there'll be freedom for me.[77]

During his research, Durham found a wanted ad for the escaped slave that described Attucks as a man whose "knees were slightly closer to each other than knees are ordinary." Durham humorously illustrates this fact in a scene in which Attucks is fitted for pants for his new job on the whaling ship.

SKIPPER: Stand up straight, man so I can measure you. (*Impatient.*) Can't you stand straight?

ATTUCKS: (*At loss.*) I am standing straight, sir.

SKIPPER: (*Peeved.*) No such thing! Are you trying to make a fool of me?

MATE: Why Skipper—no wonder he ain't standin' straight—(*Dawns on him.*)—he's got knock-knees.

SKIPPER: Got what?

MATE: Knock-knees. (*Up.*) Hey boys, take a look at these knock-knees.

SKIPPER: (*Sees.*) Well bless my soul. He stands like an "X," he does. (*Starts a short laugh and finally goes at it full.*)

NARRATOR: The knock-kneed man looked down at his own legs—and he too began to laugh.[78]

The script's narrator explains how the laughter of Crispus Attucks and his fellow whalers "rolled out across the docks. The laughter rolled out and tied the men together. Laughter rolled out in the grog shops, in the town square, in the streets." Durham claims that the laughter rolled on for "20 years," until the day a British officer orders the men to stop because he detects "rebellion in your brain." The British officer declares, "I'm here to see that [rebellion] doesn't spread to other ports."[79]

But rebellion does spread. As resistance to England's increasingly repressive grip on the American colonies intensifies, Attucks says: "Once when I was a slave I used to dream of freedom at night. But in the morning I would wake up still a slave. Then one day I dreamed I could give my life for freedom and when I woke up I was unafraid and nothing stood in my way. Nothing could stop me from helping others win freedom. I could see that if everyone had freedom—no one would need steal it from another man. Only then would we all be safe."[80]

On a fateful night in 1770, Attucks leads a citizens' protest against the occupation of a Boston square by British troops—Durham's nod to the site of the infamous Boston Massacre, birthplace of the American Revolution. In Durham's interpretation, Attucks consciously "picked his own destiny," giving his life for freedom. Before being shot by British soldiers, Attucks commands the protesters behind him: "Go on. You who want to be free—strike—the first blow!" Accompanied by the sounds of an angry crowd, guns shots, and music, Durham's narrator declares near the script's finale:

NARRATOR: In Boston, the people took up the body of the black man with knock-knees and the bodies of white men and planted them like seeds in the same grave. In Monticello, [Thomas] Jefferson dreamed of a Declaration of Independence. In Boston, Crispus Attucks and his followers had already declared it."[81]

WMAQ and the NBC officials were very happy with Durham's first script.[82] Yet conflict—like an uninvited interloper—lurked in the background, threatening to disrupt the series at will.

Before the series' debut, Durham failed to meet initial script deadlines, a problem he would repeat at other times during the show's run. As a result, *Destination Freedom*'s inaugural show had to be delayed one week.[83] Meanwhile, Durham, Du Bois Theater Guild actors, along with WMAQ's technical staff, diligently worked to fine-tune the first show.

During a run-through of the Crispus Attucks script, Durham took issue with Homer Heck's directing. In Durham's opinion, Heck, a white man in his thirties, encouraged a stereotypical portrayal of his main character. Durham wrote: "None of the Negro characters can be portrayed in the stereotypical manner because none of the situations contained in these dramas will be derived from stereotypical situations."[84] In an impassioned, single-spaced, typed letter, Durham complained to Heck that he had directed the actor playing Attucks to take a humble approach.[85] As a result, Durham said that Attucks's character "turned out to be the most insignificant of them all—although he was what the show was all about."

"Perhaps the actor went too far in the direction," Durham conceded. "Nevertheless, I think when you examine the record you'll find him so humble as to be inconsistent with a fiery rebel—which he was." Durham further claimed, "There are times when any man may be written as humble, but with the Negro it's simply overworked—phoney—and in some cases a perversion." Durham's indignation pushed him to add:

A good many white people have cushioned themselves into dreaming that Negroes are not self-assertive, confident and never leave the realm of fear or subservience—to portray them as they are will give a great education [to white listeners] than a dozen lectures. A Negro character will be rebellious, biting, scornful, angry, cocky as the occasion calls for—not forever humble, meek, etc. as some would like to imagine.[86]

Negro characters like Attucks were "leaders and initiators of historical movements—not accidents," Durham wrote, adding that these black men and women "led white as well as Negro groups." Durham also wanted his female characters to be presented "as so many Negro women are, dauntless, determined, who have a healthy contempt for people who live by race prejudice and who are quick to recognize and extend a warm hand to other humans. [Such portrayals] would be an honest, but for radio, radical approach."[87] Durham concluded his letter, stating, "Negroes in general believe that their complete, full scale emancipation is inevitable. No amount of demands for abnormal subservience, segregation or denials can stop it. They take equality (which in some circles is still controversial) as a matter of fact."[88]

Talking about *Destination Freedom* years later, Homer Heck admitted: "I had never worked with blacks. I had no idea what they were like . . . although I had some hint from what was going on [in society]." As in former presidential candidate Thomas Dewey's Michigan hometown, Negroes couldn't stay overnight in Heck's birthplace, Norman, Oklahoma. "Blacks who came in to work had to leave by sundown," Heck said. "And I always felt, though I had no association with any of them . . . that would be rough." However, Heck said that he was excited, very curious, and delighted to be associated with *Destination Freedom*. "It was sort of a significant thing to be doing," Heck said, adding that Durham wrote some "pretty damn good scripts."[89]

Regarding Durham's objections to Heck's directorial approach on the Attucks script, "I'm not sure if all his arguments held sway," Clarice Durham said. Yet her husband held his ground concerning his characters' portrayals on later shows.[90] Still, on June 27, 1948, at exactly 10 A.M., Durham's *Destination Freedom* moved into broadcast history on Crispus Attucks's broad shoulders and knocked knees.

• • •

Because Richard missed his first script deadline, NBC executive William J. Murphy imposed stricter schedules. Murphy required Durham to submit scripts at least ten days before their broadcast dates; as well, he drafted a new production schedule using six additional writers, including himself.[91] Durham would be responsible for writing only four of the next ten shows.

The schedule landed on Durham's desk with a thud.

In a controlled rage, Durham fired off a letter to Murphy on July 7, 1948, indicating in it that he was both "surprised and amazed" that Murphy had "taken the license to assign other writers to write my show *Destination Freedom*, without asking for either my permission or position on the matter."[92] Durham added:

> The format, premise and title of *Destination Freedom* is the sole property of this writer and application for its copyright is on file with the U.S. Government. Naturally any violation of this copyright will be considered willful and deliberate and I will be compelled to put the matter in the hands of the legal authorities of the Radio Writers Guild.[93]

Durham was an active member and officer in the Radio Writers Guild, a union created in 1937 to protect the rights of its members.[94] He also complained to

Charles Browning about Murphy's actions and bemoaned the fact that three weeks into production, "I have not received a single penny in payment for the use of these scripts." So Durham delivered an ultimatum: "Unless this matter is cleaned up in full by Friday of this week [July 7, 1948] you are advised, and I shall advise WMAQ not to use the script which I have prepared for next Sunday's broadcast and that no further broadcasts shall be made under the title and format of *Destination Freedom*."[95]

Durham's letters did the trick. He regained his sole author duties, and *Destination Freedom's* modified ten-week schedule in summer 1948 included an eclectic mix of fiery abolitionists, brave explorers, and contemporary trendsetters:[96]

Harriet Tubman	July 4
Dark Explorers	July 11
Denmark Vesey	July 18
Frederick Douglass (Part I)	July 25
Frederick Douglass (Part II)	August 1
Dr. Daniel Hale Williams	August 8
Sojourner Truth	August 15
Matthew Henson	August 22
Charles Caldwell	August 29
James Weldon Johnson	September 5

While Murphy, Browning, and Durham haggled over script assignment and compensation issues, Durham's former *Democracy USA* writing partner, Perry "Skee" Wolf, completed the Frederick Douglass script Murphy had asked him to write. Therefore, Murphy asked Browning to pay Wolf the agreed $125 fee.[97] This seemingly simple request became the genesis of what turned into a strained relationship between WMAQ and the *Defender*.

By late July 1948, William Murphy told Charles Browning that WMAQ was still waiting for the *Defender* to pay *Destination Freedom's* actors and Durham—costs that averaged between $250 and $300 per week. Browning acknowledged that the *Defender* had agreed to pay talent costs, but he requested that the station consider evenly splitting those fees. In a further attempt to keep costs down, Browning asked Durham to limit the number of actors to about five per show. Nevertheless, Durham populated his scripts with between thirteen and twenty-four characters as he tackled the monumental task of churning out weekly half-hour dramas.[98]

"What he was accomplishing was just absolutely impossible, except he did it. He had to," Oscar Brown Jr. said. "He didn't know it was impossible. So he accomplished it, you know, every week."[99] Actually, after working with Robert Lucas, Perry Wolf, and Irna Phillips, Durham knew that sharing scriptwriting duties could be less stressful. Durham's insistence on exclusive authorship of *Destination Freedom* had more to do with his desire to maintain creative control

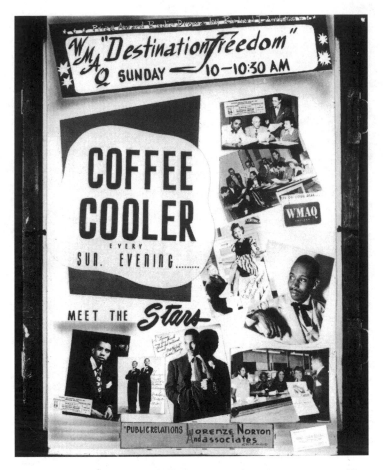

FIGURE 7. A publicity flyer, circa the late 1940s, advertising a weekly social that supported *Destination Freedom* and other Chicago-based shows and entertainers. Oscar Brown Jr. is pictured in the bottom left corner. Richard Durham Papers, Vivian G. Harsh Research Collection, Chicago Public Library.

over his series. As a result, Durham's series would have a powerful, consistent viewpoint and a lyrically signature tone.

Still, Durham scrambled to keep up with the show's demanding production schedule. To help her husband meet his weekly deadlines, Clarice typed his scripts. "I had to read his terrible handwriting," Clarice smiled, remembering Dick's large, often-hard-to-decipher scrawl. Sometimes as Clarice typed a script's last page, Dick snatched it out of the typewriter and dashed out the door with it.[100]

FIGURE 8. Chanie Durham sits with her eldest daughter Claudia Marie along with Richard and his son's dog, Patch, during the late 1960s. Courtesy of Clarice Durham.

Throughout this process, however, Durham's family was supportive. His parents bragged about their former wayward son "all over the place," Earl Durham said. "They'd say, 'That's my son! Be sure to listen on Sunday!'"

In Earl's view, Dick "got to be the star of the family," since Earl believed that he and his siblings pursued "ordinary" professions.[101] But there was nothing ordinary about the fact that Claudia Marie became a respected nurse and supervisor in Chicago's Providence Hospital, or that Clotilde's love of science led her to work as chief of bacteriology at Howard University Hospital in Washington, D.C. Winifred became a Chicago Public School counselor, and Caldwell served as an engineer with a defense contractor in Los Angeles. Earl taught sociology at the prestigious University of Chicago. The only Durham sibling surviving on a blue-collar job was CG.[102] Clearly, Curtis and Chanie's dream of a better life through education for their children had come true.

And by the time Durham's *Destination Freedom* hit Chicago's radio airwaves, his wife had realized her dream of becoming a kindergarten teacher.[103] For both Clarice and Richard, the future looked particularly bright.

CHAPTER 7

Freedom

"Railway to Freedom"

> VOICE: (*Slight echo. Longing, searching, lonesome.*)
> Oh H-a-r-r-i-e-t!
> MUSIC: Imitate intonations "Oh Harriet"
> HARRIET: (*On cue. Listening, intense, with depth, warmth
> and slight touch of the mystic.*) I'm Harriet Tub-
> man. I lived in the shadows out of sight of the
> light of Liberty. I heard their voices call out to
> me in the dark. . . They were the voices of slaves.
> They were the voices of my people. When I heard
> them the earth moved under me. Rockets burst in
> my head. They were the voices of God! (*Quieter.*)
> I—was Moses.
> SINGER: (*On cue.*) Go Down Moses
> Way down in Egypt land
> Tell ole Pharoah
> To let my people go[1]
> —Richard Durham, July 4, 1948, *Destination Freedom*

Richard Durham surrounded himself with giants.

Harriet Tubman. Benjamin Banneker. Katherine Dunham. Toussaint L'Ouver-
ture. Black leaders like these spoke to him, hour after hour, as he sifted through
the mounds of materials that Vivian G. Harsh, head of the Hall Branch Library,

and her staff provided. Sitting in the library's airy special collections reading room, with its dark oak floors and pale green walls, Durham read historical documents about a potpourri of Negro history makers.[2] He learned about their triumphs. Their failures. Their idiosyncrasies. He then decided how to best shape the dramas documenting their lives within *Destination Freedom's* half-hour timeframe.

Durham varied his storytelling approach, alternating between straightforward dramatic narratives and more whimsical or comical takes. Whatever the form, Durham created eloquent, politically outspoken scripts. *Destination Freedom's* multiracial cast and crew then transformed those scripts into the aural equivalent of a page-turning novel.

Never circumspect about his intentions, Durham told an interviewer during the series' run that "the job cut out for writers, actors and directors working with Negro material" called for breaking through stereotypes, shattering "the conventions and traditions which have prevented us from dramatizing the infinite store of material from the history and current struggles for freedom." Such struggles defined what Durham called "the truly universal people"—individuals whose experiences held "the key to the essential meaning of life for men and women of our day."[3]

In Durham's presentation of progressive blacks "as heroes fighting white supremacy," scholar Judith E. Smith called *Destination Freedom* a "powerful expression of racially inclusive universalism." Smith believed that Durham "reversed" Hollywood stereotypes by demonstrating that nonwhite protagonists, perceived to be "different" because of their race, were actually just like everyone else.[4]

Universalism was one of Durham's abiding philosophies. "I think the Afro-American represents that particular microcosm of the entire world," Durham said years later. "And by using that particular microcosm you can reveal the human condition of the main body of people of the world."[5] In Durham's opinion, oppression combined with poverty, inadequate education, and insufficient healthcare adversely affected most of the world's population. Therefore, he believed that an American Negro's sharecropping experience "is instantly recognizable to 500,000,000 Chinese people who have undergone the same experiences under imperialism for 300 years. A Negro character confused by the caste system in the land of his birth, is instantly identifiable to 450,000,000 Indians in Asia [or] 150,000,000 Africans in Africa."[6] The same connection, Durham said, could be made with Malaysians in Burma, with Jewish people struggling to create the new nation of Israel in 1948, and "with the millions of Europeans and white Americans who also want to uproot poverty and prejudice." In addition, Durham believed that women "of all races and creeds in their upward swing towards a real emancipation, find it natural to identify their striving with the direction and emotional realism in Negro life today."[7]

Destination Freedom's protagonists stood up for their rights while championing equality and justice for their fellow citizens. Yet historian J. Fred MacDonald contended that Durham's characters, "were never able to forget the fragile quality of their triumphs. . . . Durham poignantly illustrated that all blacks must be prepared to encounter the interference of race prejudice in any career."[8] For example, despite singer/actress Lena Horne's considerable fame, a Southern restaurant refused to serve her because of her race. And women's suffrage activist Mary Church Terrell was forcibly ejected from a public bus in the nation's capital because she refused to move to the rear where blacks were relegated to sit based on Jim Crow dictates.[9] According to director Homer Heck, "There was a certain sameness to the point of view" in *Destination Freedom*'s episodes. "The details of the stories were different of course, but I remember the whole experience with considerable pleasure. The Harriet Tubman script was one that comes to mind quickly."[10]

In "Railway to Freedom," Durham's Tubman character narrates her own story. At the beginning of the script, Harriet Tubman is a young slave, growing "wild like a weed" on a Maryland plantation.[11] One day a fellow slave runs past her, trying to escape from the plantation. Tubman blocks their owner's attempt to catch the fleeing slave. The owner threatens to hit her with the heavy iron bar he's holding if she doesn't move.

Durham's Harriet states: "I was afraid, but I wouldn't move. I wouldn't move! I saw him lift the iron bar. Then his hand struck down!"[12] Tubman collapses. Ethereal sound effects indicate her semi-conscious thoughts. "The earth moved and rockets burst in my head," Tubman says. Durham returns often to this earth/rocket metaphor, using it to represent the painful headaches, seizures, and loss of consciousness Tubman endures for the rest of her life because of her owner's blow.[13]

Once Tubman emerges from her wound-induced coma, she fervently desires freedom. "There are two things I have a right to—liberty or death," she declares. "One or the other I mean to have. I shall fight for my liberty."[14] Thenceforth, Harriet Tubman becomes fascinated with the Underground Railroad, a clandestine network of secular and religious organizations and individuals—black and white—who serve as the railway's conductors or agents. They secretly provide food, shelter, or financial assistance to escaping slaves—the railroad's passengers.[15]

Tubman eventually rides the Underground Railroad to freedom. However, she soon realizes that she wants family members and other slaves to taste the sweetness of liberty. Tubman becomes an Underground Railroad conductor, and her numerous liberation trips back into and out of the South are rife with danger. Tubman and her passengers could be caught and dragged back into slavery at any turn. While the exact number of slaves Tubman spirited away is in dispute, she courageously led many of her people to freedom.[16]

A couple of weeks after "Railway to Freedom" aired on Independence Day 1948, Durham wanted to bring Nat Turner's story to the airwaves. Turner, a Virginia-based slave, led a violent revolt in August 1831. But Durham indicated that NBC officials "rejected out of hand" this suggestion. They questioned how Durham would deal with the fact that Turner's rebellion caused the deaths of at least fifty-three white slave owners and their families.[17] Durham compared Turner's tale to that of Spartacus, the former soldier and slave who organized thousands of enslaved citizens and led an uprising against the Roman Empire. "How many slaveholders did Spartacus kill?" Durham rhetorically asked. "I don't know, but [his actions] added to the freedom of the world." Durham's argument didn't sway WMAQ executives.[18]

Instead, Durham turned to the story of Denmark Vesey, a former slave who masterminded a revolt nine years before Nat Turner. Vesey's 1822 slave revolt in South Carolina reportedly involved about nine thousand conspirators.[19] Although Vesey's uprising was foiled before it gained traction, his disciplined actions frightened slaveholders. They realized that Negroes were capable of taking whatever steps they felt necessary to obtain freedom. "The organization of [Vesey's rebellion] had taken a number of years," Durham explained. "And because the subsequent trial went on so long, there was quite a bit of material as to how it was organized."[20]

In order for a drama to be compelling, Durham believed that its hero needed to possess attributes the average listener also desired. "One of those attributes is courage," Durham said. In spite of the real possibility of being thrust back into the prison of slavery, Denmark Vesey refused to move north to a more welcoming environment after paying for his freedom with money he won in a lottery. He courageously stayed in the South, inspiring his people to tear down a system that oppressed them.

In this episode, a deep-voiced narrator leads listeners through Vesey's evolution. Durham's script starts with his main character's post-revolt criminal trial.

> **NARRATOR:** They say slaveholder's court was crowded that day in Charleston. They say the culprit was caught in the act—had conceded the crime. They say all was over but the hanging, and soon the masters could sleep, could rest.[21]

The script then flashes back to how Vesey wins his freedom and subsequently recruits followers. One supporter is a black woman who sells cherries in the town's marketplace. She agrees to alert the conspirators if danger approaches. When the militia swoops in to crush the revolt, the woman hawks the agreed upon signal, "Blood Red Cherries." She is killed, and Vesey is captured. Durham's script ends where it began, at Vesey's trial for treachery against the state of South Carolina.[22] After the judge castigates the former slave for his crimes, Denmark Vesey responds with a statement that is stunning in its militancy—especially its last line—for radio of the 1940s:

DENMARK: You speak of my "crimes." I feel no guilt. I felt to be idle while other men fought to be free was a crime. I was not idle. Others talked. I acted. I'd act again!

CROWD: (*Slight murmurs of unrest. "Hang him," etc.*)

JUDGE: (*Gravel raps.*) Order! Order! Is that all you can say to explain your treachery?

DENMARK: (*Thoughtfully.*) No. My treachery began when I read the Declaration of Independence . . . it said "All men are created equal." It grew when I read that black Crispus Attucks died to help the colonies be free. Did he die just to free white men or all men? Then I read what Ben Franklin, Tom Paine, LaFayette and Jefferson had said and their words warmed my blood. They wanted their revolution to make all men free and equal. They stopped with some men free and some men slaves. I took up where they left off. (*Slower.*) I found my price when I was a slave . . . I paid it. If my life is the price I pay to be free . . . take it. I'll pay it. Until all men are free, the revolution goes on![23]

This statement constitutes "one of the most damning critiques of racial abuse ever heard on U.S. radio," historian J. Fred MacDonald wrote.[24] Certainly, Durham's Denmark Vesey was unlike any black man normally heard on a medium where comic and subservient Negro characters ruled the day. Such characters included Rochester, played by actor Eddie Anderson on the popular *Jack Benny Show*, and Eddie Green on *Duffy's Tavern*. The black protagonists on the still popular *Amos 'n' Andy Show* continued to be played by their white creators, Freeman Gosden and Charles Correll.

So why did WMAQ and NBC allow *Destination Freedom*'s progressive sentiments and rebellious Negro characters on the air? One explanation may be that *Destination Freedom* could be heard only in Chicago. NBC officials claimed that Southern affiliates would bristle at its content and refuse to air it.[25] Realistically, an affiliate station near Durham's Mississippi birthplace or in South Carolina would have strenuously objected to the series' dramatizations.

Radio networks treated shows about racial issues like a "tale of caution and restriction," historian Barbara Savage asserted. The networks feared that programs about race would alienate listeners and damage their ability to attract and retain advertisers. Yet more liberal approaches to the race question seemed to emerge in the post–World War II era, especially "after President Harry Truman's embrace of the rhetoric of racial equality," and after protests by black Americans "pushed the issue onto the public airwaves," Savage suggested.[26]

• • •

Richard Durham believed that people should have the opportunity—the free-dom—to pursue their passions, whether as an explorer, a scientist, or an artist. For example, in his show about famed musician/composer W. C. Handy, Durham first presents Handy as a naive teenager who is fascinated by the blues.[27] Working as a water boy for a prison chain gang, Handy carries water to a prisoner named Lemon—Durham's salute to the great blues singer/guitarist Blind Lemon Jefferson. Young Handy asks Lemon what the blues are all about. Lemon replies:

> LEMON: Blues, Water Boy, is your heart. It's a train callin' you. It's a woman minus a man. It's talk turned into music. It's music that gets down to the rocky bottom. Sometimes it's a sad song.[28]
> HANDY: Then why you sing it?
> LEMON: The blues regenerates a man, Water Boy.
> HANDY: Will it regenerate me?
> LEMON: (*Laughs.*) Get yourself a good guitar. Maybe I'll teach you to see for yourself."[29]

Handy saves his earnings and buys a guitar. But Handy's religious mother and father discourage his blues infatuation. In a clever turn, Durham's narrator states: "Mrs. Handy called in Professor Bach, a doctor of music, who examined the patient from bass to treble clef and diagnosed his ailment." The professor finds that young Handy "is suffering from a severe dis-temperment of the pentatonic scales," with "an overgrowth of the minor chords tending towards dissonance"—Durham's creative description of the musical elements that make up the blues.[30] Professor Bach recommends that Handy study music's "proper"—translate classical—elements.

During the next twenty years, Handy masters those musical elements. But the draw of the music of his people remains strong, pushing Handy to search for a "good, rich music that's got a language and body." One cool evening, he lands in St. Louis and hears a woman humming "an odd tune." Handy asks about the song and she starts by saying, "I hate to see the evenin' sun go down." This line opens "The St. Louis Blues," the tune most associated with W. C. Handy.[31] Because of his prolific composing and arranging, Handy becomes known as the father of the blues.

"Dick had this talent of capturing the idiom, not just the African American, [but also] the American idiom," writer Studs Terkel said. "He was just gifted."[32] Exercising his acting muscles, Terkel played several characters in *Destination Freedom*. He was a sheriff in one episode and a plantation overseer in another. Perhaps Terkel's most memorable role was in "The Rime of the Ancient Dodger," Durham's whimsical homage to Jackie Robinson. Robinson integrated baseball's lily-white major leagues in 1947.

Studs Terkel played Sammy the Whammy, a comical, all-knowing, Brooklyn-accented narrator who loves his "beautiful Bums"—his homegrown Brooklyn Dodgers team. Sammy witnesses and condemns the racism that levies two strikes against Jackie Robinson before he steps onto a baseball field simply because he's a Negro. By hiring the major league's first black player, his Bums, Sammy claims, "outlawed the second strike! . . . when other teams balked, the Dodgers risked it."[33]

Durham even takes a satirical swipe—in rhyme—at the House Un-American Activities Committee and its search for Communist subversives throughout America.[34] Sammy admonishes Babe, a Brooklyn Dodgers fan, for missing Robinson's debut:

SAMMY: You mean you missed the Dodgers game today?
BABE: Didn't I say so?
SAMMY: Didja mother die? Didja have a stroke? Or wuz you just flat broke?
BABE: Neither. I wuz getting' married to Timothy Rodgers.
SAMMY: You mean you've gone an' divorced the Dodgers?
BABE: So what! Who in the devil are you to bother?
SAMMY: (*Hates to tell her.*) Babe, I'm Sammy the Whammy.
BABE: Well Scrammy, Sammy!
SAMMY: Babe, I'm from the Un-Brooklyn Activities Committee. For bein' so disloyal, I could have you boiled in oil!"[35]

When Terkel's character calms downs, he tells Babe about how his "whammy" eye lets him see what racial discrimination looks like in baseball and Jackie Robinson's dignified response to it. "See, his way of writing was not complicated," Studs Terkel said. "He was looking for clarity. It is easy to write something complex and let it go at that, but to do something such as *Destination Freedom* clearly . . . How can you go wrong with that?"[36]

Clarity, a strong philosophical base, and inventiveness defined the *Destination Freedom* series. In some shows Durham brought inanimate objects to life. Louis Armstrong's trumpet guides listeners through the talented musician's childhood in one show. A slow talking, ominous-sounding character embodies "Ghetto Slums" in the episode about Chicago preacher and politician Archibald Carey.[37] And in "The Story of 1875" Durham takes listeners through twelve months in the life of Reconstruction-era, Mississippi-based congressman Charles Caldwell, allowing the year to serve as narrator. Because Caldwell actively lobbies for voting rights and equality, Ku Klux Klan–like characters threaten the congressman on the first day of 1875's existence. On the year's last day, Caldwell is assassinated for his activism.[38]

In "The Heart of George Cotton," Durham expands the program he first created for *Democracy USA*, chronicling the innovations of Negro surgeons Dr. Daniel Hale Williams and his protégé, Dr. Ulysses Grant Dailey. Durham revisited other shows he'd written for *Democracy USA*, adding more bite to storylines for characters like J. Ernest Wilkins, the young mathematician who helped to develop the atomic bomb, and NAACP head Walter White.[39] Durham also created episodes about several of his literary heroes, including W. E. B. Du Bois, Richard Wright, and James Weldon Johnson.

Honoring his friend Langston Hughes, Durham christened one program *Shakespeare of Harlem*, inspired by the title of one of Hughes's books of poetry.[40] On September 20, 1948, Durham sent Hughes an urgent message asking if he could use Langston's "Freedom Train" and "Democracy" poems in the show scheduled for the end of the month.[41] Hughes granted permission and subsequently wrote to Durham: "I hear that the radio program about me was very good indeed, and I would love very much to have a copy of the script—or two copies if you can spare them."[42]

Hughes also told his buddy that he'd recommended him for a writing job. Both the CBS and NBC networks planned on airing a NAACP-sponsored show on Emancipation Day. "I was commissioned to do one of the scripts and I suggested that they secure you to do the other one," Hughes wrote. "But something went wrong with the plan and although I have been paid for my script, just whether there will be one or two or no programs is not yet clear. But if you do hear from them you will know what it is all about."[43]

Yet by the time he received Hughes's missive in early October, Richard Durham was swimming in some extremely murky waters. *Destination Freedom*'s continued survival was in serious jeopardy.

• • •

Back in early September 1948, the *Chicago Defender* had suggested that WMAQ discontinue *Destination Freedom* after thirteen weeks. The paper's public relations executive, Charles Browning, proposed that WMAQ and the *Defender* "evaluate the show . . . and plan another series to begin within six weeks after [*Destination Freedom*] is concluded."[44] Given the largely positive response the show generated, especially in Chicago's Negro communities, the *Defender*'s suggestion seemed counterintuitive.[45] However, Browning's proposal was rooted in politics. The *Defender* had endorsed a Democratic contender to a state legislative seat. *Destination Freedom* cast member Oscar Brown Jr. was vying for the same seat as a Progressive Party candidate. *Defender* officials apparently objected to Brown's name being mentioned each Sunday during the series' broadcasts, and Durham believed that the paper wanted to discontinue the show and its association with Brown until after the campaign season ended.[46]

Not inclined to disrupt the series' continuity, WMAQ program manager Arthur Jacobson offered to assume a portion of the show's talent costs.[47] Charles Browning lobbed a bombshell in his reply. "I regret very deeply to inform you that we will have to conclude the radio show as of this Sunday, October 17," Browning wrote.[48] The *Chicago Defender* was immediately ending its financial support of *Destination Freedom*.

WMAQ scrambled to find another sponsor. Chicago's Negro Insurance Association expressed interest. But Arthur Jacobson was not impressed with the response he received about the organization from the Better Business Bureau. Therefore, Jacobson told director Homer Heck that *Destination Freedom* would "become a sustaining program and we will pay all of the talent thereon."[49] This included the actors, limited to approximately seven each week, and Richard Durham. The October 31 show was a repeat performance of "The Heart of George Cotton." New programming resumed on November 7 with an episode about composer, bandleader, and pianist Duke Ellington.[50]

Durham maintained his weekly jaunts to the Hall Branch Library and his daily stints in front of his home typewriter. Yet he did not know how long *Destination Freedom*'s heartbeat would last. In a mid-November memo to WMAQ's accounting department, Arthur Jacobson indicated: "*Destination Freedom* is costing us from $300 to $350 per week . . . it seems to me that we might consider carrying the program through the end of this year only."[51]

In the midst of these program survival concerns, Durham's personal life also was shifting. Dick and Clarice's relationship had survived their rocky first years, and they had been trying—without success—to start a family. After six years of marriage, the couple worried about their inability to get pregnant. "We had even gone to a fertility clinic to get advice," Clarice said, "but they couldn't find anything wrong and told us to just keep trying."[52] Persistence and love eventually paid off. Clarice began experiencing bouts of increased fatigue and queasiness in late fall 1948. She was pregnant, and the couple's baby was due in August.[53]

As they prepared for this new addition to their lives, Durham maintained his demanding work schedule. "Dick was out of sight!" friend Oscar Brown Jr. remembered admiringly. "He was always at the typewriter and in the George Cleveland Hall Library. . . . You'd go over to his house and he'd have a pencil in his mouth and he'd peck away at the typewriter. He'd write that way, scratching out, scratching out, scratching out. I used to watch him and I started doing that." Dick was trying to keep up with constant deadlines. "It was a feverish kind of thing," Brown said.[54]

Every Thursday afternoon, Durham, Homer Heck, and the show's cast and crew met at the station to "rehearse for about three hours," Oscar Brown Jr. recalled. "That was a read-through at the table with corrections on the script."[55]

The actors performed the script in front of microphones and rehearsed once more with sound effects. Durham and the actors subsequently returned to WMAQ around 7 A.M. each Sunday. "We might have two more [rehearsal] run-

```
                          -6-
1  VESEY:    (GERMAN. MIDDLE AGED. TALKS STACATTO. ..PRESSION OF
2            BEING A POWERFULLY BUILT MAN  BUT WITH TOUCH OF
3            DESPERATION.  DRINK DOESN'T AFFECT HIM NOTICEABLY)
4            Denmock? (UP) Denmock, is that you?  You finished the
5            hatches? You made the doors? You done your work?
6            What you come here for?
7  DENMARK:  Master--how much am I worth?
8  VESEY:    (HE'S BEEN THROUGH THAT BEFORE) Ach! it's that talk
9            again. Be useful; pour me a drink. (PAUSE) I warn
10           you once; I warn you again--get that out of your head.
11 DENMARK:  I'm asking--
12 VESEY:    I'm telling you. You're the ship's carpenter, be
13           satisfied (DOESN'T KNOW HOW TO DESCRIBE IT) This
14           freedom is a sickness. It's unbecoming to a slave.
15 DENMARK:  Master---
16 VESEY:    (CUT IN) Get it out of your mind!! It's those books
17           you read that turn your head. You read and read. All
18           night in the cabin you read, read. We stop in a port
19           in Spain, France, Holland, you bring on more books.
20           A slave shouldn't read too much. You should drink
21           here.
22 DENMARK:  No, I thank you--
23 VESEY:    (OVER) Pour me another. You're a planner, Denmock, I
24           know. You're mad and you've got a method to it,
25           but you'll get nowhere. I've watched you talk to
             people in the market. You tell the slaves they're
             born equal. Ach! Nonsense!
```

FIGURE 9. An edited page from Durham's "Denmark Vesey" script, dated July 18, 1948. Courtesy of J. Fred MacDonald.

throughs on Sunday morning before the actual show, which was live," Brown said. "We would have been through the script probably four or five times before we actually aired it."[56]

Studs Terkel believed that WMAQ's white employees did not know what to make of the *Destination Freedom* cast. "The only thing they knew before that was *Amos 'n' Andy*, white guys in minstrel make-up, you see." Instead, Terkel said, "here was this group of black actors and occasional white actor[s] such as myself."[57] Terkel's comments confirmed radio historian John Dunning's assertion that "radio in the '40s was a white actor's playground."[58] "There were no blacks in [serious] dramatic radio at that time," recalled Arthur Peterson, a white character actor who worked on *Destination Freedom* with his wife, Norma Ransom. The couple said that the show *It Can Be Done* was the one other series about blacks that aired locally in Chicago. But white actors played all the roles.[59]

Durham would later complain that WMAQ shut Negroes out of salaried positions. Durham essentially remained a freelancer, working full-time hours for low contractual pay during *Destination Freedom*'s run. When he approached Homer Heck about this, Heck allegedly told Durham that Heck "didn't see that changing during his time."[60] Actors Oscar Brown Jr. and Fred Pinkard complained about not being allowed to audition for better-paying roles on shows broadcast nationwide by NBC. According to Brown, Heck claimed that Southern affiliate stations would object to having Negro actors in the cast. Oscar replied, "It's radio. They would never see us or know we were colored."[61]

· · ·

By the end of 1948 Durham still had no idea how long *Destination Freedom* might survive. In later years, Durham claimed that the show's quality kept it alive. "Once [network executives] took to the show, and that included Homer Heck, they defended it very strongly," Durham said. "They became very proud of it."[62] Durham also noted that Heck "had a tremendous demand for quality. He had a sense of the beauty your characters could bring about."[63]

Starting in February 1949, Durham began reaping some benefits from his hard work. The series won several awards. For its "splendid contribution . . . towards the advance of Democracy in our time and towards the preservation of this production on records and in script as a heritage for future generations," Chicago's South Central Association presented its first award to a radio program.[64] In early May *Destination Freedom* snagged a first-place prize at the Thirteenth American Exhibition of Educational Radio Programs, sponsored by the Institute for Education by Radio at Ohio State University. The Institute praised *Destination Freedom* for its "vital, compelling use of radio technique in presenting contributions of Negroes to the development of democratic traditions and the American way of life."[65] Durham said that WMAQ and NBC officials were particularly impressed with this award because *Destination Freedom* had competed against other dramatic radio shows—and won.[66]

In late May, still high on *Destination Freedom*'s recent successes, Dick and Clarice entertained guests in their home during the Memorial Day weekend. Shortly thereafter, and completely unexpectedly, Clarice's water broke. Their baby was on its way, two months ahead of schedule.[67] On Wednesday, June 3, 1949, Mark Adam Durham, all four pounds, thirteen ounces of him, arrived. Clarice's doctor determined that the infant's weight was close enough to the normal birth weight—about five pounds—for newborns. So rather than spending his first hours in an incubator like many premature babies, Mark's strong cry could be heard in the hospital's regular nursery.

"Dick was happy, but cool, too," Clarice remembered. "He didn't show a lot of excitement."[68] Viewing the baby's still forming features, Dick would later tell Langston Hughes that the baby "look[s] like nobody I ever seen in my goddam life."[69] Mark did develop into a fresh-faced clone of his father. But immediately after his son's birth, Dick was concerned about how he and Clarice would care for this tiny, seemingly fragile infant who had arrived so much earlier than expected. As a result, Dick "insisted on our getting domestic help," Clarice said. They hired a woman who helped Clarice take care of Mark.[70] However, the new parents soon found out that their son was a strong, vocal baby.

"He cried a lot—he might have had colic—and it was hard to pacify him," Clarice remembered. To get Mark to go to sleep, Dick and Clarice sometimes put their child in his pajamas and rode around with him in their car. On Chicago's wide streets and flat terrain, the car's motion lulled the baby to sleep. At other times a next-door neighbor, mother of an infant as well, took a fussing Mark into her arms, and he quieted down. The baby's cries resumed when the neighbor handed Mark back to his mother. Clarice said that she "may have been tense and Mark felt it." Still, Dick and Clarice pampered their son. "And that's why I didn't get to the anniversary celebration for *Destination Freedom*. I had to stay home with this 'fragile' child," Clarice recalled, smiling.[71]

Destination Freedom celebrated its first birthday on June 26, 1949, with the broadcast of *Harriet's Children*, a recap of some of the best segments from the series.[72] Illinois Governor Adlai Stevenson praised the show for its "promotion of understanding and tolerance among the American people" and for doing its part "to familiarize us with the many contributions which Negroes have made to American life." Following the broadcast, a brunch, sponsored by a group called the Friends of the Negro Writer, honored Durham. He and his cast members then attended a celebratory dinner that evening at the South Side's Parkway Community House.[73]

• • •

In subsequent months, *Destination Freedom* earned awards from the Chicago Commission on Human Relations, the National Negro Museum and Historical Foundation, and the National Conference of Christians and Jews.[74] Durham's scripts continued to profile contemporary and historical black leaders—although occasionally he railed against housing discrimination and racial prejudice in thematic shows. Durham even explored the mythic tales of black folk heroes John Henry, the towering, muscle-bound steel driver, and Stackalee, the man known as the Negro Paul Bunyan.[75]

Oscar Brown Jr. called his friend a feminist. "Before there was any National Organization for Women or anything like that," Brown said, Durham's scripts advocated "equal pay for equal work" for women. "His characterization of Harriet Tubman or of Sojourner Truth," Brown added, extolled "the virtues of black women."[76] In general, Durham thought women were more progressive than men, and that many women exhibited strength of character under pressure. He believed that plenty of "Joan of Arcs and Florence Nightingales" existed in the world.[77]

Durham considered his Ida B. Wells script to be one of *Destination Freedom*'s best. In it he described the outspoken journalist as "a stormy woman. Restless like a river and a tongue like a flamin' sword." Durham's Wells believed that "resistance to tyranny is obedience to God," and that a freedom that "allowed the bigoted or the powerful to restrict the freedom of others was no freedom at all." A vociferous antilynching campaigner, Wells left behind a treasure trove of writings. Therefore, Durham said he took the "least dramatic license" in documenting her life, and he hoped listeners would connect with Wells's story of struggle and triumph in a man's world.[78]

"A good dramatist [tries] to make an audience feel something," Durham explained. "That's why the hero has to be intelligent. Whether it's a woman like Ida B. Wells or Mary Church Terrell, they must appear [to be] very intelligent . . . then people will identify." Several of Durham's *Destination Freedom* protagonists—including Sojourner Truth and her antislavery advocacy, Ralph Bunche's international diplomacy, and the political activism of Adam Clayton Powell Senior and Adam Clayton Powell Junior—embodied the characteristics of intelligence, courage, and passion in order to touch listeners who Durham believed were also intelligent.[79]

• • •

As with any series, not all *Destination Freedom* episodes were homeruns. Durham acknowledged, for instance, that his "Dark Explorers" show fell flat. This script focused on the black men who accompanied well-known European explorers Christopher Columbus, Vasco Núñez de Balboa, and Hernán Cortés in their search for a new world. "I was not very happy with it at all," Durham said, calling the script a "hodgepodge" that lacked "any dramatic highlight."[80] A listener could arrive at the same conclusion about Durham's show on brotherhood. However, this script revealed Durham's belief that "racial animosity is essentially an artificial thing. . . . There has to be a constant resupplying of some motivation for the animosity, or for the separation, or for the isolation of a particular group. Otherwise it will break down."[81]

Poet Gwendolyn Brooks, Durham's former Willard Elementary School and briefly his Hyde Park High School mate, was concerned about her portrayal in *Destination Freedom*. Two weeks before the show about her life aired, Brooks told a friend: "My life has had very little drama in it, and I'll be interested to see what manipulations they make with so little material." George Kent, Brooks's biographer, thought that Durham faithfully represented the employment discrimination Brooks faced, "using the raw, broad contrasts often favored by radio drama of the time."[82] But Durham erred "outright," Kent said, in his characterizations of Gwendolyn's mother, older poet James Weldon Johnson, and her teachers, as people who misunderstood Brooks's artistic passion. Although she was concerned "about the play's false spots," Brooks read one of her poems at the end of the drama.[83]

As with Durham's Nat Turner proposal, NBC rejected a few other *Destination Freedom* script ideas. Durham wanted to spotlight Paul Robeson, the singer, actor, and outspoken activist Durham greatly admired. However, he claimed, "I wasn't as unhappy with not being allowed to put Paul Robeson on because frankly, I didn't think that I could get it done. Some subjects have more electricity than others by virtue of the fact that people know about them or have already established a certain outlook on them."[84] In the same vein, NBC considered "not suitable" for broadcast Durham's proposed script about the deadly atomic bombs America's World War II military dropped on the Japanese cities of Hiroshima and Nagasaki in August 1945.[85]

Sometimes, potential subjects refused to be featured. Durham told Langston Hughes that NBC asked novelist and former IWP writer Frank Yerby for permission to document his life on *Destination Freedom*. Yerby's bestselling historical romances, including *The Foxes of Harrow* and *The Vixens*, followed the exploits of heroic white male protagonists in the antebellum South. But Yerby's agent refused to let the writer be featured on *Destination Freedom*. "NBC's impression here was that they don't want it generally publicized that Yerby is Negro. . . . Too bad," Durham told Hughes.[86]

Durham's series also had detractors. Some members of the American Legion veterans' group protested certain episodes.[87] And one day as Durham entered the Merchandise Mart, Chicago's imposing, twenty-five-story commercial building that stretched across two city blocks and housed WMAQ's studios, he saw "a parade of picketers from the white Knights of Columbus. I was quite startled because they suddenly just appeared out of nowhere." The protesters held vigil "for about three or four weeks, about 15 or 20 of them, marching across the door . . . denouncing the show," Durham said. WMAQ also received letters of complaint about the show during a certain period, although Durham did not specify when those letters arrived. "But generally," Durham said, "the supporters on the other side were quite heavy."[88]

Inside WMAQ, censorship sometimes reared its head unexpectedly. A line in his "Segregation, Incorporated" show was cut because Durham equated segregation in Washington, D.C., with a "master race" philosophy.[89] NBC officials edited Durham's Frederick Douglass script so severely that it would have lasted only about twenty minutes. Cast members vigorously protested the cuts, and station officials restored the edited lines.[90] "Recently I took the tactic of point-blank refusing to blue-pencil anything that I felt was healthy for inspiring Negroes to a more militant struggle," Durham told Langston Hughes. WMAQ executives "threatened and cajoled, but I held pat," he said. "Then they said I 'must be a Red.' Can you imagine that? White folks will call you 'Red' in a minute, won't they?"[91]

Despite the real danger of losing his livelihood if he was publically identified as a Communist or a "Red," Durham defiantly stayed on his crusading path. For instance, Durham wrote in his script about Mary Church Terrell, "Once a white woman bows down before white masculism . . . she is ready for slavery." Dick claimed that as long as the series' white actors were being paid, they didn't seem to mind his radical statements. "However, I admit I'm forced to throw in some neutral characters now and then," Durham told Langston Hughes. One example was his script about mild-mannered Harlem native Dean Dixon—the first black to conduct the New York Philharmonic Orchestra.[92]

At times, some of *Destination Freedom*'s dramatic scenarios developed or resolved themselves too abruptly—the same criticism Durham received about a few of his *Here Comes Tomorrow* and Illinois Writers' Project scripts. But such awkward, dramatic shifts were not as frequent as in his earlier writing. And Durham found ways to link segregation with economics in *Destination Freedom*. In the episode documenting segregation in the nation's capital, Durham wrote: "Some realtors and some of the investment people here in Washington like to build up 'exclusive' neighborhoods. . . . You keep out Jews here, Catholics over there, Mexicans here and Negroes everywhere and you get what they call a select neighborhood"—a place, Durham added, where realtors can demand exclusive prices. In Durham's script about NAACP leader Walter White, White's father proclaimed: "As long as there's segregation, and profit to be made outta prejudice, it'll rise up again."[93]

Yet historian J. Fred MacDonald said that Durham's sporadic focus on economic issues needed a more nuanced interpretation. MacDonald wished, for example, that Durham had elaborated on the economic and societal relationships he raised in his Ida B. Wells script. Durham had written:

WELLS: The real motives behind all lynching was not the moral issue pretended—but underneath it was a matter of murder for money and jobs. The base of all race terror pounded itself into my head as a weapon to enslave a people at the bottom of the economic scale—and the moral charges were just the envelope of the letter.[94]

Durham tended to avoid, MacDonald said, "radical responses to the economic distortions which as he intimated, might have been the root causes of the political discrimination he openly assailed." For MacDonald, Durham's scripts revealed the philosophy of an optimistic reformer who believed "where there is injustice within a society dedicated to political freedom, such a condition emanates . . . from the personal culpability of the men who operate that system and those who tolerate such inequities."[95]

．．．

In mid-November 1949 Durham wrote to Langston Hughes, not about *Destination Freedom* but about the Du Bois Theater Guild. The guild had hoped to mount "Little Ham," a play Hughes gave the group during an earlier Chicago visit. But Durham was returning the play because the group's South Side headquarters had been "sold out from under us" and other venues refused "to allow any play on its stage," Durham explained. "That's the crying shame of theater in Chicago—little theater, that is—no place to operate."[96]

Traces of frustration, if not despondency, crept into Dick's letter. "Nothing good is going my way," Durham wrote. He wanted to find a publisher who might be interested in his *Destination Freedom*'s scripts, "especially those I've done on Aesop, Attucks, Satchel Paige, Joe Louis, Denmark Vesey," Durham said. "But I don't have any contacts."[97] However, Durham's stubborn, resilient constitution wouldn't allow him to wallow long in depression. He started to pursue other creative possibilities as 1950 approached.

Meanwhile, from WMAQ's vantage point, *Destination Freedom*'s production costs remained an issue. The station spent between $15,000 and $18,000 a year on the series. In early January 1950 WMAQ finally secured an external sponsor—the Chicago Urban League.[98] Durham was a little miffed that the NBC affiliate brought the black organization in without first consulting him, but the league agreed to pay Durham $125 per script. However, this new financial arrangement quickly turned problematic. After several weeks, Durham complained that he had not been paid.[99]

He also argued with Heck about the fact that WMAQ had yet to hire "a single Negro in any capacity except shoeshine boy." Durham claimed that Heck "ruled me out because I was late with scripts."[100] He admitted to missing a few script deadlines, and Durham certainly could have collaborated with other writers to ease his substantial research and writing burdens. But he wanted to retain as much control over his series as possible.[101]

Sometime during this period Homer Heck moved up the corporate ladder, becoming WMAQ's program manager. Heck hired a man named John Keown to direct Durham's series, but Keown's "massacre of [my] scripts was butchery I could no longer endure," Durham declared.[102] He decided to pull the plug on his series.

Years later, Durham acknowledged that he had only "scratched the surface" of his broad subject during *Destination Freedom*'s two-year run.[103] But with one-year-old Mark now padding around Dick and Clarice's small apartment, Durham planned to take advantage of other opportunities that might allow him to better support his family. The new mass medium called television, with its grainy black-and-white images and growing appeal, seemed poised to provide more scriptwriting possibilities.

So on August 13, 1950, *Destination Freedom* unceremoniously ended its broadcast life on WMAQ. Durham, then age thirty-two, walked away from Chicago's NBC affiliate determined to fashion his own form of creative freedom.

CHAPTER 8

Moving On

Time

A wild autumn evening, near the death of the
19th century.

Place

The thriving but rugged town of Auburn, New York.

Scene

Cross-section of two simple frame houses, houses
inhabited by ex-slaves and freedmen, houses almost
hand-made-like in their simplicity, with their roofs
pointing toward the North Star.

Act

A long, lonesome call of a train floats across the
houses. A thin, aged Black woman who had stood
in her doorway listening, spins around and suddenly
begins beating at her head in agony as though
thunderous explosions had been set off in her brain
. . . her hands reach out toward the stars . . . She
calls in pain, "Sarah—is that you Sarah? I'm coming
for you Sarah, I'm coming."[1]

—Harriet Tubman play draft, Richard Durham, 1951

Richard Durham strolled into his post–*Destination Freedom* life with confidence.

Perhaps inspired by his involvement with the Du Bois Theater Guild, Durham planned on writing "a major play" about Underground Railroad conductor Harriet Tubman. He wanted to present Tubman's life "in a forceful, exciting drama so that America might better understand her heritage of freedom."[2] To support this goal, Durham received a $3,000 fellowship from the New York–based John Hay Whitney Foundation.

As conceived by millionaire philanthropist John Hay Whitney, his foundation's Opportunity Fellowships supported promising, "underprivileged" young people of Negro, Latino, Asian, and Native American backgrounds, along with impoverished residents of the Appalachian foothills. The foundation's senior consultant, Ester Raushenbush, explained that during its twenty-one years, 1950 through 1971, Opportunity Fellowships went to 953 people who "encountered unusual barriers" to their professional or educational careers. Fellows could use their yearlong grants for projects or studies in the arts, the humanities, or the social sciences.[3]

In July 1950 Durham joined a highly select group of forty-two Whitney Opportunity fellows that included economist (and future Federal Reserve Board member) Andrew Brimmer and gifted opera singer Mattiwilda Dobbs.[4] Although Durham had dramatized Tubman's life in *Destination Freedom*, he hoped that extensive research in public and private libraries nationwide during his fellowship year might "ferret out the contradictions and incongruities presented in biographical and autobiographical data concerning [Tubman]."[5]

Durham also viewed his $3,000 fellowship stipend as more "inspiration" than "livelihood," since it brought in about half of the $500 monthly income he earned at WMAQ.[6] So Durham was determined to find a profitable new home for *Destination Freedom*.

• • •

Throughout America during the early 1950s, television sets—those small screens encased in wooden cabinets with black and white moving images and rather tinny sound—were becoming more affordable and fast replacing radios as the entertainment focal point in American homes.[7] Durham promoted *Destination Freedom* as: "A half-hour radio or television program dramatizing the lives and adventures of peoples of all races who have contributed to the American tradition and our present cultural heritage."[8] Two companies Durham had previously worked with—the Metropolitan Mutual Assurance Company and the Davis, Fouche, and Powell Advertising Agency—signed on. The Davis, Fouche, and Powell Agency agreed to sell the show's national transcription rights. Durham and Allen Harris, Metropolitan Mutual's advertising director, settled on a $20,000 budget; Durham would earn half of that amount as the show's producer/writer.[9] Finally, Durham seemed poised to be properly compensated for his creative efforts. Just as important, Durham's message of freedom, equality, and justice would reach millions of Americans nationwide.

Yet as the leaves on Chicago's trees turned to glistening shades of red, orange, or yellow and dropped from their branches, Durham was floored by a maddening turn of events.

An October 11, 1950, WMAQ press release, followed by ads in local newspapers, trumpeted the return of an award-winning program series featuring a "new dramatic approach to the dangers which beset the American democratic way of life."[10] The station was reviving Durham's *Destination Freedom* series *without* his consent or input. Produced by Homer Heck and directed by John Keown, this *Destination Freedom* was a show almost exclusively about white, patriotic heroes—a version that had little in common with Durham's philosophical and political thrust. WMAQ planned on airing its *Destination Freedom* during the series' original day and time slot, Sunday at 10 A.M., beginning in late October.

Richard was incensed. How dare WMAQ and NBC officials revive his series without attempting to negotiate the program's copyright and title with him?

Durham immediately sent a cease and desist order.[11] But station officials claimed that the series had been created and named by them and merely authored by "staff writer" Richard Durham.[12] Durham saw this claim as more than a bit ludicrous. Throughout *Destination Freedom*'s run, he had lobbied, without success, to be hired as a full-time staffer, and the series' title grew out of a brainstorming session between Durham and his friends.

WMAQ and NBC also downplayed *Destination Freedom*'s significance, calling it "just another sustaining public service show" that promised little in the way of revenue.[13] "Pure bullshit," Durham fumed. He said that many top-rated national programs started as a public service or sustaining show. "These shows are always good bait for sponsors and advertisers," Durham said, pointing out that programs like *Dragnet, Cavalcade of America, Life with Luigi*, and *The Big Story* were sustaining shows until they "hooked" a sponsor and became popular national shows.[14]

So Durham considered his options. He consulted with his wife and close friends about whether he should sue NBC and its Chicago affiliate. They all knew that a lawsuit would torpedo his radio career and stymie his efforts to move into television.

But *Destination Freedom* had been Richard's baby. He'd birthed and nurtured it for a little more than two years. He'd agonized over its challenges and basked in its successes. Just as his radio characters bravely challenged injustice, Durham refused to allow WMAQ to stake its claim as the series' creator and owner.

He decided to sue.

Durham retained the services of local attorney Louis Friedman. Durham told Friedman:

> I have existed on my ability to create packages which could be controlled by myself, written by myself and which could be attractive to stations for quality and showmanship and groomed for sponsorship. Now due to the fraudulent and deliberate malice of NBC officials in claiming my show as "staff produced," I face loss of job possibilities as well as direct contract cancellations.[15]

In his downtown office at 11 South LaSalle Street, attorney Friedman arranged a meeting with Durham, Homer Heck, Judith Waller, and WMAQ lawyer Tom Compere. Friedman also brought in attorney John Moser, who Friedman said was knowledgeable about radio law. Friedman presented the evidence supporting Durham's complaint, including certificates documenting Durham's copyright of *Destination Freedom* and evidence that after he'd left the station, WMAQ won prizes in national contests using Durham's scripts. Additionally, Friedman noted that WMAQ had yet to pay Durham the money he was owed from the failed Urban League sponsorship.[16] WMAQ's officials offered extremely weak rebuttals, and Durham reported that their lawyer finally threw his hands up in the air and asked Friedman, "How much do you want?"[17]

Yet in subsequent meetings, attorney Moser claimed that WMAQ's ownership and title claims were "done more or less accidentally." Moser argued that a lawsuit by Durham could jeopardize the reputations of the highly respected Judith Waller and Homer Heck. In addition, Moser said that Durham's copyright appeared to be "faulty" and "improperly processed."[18]

However, it was pretty hard to argue with evidence, still available in the Library of Congress, documenting two separate copyright certificates issued by the U.S. Copyright Office on July 4, 1948, to Richard Durham for *Destination Freedom*. Durham also provided a receipt proving that the Chicago division of the Radio Writers Guild issued Durham a script registry receipt for *Destination Freedom* on July 29, 1948.[19] Moser said that should Durham win his case, NBC "would and could appeal [the decision] again and again," actions which might "break" Moser and Friedman.[20]

Durham stood firm. He planned to move forward with his lawsuit—with or without Friedman and Moser's representation.

In the meantime, Durham's search for more details about Harriet Tubman's life and times continued. He also lent a hand to his mentor, "Doc" Lochard, who had ambitiously established a black weekly called the *Chicago Globe*. Durham wrote articles for this fledgling newspaper as it struggled for air—and advertisers—in Chicago's competitive media marketplace. Unfortunately, cash-flow problems drove the *Globe* out of business fairly quickly. Lochard returned to the *Defender*.[21]

But Durham chose not to follow Lochard back to his first journalistic stomping ground. He still believed that national broadcasts of his *Destination Freedom* series would improve his finances and provide a broader platform for his artistic and political visions.

First, Durham had to concentrate on damage control.

He assured Metropolitan Mutual officials that he had created *Destination Freedom* and retained its copyright. However, on February 19, 1951, Durham received a disheartening letter from the company's advertising director. Allen G. Harris indicated that although he had "looked forward" to working with Durham, his company could not "entertain the idea of sponsoring *Destination Freedom* at this time" because of the conflicting ownership/copyright claims between WMAQ/ NBC and Durham.[22]

Adding to his woes, Durham received what he called "another aggravated letter" from the John Hay Whitney Foundation office. He told attorney Friedman that an Opportunity Fellowship representative, likely director Robert Weaver, planned to check on Durham's *Destination Freedom* ownership claims in person. Durham believed that "the evidence of [his] copyrights with the patent office" would satisfy the foundation.[23]

But he could barely contain his anger. Durham interpreted NBC's refusal to admit that it had stolen his creative property as a continuation of the network's "slimy, white supremacy arrogance, which seeks to recognize no rights to a title if held by a Negro." Durham raged:

> Only such blind arrogance could have inspired Homer Heck to ignore all facts in the matter and to go back on the air with *Destination Freedom* without even the decency to bargain for the rights. If there was ever a case where malice was involved, and where the steal was made deliberately and in defiance of legality, this is it.
>
> While this is certainly not a free and equal democracy insofar as Negro rights are concerned—I am quite convinced that there remains enough democracy scattered around for me to get something akin to an equitable settlement in this matter—even if the case were tried in my home state of Mississippi.[24]

Durham was well aware that his lawsuit against WMAQ and NBC had the potential, as attorney Moser had indicated, to go the long haul. He had no choice, then, but to pursue alternate employment. Some of Dick's friends thought that his lawsuit and his leftist sympathies also landed Durham on the blacklist.[25]

By the early 1950s, anti-Communist investigations into the media and entertainment industries had intensified. For instance, the publication *Red Channels: The Report of Communist Influence in Radio and Television* identified 151 so-called "red fascist" artists, directors, and producers who "transmit pro-Sovietism to the

American public" via the "radios in most American homes and . . . approximately five million TV sets in use."[26] White artists like composer Aaron Copland, radio scriptwriter/producer Norman Corwin, and actor Edward G. Robinson found themselves in *Red Channels*' crosshairs, along with Negro artists Lena Horne, Hazel Scott, and Durham's good friend Langston Hughes.

Blacklisting created what artist Romare Beardon and writer Harry Henderson called "a paralyzing 1950 atmosphere of guilt by association and faceless accusers."[27] Whether or not he was officially blacklisted, Durham had to deal, as best he could, with the consequences of his lawsuit against NBC. With his Opportunity Fellowship ending on June 30, 1951, Durham lobbied for another year of funding.[28] He had not completed his Harriet Tubman play.

Fellowship director Robert Weaver assured Durham that his renewal application had been carefully considered. Still, the selection committee "decided against favorable action on it," based mostly on policy considerations. Weaver said that the foundation preferred supporting new applicants.[29] The organization probably also wanted to avoid being drawn into Durham's dispute with WMAQ/NBC.

Thus, Durham found himself on the job search treadmill once more. He checked in with Langston Hughes, telling him that it appeared he had "squeezed Chicago dry of any more writing jobs. If you hear of anything in New York, please let me know." In the meantime, his wife's teaching salary stabilized the family.[30]

• • •

As during his IWP days, Dick and Clarice's small apartment occasionally served as a gathering place for his politically active friends. They also frequently visited the South Side offices, at Forty-Eighth Street and South Wabash Avenue, of the United Packinghouse Workers of America (UPWA). The UPWA, journalist Vernon Jarrett explained, "was one of the most progressive unions in this city and we tended to hang out there. They had a lot of down-to-earth Southern blacks in it," he said. "I don't know what the proportion of black membership was, but it was very high. Consequently, the black leadership was pretty high."[31]

Unlike the predominately white and in some cases all-white meatpacking centers in other parts of the country, approximately two-thirds of Chicago's packinghouse workers were Negro and Mexican.[32] Historian Roger Horowitz observed that an alliance between the UPWA's "militant generation of black workers who entered the packinghouse during WWII," and workers affiliated with the Communist Party helped "impel the Chicago UPWA to the forefront of the national union's civil rights activity in the 1950s."[33]

Possibly as a result of his contacts with friends or Communist Party comrades working in the UPWA, Durham landed a two-month contract with the union. The organization needed a writer who could translate studies conducted by Fisk

University scholars about the union's antidiscrimination activities into a digestible brochure for the rank and file.[34] Starting his contractual work on January 7, 1952, Durham entered a world that had been evolving in Chicago since the mid-1800s. This universe had grown so substantially that it earned the city its "hog butcher to the world" moniker.[35]

Chicago's stockyards—the heartbeat of America's massive meat slaughtering and packing industries—sat about fifteen blocks north and twenty or so blocks west of Dick and Clarice's apartment. In one square mile on Chicago's Southwest Side—bordered by Thirty-Ninth and Forty-Seventh Streets, and Ashland and Halsted Streets—a maze of train tracks, stone roadways, and animal pens crisscrossed the stockyards' landscape.[36] The Illinois Central, Rock Island, and Santa Fe Railroads brought in thousands of "noisy, bleating, bellowing or mute, intimidated cattle, hogs and sheep, in a seemingly interminable procession" from farms throughout the Midwest, writer Alma Herbst reported.[37]

Imposing buildings, some eight or so stories high, housed the various departments that turned livestock into the neat packages lining grocery store meat bins. The killing floors of these production plants were near the buildings' upper levels, positioned such that gravity could move the animals more easily down the slaughter assembly line.[38] In his visits to the stockyards, Durham would have seen some of the thousands of workers who performed the same, repetitive meat-processing tasks day after day.

A little more than a half-million people, including almost forty-five thousand in the Chicago area, toiled in the industries that produced meat and its byproducts during the early 1950s.[39] Some stockyard workers immigrated from Poland or Ireland, Mexico or Lithuania, Italy or Ukraine. Others were American-born whites or blacks. They may have been Democrat or Republican, Communist or apolitical.[40] The United Packinghouse Workers of America sought to represent them all.

Certainly, Durham appreciated the union's logo. A black hand and a white hand clasped in a handshake went along with the UPWA's slogan, "Negro and White, Unite and Fight!"[41] Addie Wyatt, the first black woman to become president of her Chicago local UPWA union, liked to quote an axiom from well-known Negro labor leader A. Phillip Randolph when she spoke to her members. "We used to say to them the struggle is never really won," Wyatt explained. "We said, whatever you won today can be made null and void by a stroke of the pen if you don't keep on struggling."[42] Addie Wyatt and Richard Durham believed that workers should not only unite and fight, but that they should also "hold onto what you're able to win," Wyatt added, "and share it."

There was plenty to share and fight about regarding working conditions in meatpacking plants. During the earliest days of the industry, meatpacking companies assigned the most dangerous and least desirable jobs to newly arrived European immigrants.[43] Negroes and other people of color found themselves in similar positions as their numbers in the industry swelled. Black men, for example, toiled on the dangerous killing floors.[44] "And those guys," former UPWA steward Rosie Simpson recalled, "I don't know how they slept at night, standing all day in a pool of blood, and you know how slippery that can be." Simpson said that some meatpacking companies didn't provide insurance to protect injured employees, and workers on some fast-moving assembly lines were treated like prisoners. "All those kinds of things were what the whole fight and struggle was about. The conditions," Simpson asserted.[45]

Durham's new employer came into existence in October 1943. Formed under the auspices of the Congress of Industrial Organizations (CIO), the United Packinghouse Workers of America represented employees in hundreds of plants organized into regional districts throughout North America.[46] The union's Chicago-based headquarters covered District I workers living in Illinois and Wisconsin.

UPWA president and experienced labor lawyer Ralph Helstein refused to sign any contract with meatpacking companies that did not contain the union's clause barring discrimination against all employees and applicants.[47] According to historian Roger Horowitz, Helstein "expressed a deep liberal belief that all groups deserved equal rights and civil liberties," and he encouraged union support for social reform movements.[48] One outcome of the findings from the Fisk University studies resulted in the creation of an Anti-Discrimination Department headed by Negro vice president Russell Lasley.[49] Durham reported to Lasley regarding the brochure he was under contract to create.

Meanwhile, finding little redress for his case against WMAQ and NBC at the local level, Durham hired Donner and Kinoy, a progressive law firm based in NBC's New York City hometown. Durham's new lawyers drafted an eleven-page brief containing twenty-five itemized complaints against the network. On June 2, 1952, Donner and Kinoy filed the document with the New York Supreme Court. Durham demanded $250,000 in damages from the network.[50] NBC officials probably marveled at Durham's audacity.

While his lawsuit crawled through the legal system, Durham continued his work with the UPWA. He even helped Oscar Brown Jr. get hired as a union coordinator.[51] Brown noted that Durham impressed his supervisors, particularly Vice President Tony Stephens. Durham eventually parlayed his relationships with VPs Stephens and Lasley, along with his own hard work, into a full-time position as coordinator of the union's Anti-Discrimination Department. Such maneuvering did not surprise people who knew Durham well. "Dick got to be very skillful, both in terms of his craft, as well as his ability to manipulate the system," Durham's brother Earl explained. "He knew which white [and black] folks to talk to and which ones not to rely on; how to use them before they used him and all that kind of stuff."[52]

Durham eventually produced a twenty-one-page brochure titled *Action against Jim Crow: UPWA's Fight for Equal Rights*. Printed on heavy, 8½-by-11-inch stock, the brochure married photos of black and white union members and their leaders with Durham's attention-grabbing copy. Durham wrote:

> At daybreak on November 30, 1950, a young Negro mother left her three children with their grandmother and hurried out into the cold Chicago dawn to catch a street-car.
> She was Mrs. Pauline Wilson and she needed a job.
> She was an experienced packinghouse worker and she knew they were hiring at Swift and Company.[53]

Swift—like the Wilson, Armour, and Cudahy companies—operated the nation's largest meat processing plants.[54] Durham's copy continued:

> At 7 A.M. [Mrs. Wilson] was rushing unnoticed down the crowded, cobblestone streets of the world's biggest packing center, and at 7:30 A.M. she was inside the employment office of the biggest packer. It was the third anxious morning she had raced to be among the first to apply.
> "*Oh-h-h-h you're just a little bit too late,*" one of the clerks shook a sad head. "*We're not hiring anymore women. Just men.*"[55]

Durham then introduced Ruth Merson, a white job seeker who rushed down the same cobblestone streets to the same company on that same November morning. Yet Merson was directed to a back office and hired with every other white woman who applied that day. Swift foreman Bill Cummings encouraged Merson to send her friends because he thought she "looked like a good worker." Durham conceded, "He was right. She was even better than he thought. He had hired a field representative of UPWA on assignment for its Anti-Discrimination Department, a symbol of the Negro and white unity which has made the UPWA-CIO, the most important packinghouse union in the world."[56] Once an arbitrator heard Merson's and other white and black women's testimonies, he ruled that Mrs. Wilson and twelve other Negro women "were entitled to reach into Mr. Swift's pockets for $2,600 in back pay," Durham wrote. Additionally, Swift had to hire those black women with a year's worth of seniority.[57]

Leslie Orear, editor of the UPWA's monthly newspaper, said that as a result of this "cause célèbre," the "silent color line" among women employees and applicants at Swift had been broken. Orear praised Durham's writing as well as his "excellent" work in pulling off this sting-like operation—another example of what Oscar Brown Jr. called Durham's ability "to scheme and get things done."[58]

. . .

In the UPWA's Anti-Discrimination Department, Durham found an outlet for his crusading desire to eradicate inequality and promote justice. His department sponsored a national antidiscrimination conference in fall 1953, calling it the first such conference sponsored by an American labor union. Five hundred American, Canadian, and Puerto Rican delegates came together to discuss antidiscrimination education, legislation, and political action strategies.[59] Durham could also satisfy his wanderlust in his new position. He motored to nearby plants in his blue Plymouth, coordinating a range of antidiscrimination activities.

One particular organizing trip typified what interstate travel was like for black Americans during the 1950s. Durham asked for permission to rent a car during a September 1952 trip to Kansas City, Kansas. President Helstein rejected the request, stating that there were "sufficient staff people" in Kansas City to take care of his transportation needs.[60] In reality, Durham had to use taxicabs. When he sought reimbursement for one particularly high cab fare, Helstein refused to pay. In his strong rebuttal, Vice President Lasley reminded President Helstein about the cost of doing business in segregated America.

> Durham's expenses show a $42.45 taxi bill because I directed him not to attempt to use segregated facilities or subject himself to that type of humiliation. . . . As you possibly know, white hotels in Kansas and Missouri refuse to house Negroes. We are obliged to either stay in Negro hotels which are rat-traps, or find housing in some individual home which is in an outlying region from the [UPWA] district and organizational offices. Your refusal to pay this bill may be the easy way out, but it sure in hell is not the answer to this problem.[61]

A couple of years later, Durham argued his own case regarding travel and housing disparities. His February 1954 memo to President Helstein stated:

> I learned that the forthcoming District No. 9 convention in Memphis, Tennessee, will have Negro delegates housed in private homes and a run-down, Jim Crow hotel, while white delegates will be housed quite properly in the best hotels in the city. . . . The policy on Jim Crow conferences apparently is still unclear, and I suggest that this be made emphatic.[62]

Durham could write with authority to the UPWA president because by March 1953 his status in the union had changed yet again. He now headed the union's newly created Program Department, with responsibility for coordinating the UPWA's educational training and civil rights advocacy activities. Vice Presidents Lasley and Stephens supervised Durham's activities.[63]

With Dick's $5,800 UPWA salary and Clarice's earnings as a teacher, the couple decided to buy a house.[64] They wanted more space for themselves and their energetic son, Mark, now approaching his fourth birthday. And the Durhams' landlord could not wait to get rid of them. "There was some problem with the apartment complex's upkeep and we started to organize the tenants to protest the conditions," Clarice smiled as she remembered. "We were asked to move and they were glad to have us leave."[65]

As Durham's mother had done thirty years earlier, Dick and Clarice searched for a South Side house they could fall in love with *and* afford—with financial assistance from Dick's father. Eventually they found it. It was a detached, two-story, A-frame house with gleaming hardwood floors and a full basement.[66] Located at 6059 South Harper, the house stood just a few blocks away from the place where Durham had tried his hand as a teenage delinquent—Hyde Park High School. The neighborhood "had been Caucasian, but was now more integrated," Clarice said. "And it was near schools we liked." Access to quality schools factored heavily in Dick and Clarice's home-buying choice, as it had for Dick's parents.

The previous owners of the Durhams' new home had converted the three second-floor bedrooms into individual rentals. Dick and Clarice kept that configuration, opting to live, as he had done with his parents and siblings during the Depression, on the home's spacious first floor. That level contained a bedroom, full bathroom, a living room, dining room, and kitchen. For several years, Dick and Clarice rented the upstairs bedrooms to various people, including Clarice's older sister Marguerite.[67]

Meanwhile, Durham's lawsuit moved at a glacial pace while the now-thirty-five-year-old writer led a unit in a very active international labor union. If Richard Durham missed being directly involved in the media during this time, he could sporadically satisfy his cravings by writing for UPWA publications. Durham also offered story suggestions to Leslie Orear, editor of the union's monthly newspaper, the *Packinghouse Worker*. However, the two men began "crossing swords," Orear said. "I thought that he was moving into my territory." At one point Durham suggested that Orear create a book review column. "Well, what book do you suggest?" Orear asked. "And so he handed me some novel."[68]

Durham had suggested a novel by John Oliver Killens. Killens would become a major literary figure in the Black Arts Movement of the 1960s and 1970s. But in fall 1954 Killens asked Durham if he could help him publicize *Youngblood*, Killens's debut novel about a Southern, black, activist family. "We are very glad you came up to the International Office, and I am sure that your book will be well received by leaders of this union," Durham told Killens.[69]

Leslie Orear read *Youngblood*: "I thought that it was totally inappropriate," he said. "It had nothing to do with the meatpacking industry or anything to do with the food industry and would not be welcomed at all by our readership. Not that

I thought that any particular novel would be appropriate to this newspaper of ours."[70] To be fair, Durham recommended more than just novels. In November 1953 he had asked a Columbia University Press manager to send a copy of its publication about race, jobs, and politics to Orear for possible review.[71]

Still, Orear said that Durham "tried to lean on me some more [about book reviews] and threatened me. I went to President Helstein and told him that this guy Durham is throwing his weight around here. . . . He wants to tell me what books I should review."[72] In his memo to Helstein, Durham noted that other labor publications featured book and even movie reviews. "I wonder," Durham wrote, "if we could give recognition to good pro-labor books and establish relationships with the major publishers who would put out more pro-labor literature if they thought they had a market."[73] Helstein ended up siding with Orear.

Durham and Orear kept bumping heads. Durham took offense at the way Orear congratulated a Negro district leader, calling him "Birthday *Boy*" [emphasis added] in one *Packinghouse Worker* issue. "So [Dick's] demanding my job, [saying] I should be fired," Leslie Orear recalled. "Helstein once again has to say, back away, Dick."[74] This incident demonstrated how tenacious Durham could be regarding any real or perceived slight. He'd whip out his boxing gloves to hammer home his point—sometimes going overboard to do so.

• • •

As the UPWA's Program Department head, Durham interacted with union leadership, rank-and-file members, and nonunion community members about issues as varied as local farm-labor disputes and national politics. He reached out to a wide range of leaders, soliciting their participation in UPWA-sponsored conferences, training workshops, or political action campaigns. In his sights were Kenyan liberation leader Jomo Kenyatta, progressive Chicago lawyer Earl Dickerson, Howard University President Mordecai Johnson, and his former IWP buddy, Studs Terkel.[75]

Durham also championed women's rights issues. Black women and white women were noticeably absent from top UPWA policymaking positions. In addition, women suffered from salary inequalities. UPWA local president Addie Wyatt said there was an hourly difference between the pay for men and women of at least fourteen cents. That "differential" disappeared by the late 1950s, progress Wyatt attributed to UPWA's International Office and Dick Durham: "[Durham] seemed to have known the kinds of struggles that a little black woman like me would have fighting against the white giants," Addie Wyatt said. He "was there to encourage you, but also to feed you with information that you'd need so that when you spoke or you wrote you'd have the facts and figures there to work with."

So I was always impressed," Wyatt concluded, "because he was not fearful of our struggle. He embraced it."[76]

Durham also embraced the union's activist role outside the packinghouse universe. One example involved the gruesome murder of fourteen-year-old Chicagoan, Emmett Till. While visiting Mississippi relatives in late August 1955, the teenager was savagely beaten, shot in the head, and dumped in the Tallahatchie River for allegedly whistling at a white woman named Carolyn Bryant. Till's mother, Mamie Till Bradley, courageously allowed her son's ravaged body to be photographed and displayed in the black press, "so the world can see what they did to my boy."[77] Those disturbing images inspired anger and condemnation among blacks nationwide.

Durham decided to send UPWA representatives to Mississippi to report on the trial of Till's alleged killers, Carolyn Bryant's husband Roy and his relative, J. W. Milam.[78] In mid-September, an interracial group of UPWA Ladies Auxiliary members traveled from Louisiana to Mississippi.[79] The group's dispatches to Durham detailed the poisonous atmosphere in Durham's home state. One white man threatened to kill the group members if they didn't "get the hell out of Mississippi." And of the nearly two hundred spectator seats in the courtroom, Negroes could occupy only twenty-three—all in the rear. On September 23, UPWA District 8 coordinator Jack Telfer told Durham that an all-white jury spent a little more than an hour in deliberation before rendering a "not guilty" verdict for Bryant and Milam.[80]

The UPWA delegation issued a press release decrying the "intolerable discrimination against both Negro people and the American principles of free speech and free press" in the Mississippi courtroom and the "widespread prejudice and distorted sense of what is just and right where Negro people are involved." The delegates sympathized with Mrs. Bradley's "cruel bereavement" and called upon all women, "Negro and white, North and South to join in condemning and working together to end the race discrimination out of which such crimes as this one are inspired."[81] Durham thanked delegates Lillian Pittman and Frieda Vicknair for their "courage and devotion to the cause of equality and justice." He also noted: "I am sure that the fight around the Till case has opened the eyes of millions of people and has set the climate for the fulfillment of democracy and equal rights for everyone."[82]

Durham was right. Historian Adam Green determined that Emmett Till's case "marked a crucial turn in the generations-old struggle to confront and overturn racial supremacy. African American writers, activists, and public figures routinely recall Till's lynching as an occasion of awakening, one inspiring many to commit themselves to struggles that, over time, constituted the civil rights movement."[83]

Durham and the UPWA backed another important cause in 1956. In mid-February Durham attended a meeting in the union's downtown offices with his supervisors, other union members, a local preacher, and a then-little-known Southern minister named Dr. Martin Luther King Jr. Notes from the meeting described the twenty-six-year-old Baptist minister as the "outstanding leader of a 'passive resistance' boycott" in its infancy in Montgomery, Alabama.[84]

Dr. King summarized the events leading to the Negro community's ongoing boycott of Montgomery's segregated bus system. On December 1, 1955, a respected community member, forty-two-year-old Rosa Parks, was arrested and jailed after refusing to give up her seat on a city bus to a white person. Her arrest sparked outrage. Negro community members and their religious leaders decided to stage a one-day boycott of all city buses on Monday, December 5.[85] Dr. King told Durham and his UPWA colleagues that only eight Negroes traveled by bus that day—in a city where roughly 75 percent of Montgomery's black population, about forty-seven thousand strong, used the bus system.[86] In the city's Holt Street Baptist Church that Monday evening, Dr. King delivered a fiery, eloquent speech that electrified the overflowing crowd.[87] Montgomery's Negro citizens resolved to fight on, extending the bus boycott indefinitely.

Dr. King indicated that the Montgomery Improvement Association (MIA), the organization formed in the shadow of the protest he now headed, had three main demands: more courteous white drivers, first-come-first-served seating, and the hiring of Negro drivers. After negotiations with the city broke down, the MIA sought a court injunction, demanding that segregated seating on city buses be declared unconstitutional.[88]

To support the boycott, some of Montgomery's Negro residents dusted off their shoes and walked everywhere. Some stayed home. But for the thousands of other blacks who needed it, the MIA established an alternate transportation system. Individual car owners and churches volunteered their vehicles; Negro taxi drivers reduced their fares. Dr. King said that the MIA needed about $300 a day just to pay for gas.[89]

Some funds to support the boycott came from donations received at mass meetings. Prominent souls such as Montgomery pharmacist Richard Harris and internationally acclaimed entertainer Harry Belafonte also contributed.[90] Still, Dr. King told Durham and his UPWA colleagues that unless additional aid flowed in "to boost the morale of the people," the two-month-old boycott might soon have to end.[91] Richard Durham asked Dr. King if similar boycotts in cities like Mobile, Alabama, or Sioux City, Iowa, would help MIA's plight.[92] According to sociology scholar Matthew Nichter, Durham's suggestion was based on research revealing that the corporate owners of Montgomery's bus line owned subsidiaries in several other cities throughout the United States.[93]

In solidarity with the MIA and the boycott, the UPWA executive board sent $1,000.[94] With encouragement from Durham's Program Department, union members "committed ourselves to [raising] $20,000," Addie Wyatt recalled. "They divided that [amount] up between the districts so that each one of our [nine] districts had responsibility to raise funds and send it into the international union." District 1 led the way. According to Wyatt, her district raised about $12,000 for the boycott.[95]

For nearly a year, Montgomery's Negro residents stayed away from and nearly bankrupted the city's bus system. Finally, on November 13, 1956, victory reigned. The United States Supreme Court declared Alabama's law mandating segregated buses unconstitutional.[96]

A month before America's highest court delivered this verdict, Durham set out to have his day in court. The New York State Supreme Court had placed his lawsuit against NBC on its docket for Monday, October 10, 1956.[97] Getting to this point had been a painful, six-year slog. Durham struggled with legal representation, changing lawyers several times before settling on William Rossmoore, an attorney based in Newark, New Jersey. Rossmoore and NBC's lawyers haggled over requests for supporting documents and argued about where and when witness depositions would take place and who should pay for them.

In early 1955 both sides had considered settlement possibilities. Attorney Rossmoore thought that NBC should pay at least $20,000. NBC offered a mere $500.[98] Durham rejected both amounts. "The manner in which my work was stolen deprived me of at least $75,000 in earnings over the period I have been forced to withdraw from the trade," Durham said.[99]

However, records documenting the final outcome of this lawsuit were conspicuously missing from Durham's files, and searches of NBC's files were equally frustrating. The plaintiff and defendant undoubtedly reached a confidential, out-of-court agreement requiring them not to disclose settlement terms. Clarice could not remember the details, although she knew that her husband "didn't get a quarter of a million dollars."[100] It's probably safe to speculate that Durham took home an amount somewhere between the $20,000 his lawyer had proposed and the $75,000 Durham thought was the minimum amount he had lost through the years. Durham also retained the copyright to his *Destination Freedom* scripts.[101]

· · ·

During the mid-1950s the CIO, UPWA's parent organization, engaged in merger negotiations with the much larger, less diverse, and certainly less progressive American Federation of Labor (AFL). Unions in both camps were concerned about the merger's outcome. "Dick's concern," Oscar Brown Jr. said, "was that the leadership in the [newly] merged union would have black representation."[102]

According to historian Roger Horowitz, Durham saw the UPWA as a largely black organization headed by white leaders.[103] Relying on his superb organizational powers, Durham pulled together a caucus "of all the key black guys all over the country," Oscar Brown Jr. recalled. "He did this so successfully that as the [AFL-CIO] merger was coming into being, he was able to set up the election of several black officials to the merged leadership."[104]

At the same time, Vice President Tony Stephens had started his own push to replace Ralph Helstein as UPWA's president. Stephens formed an alliance with Durham, hoping that black caucus support might help propel him to the top of the UPWA.[105] President Helstein noticed that people who owed their allegiance to Durham, rather than to him, had started surrounding Helstein. "Durham was engineering a coup," Leslie Orear said, "that would leave Helstein either a prisoner or out on the street looking for a job."[106]

Earl Durham agreed. "Dick thought he could pull off a coup and it was very controversial whether his strategy was correct of not."[107] Helstein mobilized his forces and was reelected. Stephens was out, and Program Department staff members who supported Durham—including Oscar Brown Jr.—were handed their walking papers.[108] Vice President Russell Lasley wrote to Durham: "You are hereby notified that effective as of today, March 11, 1957, your services with the International Union are terminated."[109]

Dick's union days were over. It was time, yet again, to move on.

CHAPTER 9

Empowerment

Sweet Cherries in Charleston

PETER: My son, in a revolution, one looks for the honest, not the honored. Some say Gullah Jack is crazy. Some say he's wise. But I know he's honest. Go to him.

MUSIC: (*Orchestral music transitions to rhythmic drumbeats.*)

GULLAH: Who that? . . . (*Drumbeats stop abruptly.*) Oh, it's you. Denmark Vesey, the dis-believer. Why you come here?

DENMARK: Gullah, I want you to cast a spell that'll make the slaves know the land is theirs as much as their masters. Tie together black men and white men in a common fight to free every man in Charleston . . . (*Firm.*) Listen, Gullah. I read one time of a giant who fell asleep in a foreign land. And while he slept, hordes of little men tied him with ropes and chains. And as long as the giant was sleep, he's a slave. But when he woke up, he stretched . . . the chains snapped and the ropes broke. And the little men hopped off his back like fleas and he stood up free and strong.

GULLAH: (*Interested.*) Uh huh, uh huh.

DENMARK: Now, the slaves are giants . . . the masters are the little men. When the slaves wake and stretch, they'll be free. And you can help awake them.[1]

—*CBS Radio Workshop*, Richard Durham, August 25, 1957

Richard Durham found himself adrift. For five invigorating years, he had been a behind-the-scenes powerbroker. He had shaped the United Packinghouse Workers of America's education programs and advanced the union's antidiscrimination agenda. But forced to resign after his failed power play, Durham felt betrayed. Angry. Frustrated. He fell into a funk.[2] What would he do now?

Durham turned to his typewriter to work out some of his swirling emotions. It is unclear exactly when this idea formed, but Durham decided to write a novel based on his UPWA experiences. One month after his March 1957 departure from the union, Durham asked his friend and brother-in-law, Robert Davis, if Davis could find some "good literary agents for him" in California.[3] Davis, a struggling actor, lived in Los Angeles.

"Those of us who were his friends in Chicago, like Fred [Pinkard] and Jan [Kingslow], we all expected Dick to write a novel or write a piece that would be equivalent to anything Richard Wright . . . or anybody ever did," Oscar Brown Jr. said. "But Dick was always kinda postponing that. . . . He'd say he was gonna get to that. In the meantime he had to earn a living."[4]

Perhaps now he could do both.

While he worked on his novel, Durham returned to freelancing—again relying on unpredictable assignments. On a positive note, Durham finally realized a goal he had set before the legal wrangling with NBC took hold. He found a national audience for *Destination Freedom*—or at least for a tiny portion of it. Durham reworked his "The Heart of George Cotton" and "Denmark Vesey" scripts for the highly regarded *CBS Radio Workshop*, born in 1936 as *The Columbia Workshop*. Talented writers like Norman Corwin, Dorothy Parker, and Archibald Oboler cooked up half-hour feasts for the series. Calling itself "the theater of the mind, dedicated to man's imagination," the *Workshop*'s dramas could be "anything from traditional to bizarre," radio historian John Dunning noted."[5]

Durham's episodes aired in August 1957.[6] In "The Heart of the Man," Durham again profiled Negro surgeons Dr. Daniel Hale Williams—the man who performed the first successful open heart surgery—and Williams's protégé, Dr. Ulysses Grant Dailey. But in a disturbing departure from Durham's *Destination Freedom* and *Democracy USA* scripts about these men, scenes dramatizing the racism a young Dailey faced while studying in America and abroad disappeared in this version. Additionally, white actor Martin Blaine portrayed Dr. Dailey.[7]

However, Durham's second *CBS Radio Workshop* episode, "Sweet Cherries in Charleston," more closely mirrored his *Destination Freedom* script. It obviously would have been impossible to eliminate racial references from a show about Denmark Vesey and his nineteenth-century slave revolt. It also helped that William Robson, the progressive writer/producer Durham admired and befriended during the 1940s, directed this episode.[8]

In another departure from Durham's *Destination Freedom* original version, the woman selling cherries becomes Vesey's love interest. Durham could have made this choice to further humanize Vesey, smoothing some of the leader's militant edges for the network's white listeners. While this show retained some of the original's radical statements, Vesey's "until all men are free the revolution goes on" declaration was dropped. In selling his scripts to CBS, these shows apparently fell victim to the network's fear of racial issues.[9] As a result, *CBS Radio Workshop* listeners heard technically polished but watered-down versions of Durham's earlier scripts.

• • •

Durham and his family actively pursued their individual interests during the summer of 1958. Nine-year-old Mark whooped it up in summer camp. Clarice prepared for her upcoming new job in the fall, teaching kindergarten in the Chicago Public Schools system. Dick labored on his novel, telling his brother-in-law Robert that he had "a prospect of an option on it" from a publisher.[10]

Several pages of notes for Durham's proposed novel about an unnamed protagonist and a Louisiana union strike have survived. The real intermingled with the imagined in Durham's notes. Some clearly documented machinations within the UPWA leadership; ambiguity characterized others. On one page, Durham described a union officer's ouster as "the plunge downward from the pinnacle, downward into drabness, the anonymity."[11] Durham could well have been writing about his own fall from UPWA grace.

More troubling, Durham wrote about an intense "inner cave-in," in which "the issue of suicide creeps in vaguely, then clearly."[12] Clarice said that her husband never got so depressed that he considered suicide. Whether or not Durham projected his own despair on his main character, he was fortunate that his son was a calming presence and that his wife stood by him. "Clarice is like Richard in many ways," longtime friend Timuel Black Jr. said. Like her husband, Clarice projected soft-spoken compassion, strength, and intelligence. "When Clarice and I were in high school," Black recalled, "she was so much smarter than me that I stayed away from her so I didn't get embarrassed."[13] Dick found solace in Clarice's emotional support and even-keeled personality.

Renters still occupied the second-floor bedrooms of Dick and Clarice's home, so some of the financial pressure Durham understandably worried about after losing his union job must have been eased. And Durham probably still had a modest kitty from his settlement with NBC. But as the end of the 1950s approached, Durham's proposed novel met the same fate as his Harriet Tubman play.

He never completed it.

Clues about why these projects languished could be found in a letter Durham sent to his sister Clotilde years earlier. He had encouraged Clotilde to nurture her writing talent: "You said when you saw something attractive, you 'want to run for a pencil and write about it.' Lord! If I only had that desire." Revealingly, Durham added:

> Sometimes I have to kick myself in the ass to force myself to write. I suppose in a way it's simply laziness. If that's all it is, I can conquer it . . . I hope that's all it is. If you've got that precious gift of initiative, cultivate it. Writing to you would always be a lot of fun. To me, it's too often work.[14]

Without a contract with a publisher or the pressure of deadlines, Durham moved on to the next project. And he would confront many deadlines in the tumultuous years to come.

• • •

The 1960s started innocently enough.

During the beginning of the first year of this decade, four North Carolina Agricultural and Technical College students—teenagers Ezell Blair Jr., Franklin McCain, Joseph McNeil, and David Richmond—were fed up with the daily indignities of America's apartheid system. So, like Rosa Parks and unknown others before her, these students took a stand against racial discrimination by sitting down. On Monday, February 1, 1960, the students sat on stools at a whites-only lunch counter in a Woolworth's department store in downtown Greensboro.[15]

Blair ordered coffee. "I'm sorry," the white waitress said. "But we don't serve colored here." The young men politely refused to move, staying at the lunch counter until the store closed. They returned the next day to request service and sit with twenty or so friends. Those twenty grew to more than eighty protesters the following day. By month's end, student sit-ins had spread to thirty-one cities across eight Southern states.[16]

Other antisegregation protests soon followed. On their TV screens, Richard Durham and America witnessed the frightening backlashes these protests sparked. In just one incident, a mob of angry whites firebombed a bus containing an integrated group of young people—so-called Freedom Riders—as they arrived in Anniston, Alabama.[17] White police officers in other Southern cities used excessive force—brandishing billy clubs, attack dogs, and the stinging blasts of water hoses—against peaceful black marchers armed only with freedom songs and their Christian faith.[18] And during the first two years of the 1960s, at least fifteen African and Caribbean nations—including Nigeria, Somalia, Jamaica, and Trinidad and Tobago—demanded and secured their freedom from European rule.[19]

Within this volatile atmosphere of global resistance and liberation, Durham's next full-time job emerged. The offer came from a group that saw itself as an autonomous black nation within a nation—the Nation of Islam (NOI). A shrewd, physically slight man in his mid-sixties, respectfully called the Honorable Elijah Muhammad, led the NOI faithful. Muhammad was, in his own words, the messenger of "the one God whose proper name is Allah."[20] He saw black Americans as a "Lost-Found" tribe, a people lost without knowledge of their true religion and purpose. Black people could, however, find salvation and self-determination as Muslims in the Nation of Islam.[21] Remarkably, for a man who was not religious, Durham seriously considered the Chicago-based NOI's offer to serve as editor of its newspaper, *Muhammad Speaks.*

Richard Durham would not be the paper's first non-Muslim editor; that distinction went to experienced black journalist Dan Burley in 1960.[22] Two years later, Burley died unexpectedly. While the NOI searched for Burley's replacement, Durham's name came up along with that of fellow Chicagoan Gus Savage—publisher of a West Side community newspaper. The Nation of Islam approached both men about possibly editing *Muhammad Speaks.*[23] But Clotilde and Earl Durham wondered why their brother even considered the offer.[24] Dick's siblings knew that the Nation of Islam had a mixed reputation, both within and beyond black Chicago.

Elijah Muhammad said that the Nation of Islam was formed when "Allah (God) appeared in the person of Master W. Fard Muhammad [in] July 1930."[25] Fard, a rather mysterious man with several aliases, preached his own brand of Islam to Negroes in Depression-era Detroit. His message of black economic empowerment and spiritual uplift inspired thousands. Elijah Muhammad, then known by his birth name of Elijah Poole, became Fard's prized pupil and led the NOI when Fard disappeared.[26]

Calling it "the largest and longest-lived institutionalized, nationalist movement among blacks in the U.S.," scholar Ernest Allen Jr. determined that the Nation of Islam's appeal and influence "far outstripped that of Marcus Garvey's Universal Negro Improvement Association" during the early twentieth century.[27] The NOI tended to be tight-lipped about membership figures, but estimates ranged from a few thousand to close to five hundred thousand followers.[28]

Whatever its size, some observers dismissed the NOI as little more than a strange, fanatical religious sect with racist philosophies. For example, anthropologist and modern dance pioneer Katherine Dunham, one of Durham's former Illinois Writers' Project colleagues, wrote in her 1939 study of black religious cults that "violent, anti-Caucasian sentiments [and] militant attitudes" were the "key-notes" of the Nation of Islam.[29] Elijah Muhammad declared the black man to be the world's original man—born in what the NOI called "East Asia," the region around Egypt and today's Middle East. He also anointed blacks as "the people of God's choice."[30]

Conversely, white people personified the Devil. Elijah Muhammad claimed that a brilliant though diabolical black man named Yacub created whites through genetic engineering.[31] Because of white people's evil, self-destructive nature, Elijah Muhammad decreed that white dominance would soon end. At the designated time, a huge plane with a flying-saucer appearance would hover over the earth and release smaller planes to drop bombs on the "cities of the White Devils. All those of the Faith will know how to find shelter," Katherine Dunham explained in her report.[32]

As blatant racial discrimination and inequality continued to disenfranchise black Americans, civil rights protests intensified. Within the context of this atmosphere, it is possible to understand why the Nation of Islam's rhetoric resonated with converts in about sixty-nine temples across twenty-nine states.[33] Some black non-Muslims responded as well. "I was not that interested in Islam or becoming a Muslim," former *Muhammad Speaks* reporter Darryl Cowherd said. "But the politics of *Muhammad Speaks* just kind of reached out to me. They were talking about things nobody else was."[34]

Declaring itself "Dedicated to Freedom, Justice and Equality for the so-called Negro," the national and international news coverage in *Muhammad Speaks* attracted thousands of readers.[35] The newspaper claimed a monthly circulation of 150,000 in January 1962. Readership numbers reportedly jumped to 360,000 by July, after the paper transitioned to biweekly publication.[36] Dick Durham told his youngest brother about those circulation figures, "and I could hear the wheels turning in his head," Earl Durham said. "He was thinking, now here's a chance to reach a lot of people."[37]

Durham met with the Nation of Islam's leader and decided to take the job. Dick "was very skillful in working with people and very good at building relationships," Earl recalled. "He built a relationship with Elijah Muhammad and that gave [Dick] sort of carte blanche when he was talking to the rest of the [newspaper] staff." Dick also told his brother that he hoped he could soften some of the paper's ultranationalistic sting. "I don't know what kind of arrangement he made on a trial basis, but he was determined that he could do it," Earl said.[38]

Durham became a regular visitor to Elijah Muhammad's South Side home. Over meals, Muhammad and Durham had long discussions, which Muhammad tended to dominate. "Elijah could talk for a very long time without stopping," former reporter Brenetta Howell Barrett recalled. "When Elijah was talking, everybody else was quiet."[39] Still, as a result of his interaction with Elijah Muhammad, Durham better understood the leader's mindset and the NOI's media goals and history.

. . .

During the mid-1950s Elijah Muhammad's weekly column, "Mr. Muhammad Speaks," appeared in black newspapers like the *Los Angeles Herald Dispatch, Chicago Crusader, Amsterdam News,* and most prominently in the *Pittsburgh Courier.*[40] Muslim men stood on city street corners and sold nearly one hundred thousand *Courier* newspapers "because [the Messenger's] column was in it," Nation of Islam member and journalist Askia Muhammad explained. "That boosted the circulation so that the *Pittsburgh Courier*'s circulation rivaled that of the *Chicago Defender.*"[41]

Perhaps no one was as mesmerizing—and as polarizing—a cheerleader for the Nation of Islam as the Harlem-based minister named Malcolm X. The letter X in Minister Malcolm's and other NOI members' names represented Elijah Muhammad's belief that black people should be "freed from the names imposed upon him by his former slave masters," historian Claude Andrew Clegg III explained.[42] In time, a proper Islamic name would replace the *X.*

Some people credit Malcolm X with starting *Muhammad Speaks.* In May 1960, the lanky, charismatic minister published the inaugural edition of *Mr. Muhammad Speaks,* a tabloid that borrowed its name from Elijah Muhammad's newspaper column. This paper contained reports about police brutality in New York, Elijah Muhammad's address to thousands in Chicago, and freedom struggles in Kenya and South Africa. Basically, *Mr. Muhammad Speaks* was the prototype for the type of paper *Muhammad Speaks* would become.[43]

But Malcolm X's paper generated envy among some NOI officials who felt that he exerted "too much influence," Askia Muhammad said. "So in that sense it was doomed to not succeed."[44] Elijah Muhammad moved the paper's operations to the Nation of Islam's Chicago headquarters and changed its name to *Muhammad Speaks.* He then recruited skilled writers like Richard Durham to shape the paper's journalistic voice. Employing non-Muslim editors and writers also eliminated the possibility that some ambitious Muslim follower might use the paper as a stepping stone to power—possibly even replacing Elijah Muhammad himself.[45]

Richard Durham and Gus Savage briefly worked together at *Muhammad Speaks.*[46] But as Savage moved on—he eventually spent twelve years as an Illinois congressman—he referred a woman who became one of Durham's first hires. Brenetta Howell Barrett saw Durham as "very business-like, friendly and down to earth" during her interview with him. He laughed a lot and put her at ease.[47] "He was short, stocky, powerfully built," former *Muhammad Speaks* reporter/editor John Woodford said about Durham. "He had a lot of energy, and he would come sweeping in" to the paper's headquarters, ready to tackle the day's work.[48]

Durham impressed and sometimes intimidated staff members with his still lightning-quick typing skills. "I would have to tune him out," Brenetta Howell Barrett said. "His fingers would just fly."[49] One day after their boss left the office, Darryl Cowherd peeked at Durham's typewriter. What he saw shocked him. The paper in Durham's machine contained pure gobbledygook—exactly what you'd get if you pressed the typewriter's keyboard indiscriminately. Cowherd laughed heartily. "I'm sure that for the sake of the staff he kept pounding the typewriter like that, but I think he used it as a means of thinking." Cowherd told his colleagues about his discovery and they were surprised only that Cowherd had not known that Durham sometimes worked this way.[50]

Durham "had this habit," Cowherd added. "He would be back there by himself and all of a sudden he might loudly say something like, 'Yeah, well, all right.'" Durham wasn't on the phone. Nobody sat with him at his desk. He was talking to himself. Cowherd believed that Durham had so many thoughts coursing through his brain, he at times had to talk out loud.[51]

Brenetta Howell Barrett recalled that often it was "challenging to tell a good story that wouldn't be offensive to the readers or the publishers." For instance, Elijah Muhammad and NOI members used the stock phrase "so-called Negro" when referring to black people. Howell Barrett said that they found ways to avoid using the term in their stories.[52] In essence, Durham and his non-Muslim writers walked a tightrope, delicately balancing their journalistic sensibilities with Nation of Islam desires. "Richard Durham dreamed of evolving a certain separation of church and state reportage between *Muhammad Speaks* and the Nation of Islam," novelist Leon Forrest revealed in his autobiography. As one of the paper's former reporter/editors, Forrest thought that this church-state divide "would be similar to the apparent relationship of the *Christian Science Monitor* and the Christian Science hierarchy. . . . It meant that [Durham] had to develop a very close and highly respected range of confidentialities within Elijah Muhammad's priorities."[53]

John Woodford agreed. Both the *Christian Science Monitor* and *Muhammad Speaks* included "designated space for religious messaging," Woodford said.[54] The front, centerfold, and back pages of *Muhammad Speaks* featured Elijah Muhammad's official messages. Religious editorials, illustrations, and NOI-specific articles could be found in select sections throughout the paper. "That Durham was able to convince the Messenger time and time and time again that the Muslim's best interests were served by keeping the Nation of Islam's progress sectionalized, nay segregated, from the rest of the general news was an act of the highest journalistic valor," Leon Forrest wrote. "It was also one of the reasons why the paper had such currency and respect within the black community."[55]

Yet Durham occasionally aroused his boss's wrath. In mid-April 1963, NOI national secretary John Ali reprimanded Durham for not consistently submitting the paper's layout to Elijah Muhammad for approval prior to publication.[56] Elijah Muhammad weighed in as well in his own mid-April letter to Durham: "It is not a matter of whether or not you are a follower of mine or the devils," he wrote. "The only thing we are interested in and desire of you is to use your talent as a journalist according to our wishes and satisfaction." He ended his three-paged, single-spaced directive to "Editor Durham" with the following: "Your salary of 200 dollars-per-week will remain the same if you do this for us; otherwise we have a right to cut the salary or fire a worker who will not do as we desire."[57]

Durham got the message.

And he realized that he might have to deal with other pressures as well. "It's likely that the FBI secretly put the [Muhammad Speaks] office under surveillance," Brenetta Howell Barrett correctly speculated. Declassified FBI files proved that the agency bugged NOI telephones and sought to undermine the organization.[58] Because of the high security clearance Caldwell Durham held as an engineer with a Los Angeles–based defense contractor, an FBI agent told Caldwell that the bureau had been monitoring his brother's and the NOI's activities.[59] The FBI's covert Counterintelligence Program, code named COINTELPRO, actually targeted several organizations and individuals it viewed as subversive, including the Black Panther Party and even Martin Luther King Jr.[60]

Dick Durham and Brenetta Howell Barrett's attitudes about suspected FBI surveillance was "the hell with them," Barrett said. "We wanted to do the best to help our community. The Nation was creating jobs, talking about pride and all the things we wanted to hear."[61] Meanwhile, the circulation of Muhammad Speaks reportedly grew to a half-million readers when the paper became a weekly in 1963. Well-dressed Muslim men in pressed suits, starched shirts, and bow ties stood on street corners, at major traffic intersections, and in front of businesses throughout the country, peddling the paper. The sellers had to move a certain number of papers each week, and the men met their quotas with varying degrees of success.[62] Still, journalist Askia Muhammad said that those sales tactics helped "drive up the circulation numbers" and exposed the paper to more people.[63] Muhammad Speaks readers eventually could read regular articles about one of the NOI's most popular and controversial figures—the good-looking, brash, but superbly talented young boxer born as Cassius Marcellus Clay Jr. "Soon after I accepted Islam," he would later reveal to Durham, "Mr. Muhammad gave me the name Muhammad Ali, which means "one who is worthy of praise."[64]

Muhammad Speaks supported Ali despite the fact that Elijah Muhammad had railed against the evils of sport in his October 15, 1962, column. But Ali became too public a sports figure and too potent a NOI spokesman for Elijah Muhammad to maintain that position.[65]

Muhammad Ali must have reminded Dick Durham of his own glory days in

FIGURE 10. Nation of Islam leader Elijah Muhammad addresses followers during a 1966 Savior's Day gathering in the Chicago Coliseum. Seated behind Muhammad are (from left to right) Tennessee entrepreneur Robert Karriem (with glasses), Fruit of Islam (FOI) security members, Muhammad Ali, and Louis Farrakhan. © Robert A. Sengstacke.

a sport he still loved, and the two men developed a good rapport. "This helped Dick understand the inner workings of the Black Muslims, the Fruit of Islam (the Nation's security detail) and the economics of the thing," Earl Durham said. Following its own nationalistic and entrepreneurial teachings, the NOI owned millions of dollars worth of property in Chicago and acres of farmland in other states. The Nation of Islam also operated cleaners, bakeries, restaurants, and a profitable fish import business.[66]

• • •

November 22, 1963.

Americans descended into a collective state of shock and grief. While waving to crowds of well-wishers as his motorcade rolled through the sunny streets of Dallas, Texas, President John Fitzgerald Kennedy was felled by shots from assassin Lee Harvey Oswald's rifle. Born the same year as Durham (1917), President Kennedy was only forty-six years old when he died—the youngest man ever elected to the presidency and the youngest to die in America's highest office.[67]

Elijah Muhammad directed Richard Durham to place a picture of the slain president on the front page of *Muhammad Speaks*. The NOI leader expressed his shock over Kennedy's "tragic death," even though, as historian Claude Clegg noted, Elijah Muhammad had been a vocal critic of President Kennedy's policies.[68] Worried that the Nation of Islam might somehow be implicated in Kennedy's murder, Elijah Muhammad ordered his ministers to refrain from issuing public statements about the assassination. However, while answering questions in New York nine days after Kennedy died, Malcolm X said the murder was a case of "chickens coming home to roost." He provocatively added, "Being an old farm boy myself, chickens coming home to roost never did make me sad; they've always made me glad."[69] Incensed that Malcolm X violated his gag order and concerned that such remarks might be interpreted as NOI glee over the president's death, Elijah Muhammad slapped a ninety-day suspension on his main spokesman. This suspension and his discovery of Mr. Muhammad's infidelities caused Malcolm X to leave the Nation of Islam in March 1964. He subsequently formed his own political and religious organizations.[70]

Watching Malcolm X during this period, Durham believed that the former NOI minister had grown. Dick told his brother Earl that as people like Malcolm X became more enlightened, the "mysticism" Elijah Muhammad preached would be challenged and cause more tension within the Nation of Islam.[71]

A smear campaign against Malcolm X soon played out in the Muslim sections of Muhammad Speaks. Articles by Malcolm X's brother, Minister Philbert, and a "Minister Lewis"—the man known today as Louis Farrakhan, the NOI's current leader—condemned Malcolm X's treachery. Elijah Muhammad labeled Malcolm X a hypocrite, considered to be one of the ultimate forms of insults for a Muslim.[72]

Durham counterbalanced this rhetoric with news stories that examined everything from the upsurge in Chicago's black population and continuing white flight to living conditions in Rhodesia (now Zimbabwe). The paper also regularly featured well-written profiles of historical figures. One, for example, chronicled the tale of a captured West African named Cinque who "staged a lightning strike for freedom" by leading a mutiny on the Amistad slave ship in an attempt to reset its course back to Africa.[73] By September 1964, Elijah Muhammad lavished high praise on "our editor." In a personal letter to Durham, Elijah Muhammad wrote: "Our paper seems destined to be the greatest so-called Negro paper in the country with your expert and well trained journalism and editing."[74]

Yet in one of the newspaper's final attacks against Malcolm X, Minister Louis X—Farrakhan's name at the time—wrote a scathing five-page indictment in Muhammad Speaks December 4 edition. The article included the minister's belief that "such a man as Malcolm is worthy of death."[75] Two months later, on Sunday, February 21, 1965, Malcolm X fell to assassins' bullets while speaking in a Harlem ballroom.

"That's it!" Dick told his brother Earl after Malcolm X's murder.[76] Durham suspected that retaliation from former NOI members who had supported Malcolm X might be in the making. Durham began plotting his escape from *Muhammad Speaks*. He just did not know then that it would be a few years before he could leave.

. . .

Possibly as a result of the stress her husband experienced during this period, Clarice said that Dick started having nosebleeds. The bleeding lasted longer than it should have and occurred much too often. Alarmed, Dick was hospitalized in late April 1965. But his doctors could not offer a conclusive diagnosis.[77] From his other home in Phoenix, Arizona, Elijah Muhammad wrote to express his concern about Durham's health: "We have missed you so much that we feel at a [loss] without you." He playfully promised that if Durham wasn't out of the hospital by the time he returned to Chicago in early May, "I am coming to get you, maybe (smile)."[78] Durham slowly eased back into work shortly thereafter.

During this time, *Muhammad Speaks* featured a syndicated column by Durham's good friend Langston Hughes. In one column, Hughes's Simple character humorously offered his own solution to America's escalating entanglement in the Vietnam War. "Draft all older white men first," Simple proposed. "Let them run from bombs and bullets in Viet Nam a little. Then the old white folks [won't] be so quick to want to send the young folks, white or colored, over there."[79] American soldiers had been battling Communist forces in Vietnam for nearly six years.[80] Approximately twenty-five thousand Americans fought in Vietnam in April 1965; their numbers ballooned to 184,000 by the end of the year.[81] Richard Durham made sure that *Muhammad Speaks* regularly featured articles about the war and its impact on black G.I.s.[82]

Meanwhile, Durham's only child considered his college options while attending his father's alma mater. Mark distinguished himself at Hyde Park High as a top-ranked student and member of the football team. "My parents, particularly my father, really wanted me to go to Harvard University," Mark said. Durham believed that his son could earn a "very marketable" degree there. Harvard did not interest Mark, but Dick and Clarice could not complain about the institution Mark chose: Columbia University. Mark headed to New York City in fall 1966, using a Ford Foundation–funded National Achievement Scholarship to offset some tuition costs.[83]

Around the same time, Durham resumed freelancing for Irna Phillips while carrying out his *Muhammad Speaks* duties.[84] A year or so earlier, Elijah Muhammad had playfully warned Durham, "Do not forget that our paper is advancing in such a way toward the public, that you are going to meet with many jealous and envious editors (smile)."[85]

Essentially, Elijah Muhammad's prediction came true.

A few NOI ministers resented the fact that Richard Durham, a nonbeliever and a non-Muslim, headed their paper and had a close relationship with their leader. Some probably wanted to wrest control of the paper to satisfy their leadership ambitions. According to Durham's friend Edward "Buzz" Palmer and his *Muhammad Speaks* colleague Leon Forrest, one particular incident put Durham in serious jeopardy.[86] "A group of Black Muslim ministers dedicated to Durham's immediate demise went to Elijah [Muhammad] and told him that they had evidence that Editor Durham is a Communist," Leon Forrest wrote in his autobiography. Elijah Muhammad summoned Durham to his house and asked the ministers to present their case. According to Forrest, Elijah Muhammad told the ringleader of the planned coup: "Well brother, at least Editor Durham isn't with the Devil."[87] Elijah Muhammad fully supported Durham and his editorship.

The ministers backed down. Durham's reign continued.

And although Durham was no longer a member of the Communist Party, he recommended leftist literature to his reporters. One book, *Theory and Technique of Playwriting*, came from the pen of John Howard Lawson, one of the so-called "Hollywood Ten." This group of screenwriters had been blacklisted because of their alleged, or actual, Communist Party affiliation. Durham thought that Lawson's book might help reporters identify "some intriguing contradictions" that could enhance the drama in their stories. Durham also recommended *The Role of the Individual in History*, written by nineteenth-century Russian philosopher George Plekhanov, who advocated Marxist theories of social development, believing that the activities of individuals were historically important.[88] "It was . . . as if reading these things was some sort of mental training," former reporter John Woodford said. "They stimulated you to think about yourself in a context, to have more of a historical awareness, and that people make a difference. It was humanistic in orientation."[89]

Interestingly enough, Durham did not take credit for the articles or editorials he wrote in *Muhammad Speaks*—just one of the reasons why some of Durham's colleagues and friends affectionately called him the "shadows man."[90] Writer Leon Forrest believed that Durham "wanted to be invisible to the public, but he also hungered to influence important issues of race and class, media, the arts, power and government . . . strictly from behind the scenes." In the *Muhammad Speaks* newsroom, staff members believed that "Durham was without question the best writer on the newspaper," Leon Forrest said. "I think we all learned from him. I know I certainly did."[91]

Durham led by example. When John Coltrane, the extraordinarily influential jazz saxophonist, succumbed to cancer in mid-April 1967, Durham assigned Darryl Cowherd to write a tribute. Cowherd turned in his piece and Durham thanked him. "As was his custom," Cowherd said, "you didn't know whether it was good or bad or off the charts or what." A couple of days later, Cowherd saw that Durham had rewritten his piece. "It was just awesome!" Cowherd said. "I don't remember anything that floored me like that."[92] Durham's tribute typified the kind of writing and thinking the young reporter wanted to perfect. In "On the Death of John Coltrane," Durham wrote, in part:

> If the Prime Minister of Britain gratefully acknowledges the Beatles—Britain's four white musicians who openly copied the blues and rhythms spawned in the black ghettos of America—then what should a nation have paid to John Coltrane, the black musical titan who died in New York this week? If England officially declared the Beatles to be one of its "greatest national treasurers," then what was Coltrane, in whose shadow musicians throughout the world could become famous simply by imitating his most casual concepts? . . . *Muhammad Speaks* presents this simple eulogy to this Black Colossus . . . his phenomenal performances opened special spheres for untold millions in this world and in the worlds to come.[93]

Unfortunately, death and loss personally touched Durham shortly thereafter. Langston Hughes, the writer Durham had so admired, befriended, and collaborated with for more than twenty years, died of complications from prostate surgery on May 22, 1967.[94] Hughes's unexpected death at age sixty-five shocked the literary world and shook Durham up. "We were supposed to take a trip to Europe together," Durham told an interviewer years later. "Langston was [writing] the third section of his autobiography and wanted me to work on it with him," Durham said. "[Langston] had reached the point where anything he wrote would be published or produced, and he had so much more left in him."[95]

Seven months later, Durham lost his very first role model and mentor—the man from whom he had learned about the power of observation, diligence, and generosity. Durham's eighty-seven-year-old father, Curtis George Durham, suffered a fatal heart attack on December 9. This unassuming, hardworking man had, along with his wife Chanie, encouraged his seven surviving children and fifteen grandchildren to achieve their best by pursuing knowledge and sharing it with others.[96] His father's sudden death, along with Langston Hughes's loss, caused Durham to fret about his own mortality. He talked about changing his eating habits because he did not want to "just drop" like his father or his good friend.[97]

• • •

Muhammad Speaks staffer Rose Jennings remembered that in Durham's capacity as editor, he might suggest the first few words or lead sentence for a story he needed her to rewrite. He then would tell Jennings to figure out the rest of the rewrite from there.[98] For photographer Robert Sengstacke, Durham "helped to show me myself before I even knew myself." Durham encouraged Sengstacke, grandson of *Chicago Defender* founder Robert Abbott, to creatively capture black life.[99] Several of Sengstacke's iconic photographs documented Nation of Islam members.

"[Durham] could adapt or adjust guidance for anyone, depending on what they needed," colleague John Woodford noted. "I guess once we sort of got rolling, you didn't feel like you were being guided. But he probably had set it up so you only wanted to run a certain way. He was just a master psychologist."[100]

Sometimes, however, Durham's assessments were flawed. For example, one *Muhammad Speaks* staffer had a drug addition and got sick at work one day. Darryl Cowherd escorted the man home. "Durham threatened me for helping this guy," Cowherd recalled. "He just had no compassion for him at all." Durham's attitude perplexed Cowherd. He could not understand why his boss refused to empathize with someone who clearly was suffering. Cowherd later reasoned that because Durham exercised such discipline in his own life, he had little sympathy for someone who could not control himself.[101]

"Steamed." That's how John Woodford described Durham when he got angry. "It would be just like something in a cartoon, with steam coming up off someone's head," Woodford explained. "Or he could look disgusted at you for something stupid. In the main, it was like a very paternal kind of relationship I guess we had with him, in a way that we wanted daddy to be proud and not come down on us. So I think we behaved pretty well."[102]

Residents of the "City of Big Shoulders"—another one of Chicago's many nicknames—apparently loved moving those shoulders around in big cars. Durham was no exception. "I remember this 'hog,' this Cadillac he bought," Darryl Cowherd said. "It was tan and a mile and a half long. I could almost see him with that arm on the [steering] wheel, tooling down the [road]." Durham might drive his car down Chicago's flat streets, park, and then spin yarns with the regulars at the Tiger Lounge, the bar next to the *Muhammad Speaks* South Side office. Back at his desk Durham astutely analyzed the world's sociopolitical ills.[103] Staffer Rose Jennings observed that Durham "was light years ahead of his time."[104]

Many *Muhammad Speaks* staff members saw Durham as a committed internationalist, a man intent on reporting about and supporting freedom struggles around the world. "We didn't have a heck of a lot of experience to be talking about international affairs," John Woodford noted. So Durham "was big on us researching and reading widely," Woodford added. "He just gave you confidence that there wouldn't be any subject [you couldn't write] about as long as you were interested in it yourself."[105] Historian Penny M. Von Eschen determined that *Muhammad Speaks* became "one of the most sophisticated sources of information on Africa available to Americans."[106] Actually, concerns about a variety of developing nations found voice in the paper. As Elijah Muhammad told Durham in a 1964 letter, "There is much going on outside of America that we can get the authenticity of and publish it in our paper without fear."[107] Scholar James Edward Smethurst suggested that the editorial thrust of *Muhammad Speaks* generally "was militantly antiracist and anti-imperialist (and often anti-capitalist) as well as nationalist."[108]

The paper's former Washington, D.C.–based correspondent, Ghayth Nur Kashif, said that Durham required reporters to research their stories comprehensively to avoid the impression that the paper might be "mouthing off conspiratorial theories." *Muhammad Speaks* reporters "could not and would not print even things we absolutely knew to be truth [if] we didn't have all the information," Kashif said. "Some stories we couldn't print because we couldn't get alternate sources."[109]

And Durham fully supported his reporters' attempts to obtain primary source material. For instance, in 1967 Durham heard rumors that several young black women were forcibly sterilized in a picturesque town at the foothills of the Blue Ridge Mountains. He sent Ghayth Nur Kashif, then called Lonnie 2X, to Front Royal, Virginia, where he interviewed several women who had been sterilized. Kashif also interviewed an administrator in the clinic where the procedures took place. Kashif's article, "Sterilization Clinics Built for Murder of the Black Unborn," appeared in the *Muhammad Speaks* October 13, 1967, edition. Later, Kashif wrote other news stories about unscrupulous birth control methods.[110]

Durham firmly believed that "you can't just write [about something] one time," former reporter John Woodford explained. "You have to have sort of a campaign if you really want to affect public opinion. It was a strange kind of journalism because objectivity was not necessarily anything you had to be concerned with. Your heart could be on your sleeve in the story, so long as it was sort of consistent and dramatic, because the things we were covering were crime, war, violence."[111]

The simmering cauldron that was the sixties seemed to come to a dangerous hard boil as the decade neared its end. Casualties reached staggering proportions as the Vietnam War droned on, shocking Americans with the scope of human carnage and landscape devastation from massive bombing raids, artillery attacks, and chemical warfare.[112] And in the beginning of April 1968 the man both lionized and demonized for his opposition to the war, as well as for his nonviolent stance against racial discrimination, met the same fate as John F. Kennedy and Malcolm X. A shotgun blast, allegedly fired by gunman James Earl Ray, stilled the eloquent voice of Dr. Martin Luther King Jr. as he stood on the balcony outside a motel room in Memphis. Black communities nationwide exploded in anger and pain. Riots ripped through 110 cities.[113] The ruins from those life-altering riots would blight some neighborhoods for decades.

Elijah Muhammad publically offered his condolences to the King family in *Muhammad Speaks*, describing the fallen leader as "a great and courageous black man who died in the effort to get for his people that which belonged to them—FREEDOM."[114] In the past, the NOI had denounced King because of his integrationist convictions.[115] But according to Earl Durham, Richard Durham worked to "get the Nation off King's back." In October 1964 Durham printed an article in which King analyzed the causes of Negro rage and rioting in New York and Philadelphia. In March 1966 Durham reported on a cordial meeting between Dr. King and Mr. Muhammad.[116]

Americans gasped in horror at yet another assassination a mere two months after King's death. On June 6, 1968, President Kennedy's younger brother Robert, former U.S. Attorney General and then presidential candidate, lost his life to gunman Sirhan Sirhan while campaigning in Los Angeles.[117] Later that summer, clashes between protesters and Chicago police officers added more tension to an already contentious Democratic National Convention.[118] And college campuses nationwide pulsated in discord throughout the year.[119] Durham's son even got involved in student demonstrations at Columbia University. Clarice "saw Mark on TV, hanging out of one of the [campus building's] windows and almost had a fit," Dick's sister Clotilde remembered, smiling. "Mark was taking part in a protest."[120]

During this period, the NOI purchased a state-of-the-art printing press, housing it in a building twenty-six blocks south of the Loop on Federal Street.[121] There, *Muhammad Speaks* staffers came under the direct gaze of the Fruit of Islam. The security force's ban on smoking in the building "riled our chief, Dick Durham, and the three top editor-writers who had seniority over me," John Woodford revealed. "Another irritant was the psychological atmosphere: being spied on and being glared at as if one were hopelessly fallen."[122] With this increased scrutiny, Durham was even more determined to leave *Muhammad Speaks*. An opportunity to do just that materialized during the first half of 1969.

And Richard Durham was ready for the change.

CHAPTER 10

Struggling to Fly

Jonah and the Whales

FUNKY FRANK [is] near the Jukebox, doing his inimitable Boogaloo with amazing aplomb . . . FUNKY looks up . . . instantly recognizes his visitors [and] dances over to the bar against which [SERGEANT] VINES is leaning.

FUNKY:

Lord, Lord, Lord. Look what the race riot drove in here . . .

VINES:

(*Looking over the tavern, shakes his head.*) I don't understand you.

Half the town is going up in flames, billions in property damage, jails are overflowing, and you dance.

FUNKY:

(*Sighs philosophically.*) Brother, the old world is going out and the new world is coming in. As I see it, if you weren't such an Oreo cookie, you'd be dancing too.

VINES:

(*With a touch of intensity, he speaks low, for he wants a contest only with Funky.*) The homes they burn are their own. Most of the dead will be Black, most of the heads cracked, Black, and most in the jails will be Black.

FUNKY:

(*Confidently.*) The Lord says light a candle in the dark and it makes a fire big enough for the whole world to see. Then maybe they get the message.

VINES:

(*Shaking his head.*) This one's the worst.

FUNKY:

(*He reaches for a glass, sets it down and pours a stiff drink for himself.*) Naw, I wouldn't say that. (*Optimistically.*) The worst is yet to come. Drink up . . . What the hell you want anyhow? I don't pay off the police until Friday.[1]

—*Bird of the Iron Feather*, Richard Durham, 1970

Television.

Richard Durham had been hankering to write for this popular mass medium since the early 1950s. He had to be thrilled that 1969 brought the promise of creating a unique TV series. The show, to air on noncommercial station WTTW—Channel 11, would be a soap opera about black life in the Windy City.[2]

In the past, Durham's TV scriptwriting desires had been dashed while he legally sparred with NBC. But after that fight ended, Durham served as a ghostwriter for science fiction shows like *One Step Beyond*, *Climax*, and *The Outer Limits*, as well as other TV dramas during the late 1950s.[3] Durham's name might have been removed or never attached to the scripts he authored because of the still-potent blacklists that restricted the careers of past and present Communist Party members and some leftist sympathizers. So WTTW's proposed show offered Durham an opportunity to receive on-air credit for what might be a groundbreaking series. And within certain limits, he could set the agenda for WTTW's serial about black Chicagoans.

In the 1950s Negroes had been featured so sparingly on television that black households often celebrated when a "colored" face appeared. "I'm in the age group where I remember when people would say, 'Come here! Some colored people on TV!'" Durham's longtime friend Abena Joan Brown laughingly remembered.[4]

Looking at TV from a broader perspective, Newton N. Minow, chairman of the United States Federal Communications Commission, infamously blasted television in the early 1960s. Minow called TV "a vast wasteland" because of its steady stream of violence, "unbelievable families," formulaic comedies, and "screaming, cajoling and offending" commercials. Speaking to the nation's broadcasters, Minow said, "It is not enough to cater to the nation's whims, you must also serve the nation's needs." He pressed for more imaginative, experimental, and higher-quality programming.[5]

By the time Durham began his stint with WTTW, Minow chaired the station's board of directors.[6] Blacks were becoming more visible on America's TV screens, especially in advertisements and public service announcements. Madison Avenue's advertising industry had "discovered" black Americans and their spending power—then estimated to be around $30 billion.[7] Media scholar Donald Bogle believed that TV images in general "were affected by new attitudes toward the Negro and the American system, and by black America's growing (and vocal) political disaffiliation and dissent."[8]

If racial attitudes and practices were changing in America, ongoing civil rights demands as well as the passage of the 1964 Civil Rights and 1965 Voting Rights Acts fueled the country's imperfect evolution. Lyndon Johnson, who inherited the presidency after John F. Kennedy's assassination, called the Voting Rights Act "one of the most monumental laws in the entire history of American freedom." In President Johnson's eyes, the vote was "the most powerful instrument ever devised by man for breaking down injustice and destroying the terrible walls which imprison men because they are different from other men."[9]

One of the "walls" restricting black actors' presence on television seemed to disintegrate when NBC's *I Spy* debuted in September 1965. For the first time a black man, actor/comedian Bill Cosby, co-starred with a white man, actor Robert Culp, in a dramatic series on primetime network television.[10] And Cosby's character was no uneducated, shuffling, Stepin Fetchit–like stereotype. Instead, Cosby's multilingual Alexander Scott character combined a brilliant, Rhodes-scholar mind with wicked karate and sharpshooting skills. On the surface, Scott was the trainer and best friend of tennis pro Kelly Robinson—Culp's character. Off the tennis court, Scott and Robinson tracked down nefarious types around the world as undercover agents—not unlike cinema's popular James Bond figure.[11] However, some black viewers complained that *I Spy* was just another example of a black character stuck in a subservient relationship with a more dominant white character.

Other network shows featuring highly intelligent black co-stars included *Mission Impossible*'s Greg Morris, *Star Trek*'s Nichelle Nichols, and *N.Y.P.D.*'s Robert Hooks.[12] In 1968, black actress Diahann Carroll made history by starring in her own sitcom, *Julia*. Carroll played widowed nurse Julia Baker, who was raising her young son Corey in an upscale, integrated apartment building in Los Angeles.[13] Some viewers criticized the show because of its tepid approach to race, its avoidance of contemporary social issues, and absence of strong black male figures.[14] As accomplished as Julia and many of the other black characters on network shows appeared to be, they lived in a strange bubble, often removed from contact with the black community.

Sometime either during the end of *Julia*'s first season or the beginning of its second, Durham found out about WTTW's plans to create a black soap opera. He probably heard about these plans from Irna Phillips. During an on-air interview one evening in the mid-1960s, Phillips suggested to WTTW program director Edward L. Morris that the soap opera concept might work on educational TV.[15] With input from black staff members and other station officials, the station decided to create a series exploring some of the socioeconomic problems affecting black Chicagoans. The drama would be called *More from My Life*.[16]

Station executives identified a potential funding source: the Ford Foundation, which had had set aside $5 million to establish a "New Television Programming Grant." Noncommercial TV stations or networks could apply for funds to improve their cultural, public affairs, and children's programs.[17] In its October 1968 funding proposal, WTTW asked for nearly $750,000, the maximum allowed for stations in large markets.[18] WTTW believed it could replicate the earlier programming success of KCET-TV in Los Angeles. KCET's *Cancion de la Raza* [Song of the People] was a well-regarded, sixty-five-episode soap opera about Mexican Americans. *Cancion* provided job opportunities for Chicanos, and the Ford Foundation grant funneled sorely needed dollars into that struggling noncommercial station.[19]

WTTW envisioned similar financial and critical success with its proposed black-oriented series. Station officials estimated that slightly more than one million blacks lived in the Chicago metropolitan area; approximately eight hundred thousand resided in the inner city. To attract those potential viewers, Program Director Morris said that the show would reflect middle- and lower-middle-class struggles and triumphs.[20] In spring 1969 the Ford Foundation awarded WTTW $600,000 to support the production of one hundred *More from My Life* episodes.[21]

WTTW officials interviewed several scriptwriters, but based on his "considerable experience," Richard Durham, then fifty-one years old, became the show's chief writer.[22] The station also hired other staff writers and freelancers.[23] In short order, Durham infused his philosophical sensibilities on the series. For inspiration, he turned to one of his favorite *Destination Freedom* personalities: Frederick Douglass. In an 1847 speech, Douglass asserted that black Americans, "the sons and daughters of Africa in the United States," had a history laced in struggle and blood. "They have been a bird for the hunter's gun, but a bird of iron feathers, unable to fly to freedom."[24]

Consequently, Durham transformed Channel 11's innocuous original title into *Bird of the Iron Feather*. The show's executive producer, Clarence McIntosh, said the new title "more accurately depicts the plight of the men and women forced to live out their lives amidst the countless frustrations of the ghetto."[25] *Bird* would break ground in its approach to storytelling by and about blacks, and seek, through protracted struggle, to increase black involvement in television's behind-the-camera world.

Before those battles erupted however, Durham had to figure out how to shape his story. He could have embraced the approach he took in *Here Comes Tomorrow*, exploring familial issues through the experiences of a black war veteran. Via the news coverage he oversaw at *Muhammad Speaks*, along with the graphic battlefield images broadcast on American TV screens, Durham knew that the Vietnam War was a rich incubator of heroic and tragic tales.

By summer 1968 about a half-million American soldiers had fought their way through Vietnam's jungles, rice paddies, and cities.[26] Many black Americans complained about the disproportionate number of blacks drafted into the military—men who, with their white comrades, lost their lives or portions of their humanity in this bloody conflict.[27] One prominent black man openly refused to become a war statistic, however. World heavyweight boxing champion Muhammad Ali was condemned and praised because of his refusal to be drafted into the U.S. Army. Durham could have fictionalized Ali's story and wrapped *Bird*'s plot around a black draft resister, his family, and the wider community.

But Durham chose another path.

He let the friendships he'd cultivated with police detective Jack Cole and younger officers Edward "Buzz" Palmer and Renault Robinson guide him.[28] These black men regularly spoke with Durham about the challenges of working in the Chicago Police Department (CPD)—one of the nation's more volatile law enforcement bodies. "I think he helped us in a lot of different ways," Robinson recalled. "We could trust what he had to say . . . and he would advise us on certain types of tactics that we should use to promote our cause and stay visible to the public. He wrote articles in *Muhammad Speaks* that benefited us quite a bit."[29]

Those articles were about the Afro-American Patrolmen's League (AAPL). In May 1968 Robinson, Palmer, and three of their colleagues created the AAPL—the first black police organization of its kind.[30] The league embraced a threefold mission: improve relationships between black police officers and black citizens; eliminate police brutality—a key complaint against police in black communities; and encourage a greater degree of professionalism in law enforcement overall. With Robinson at its helm, the group eventually sued the CPD, charging it with discriminatory practices in the hiring, assignment, and promotion of blacks, women, and Hispanics.[31]

Buzz Palmer saw Richard Durham as his mentor, someone with whom he could talk about some of the unsavory aspects of his job. In his unfinished memoir, Palmer described how his first CPD partner showed him how he made extra money taking bribes "without getting dirty." Palmer also said that one white sergeant never seemed to be able to tell the difference between or remember the names of two black officers—one tall and thin, the other shorter and overweight. After two years of this insensitivity, one of the officers confronted the sergeant,

FIGURE 11. *Bird of the Iron Feather* actors Curly Ellison and Louise Pruitt Dumetz Hodges enjoy a moment off camera. Courtesy of Clarice Durham.

noting that a good cop ought to be more observant. After this remark, Palmer said that his colleague was transferred to "less desirable duty."[32] At some point, Renault Robinson said, Durham realized that stories like these "might make a hell of a serial program."[33]

Bird of the Iron Feather became his vehicle.

Durham painted his protagonist, Jonah Rhodes, as an intelligent and sensitive thirty-five-year-old detective.[34] And Durham added an unexpected twist. Detective Rhodes would be dead by the time the series began—killed, Durham wrote in his script treatment, in a crossfire between black rebels and the police during a race riot on Chicago's West Side. The diary Rhodes left behind provided "fragmented but incisive notations" regarding the detective's family life as well as his inner thoughts.[35] Rhodes's personal relationships and professional dilemmas would be revealed through flashbacks and the recollections of the people whose lives he touched.

Durham molded an interesting set of characters around Jonah Rhodes, including his wife, with whom Rhodes had a loving though increasingly strained relationship; a deaf aunt and uncle battling poverty and health concerns; a politically active younger sister; and a gang-leaning younger brother. Jonah's family also included his jazz pianist father, stepmother, and grandmother, as well as his uncle Funky Frank, the hip owner of a neighborhood bar.[36]

In addition, Durham threw in plenty of police officers who either supported or sabotaged Rhodes. To make his law enforcement characters and their dilemmas as authentic as possible, Durham hired Palmer, Robinson, and Cole as script consultants.[37]

• • •

Six months.

That's how little time there was between Durham's July 7, 1969, hiring and *Bird of the Iron Feather*'s mid-January 1970 launch date.

WTTW producer Clarence McIntosh auditioned nearly five hundred actors by the end of the summer.[38] Interest in *Bird* was extremely high in Chicago's black communities, and this interest created problems neither Durham nor WTTW anticipated. In hindsight, station officials admitted they never thought that mass-producing black dramas would be "less feasible" than the similar effort and cost of KCET's *Cancion de la Raza*.[39] But WTTW woefully underestimated black Chicagoans' desire to see themselves portrayed more holistically than *Julia*, *I Spy*, or other TV shows featuring blacks offered. As word about *Bird* spread, the consensus in the black community was "if you're going to do this [TV series], you're going to do it right," director Harold C. Johnson said.[40] Of course, the various definitions of "right" clashed.

The Coalition for United Community Action, an umbrella organization of several black community and religious groups, formed a committee to articulate specific demands for and oversight of *Bird*. Coalition members wanted black men and women to be trained and hired for the show's technical jobs.[41] Few blacks worked in such positions in noncommercial or commercial TV stations throughout the country.[42]

WTTW had planned on using two white staff directors for the show. Coalition members "insisted that we have at least two black directors," actor Ira Rogers recalled. Rogers told producer Clarence McIntosh, "If you're going to [train] people, then go get Roy Inman."[43] For years, Chicagoans Inman and Rogers had performed together as a black folk act, and Inman had worked briefly at Channel 11. McIntosh called Inman, who "became one of [*Bird's*] directors," Rogers explained.[44]

Months before the series became a reality, Richard Durham told Harold Johnson, whom he knew from his thespian connections, about a unique opportunity. WGBH-TV in Boston, a growing production powerhouse in noncommercial TV, was offering a free training program in television directing. Durham suggested that Johnson, an experienced theater director, enroll in the program to prepare for the possibility of directing *Bird* episodes. "That [was] one of the things about Richard," Johnson said. "He was in on everything."[45] Johnson completed the WGBH training, returned to Chicago, and applied for a *Bird* directing job. However, the station rejected Johnson because Roy Inman had already been hired.[46]

Other issues quickly emerged. After agreeing to lead *Bird's* writing team, Durham signed a contract with the station for $500 per script. He subsequently learned that New York–based TV scriptwriters earned one and a half times more for the same work.[47] In addition, the rate of pay for *Bird* actors became an issue.

"So the coalition then got strong," Harold Johnson said. "We got the Blackstone Rangers, a street gang, and took them over to the station. I mean literally, they walked in and pulled all the cords out of the switchboard and stood around and would not let [anything] go on in the station."[48] Durham did not appreciate this show of force. He knew about this black gang's criminal activities, including alleged cases of extortion and murder, because he had assigned *Muhammad Speaks* reporters to write articles about them.[49] "Dick really frowned on the Blackstone Rangers," Ira Rogers said. He and Durham believed it was "sad" that coalition members used gang members "to threaten Channel 11 if they didn't do such and such and such a thing."[50]

Yet gang members were not the only people who stormed into WTTW demanding to be heard that day. Actor Harold Lee Rush Jr. said that most of the protesters included people like himself, honest black citizens who wanted to be considered for acting or technical jobs on this new series.[51]

The pressure produced results. WTTW hired about twelve black staff members, including camera, sound, and lighting technicians or trainees, along with production assistants and a secretary. Harold Johnson came aboard as a director, the actors' pay rates increased, and Durham's compensation doubled to $1,000 per script.[52]

But a major issue remained. WTTW still planned on using the Ford Foundation's $600,000 grant to produce one hundred episodes, generating five half-hour shows a week for six months. Coalition members balked. "We said, 'No you can't do that,'" Harold Johnson recalled. "You can't spend $6,000 and get a [high quality] dramatic program."[53] At the time, soap opera episodes on commercial TV might cost about $30,000 each.[54] The coalition pushed to reduce the number of *Bird of the Iron Feather* episodes in order to increase the quality of each show—a concept trumpeted by executive producer Clarence McIntosh with Richard Durham's backing.[55]

In the meantime Durham still had to fulfill his *Muhammad Speaks* editorial duties. "He'd come to work and edit the articles or do this stuff for the paper," former reporter John Woodford said, "but he often had other stuff he was doing, and then he left. And you didn't quite know if he might have another life. He just knew so many people."[56]

In late September 1969 Durham received a letter Elijah Muhammad had sent from an unspecified West Coast mountainside "overlooking the blue and peaceful Pacific." Muhammad praised Durham's "tremendous job" on *Muhammad Speaks* and asked him to find employees who would ensure that the Nation of Islam's new printing press ran smoothly and produced the highest quality newspaper. A bit of paranoia also crept in. Elijah Muhammad told Durham not to print anything that might cause a lawsuit. "Do not think we are not watched by enemies for such chances," the Nation of Islam leader cautioned.[57]

One section of Elijah Muhammad's letter must have given Durham pause: it revealed that the NOI's printing press was "too expensive to just print one paper. We need to print other periodicals," Muhammad added, "to get some of this money back that we have put out."[58] But taking on additional editing responsibilities definitely would not have appealed to Durham. So probably not long after he received Elijah Muhammad's missive, Durham asked for a leave from the paper. He recommended John Woodford as his replacement.[59] With Muhammad's blessing, Woodford became the paper's new non-Muslim editor—a position he would hold for nearly four years.[60]

Along with his *Bird of the Iron Feather* responsibilities, Dick had another major concern. He and Clarice had to find a new place to live. Quickly. According to Clarice, Chicago officials invoked eminent domain, intending to gobble up the Durhams' block based on pressure from the powerful nearby University of Chicago and the local Woodlawn Organization. Dick, Clarice, and their neighbors scrambled to secure new housing before wrecking crews demolished their homes.[61]

• • •

By early November 1969, Durham and WTTW executives were well aware that in just two months, *Bird of the Iron Feather* would make its maiden flight. Yet months of protests, delays, and escalating costs destroyed the serial's production schedule. The station was in no position to deliver the one hundred episodes originally promised. Therefore, Program Director Edward Morris asked the Ford

Foundation for permission to reduce the number of *Bird* shows to a maximum of 35. The foundation agreed.[62]

Bird of the Iron Feather was now set to air three nights a week, Monday, Wednesday, and Friday at 7:30 P.M. starting in mid-January 1970.[63] Bernard Ward, a professional actor from New York, would play Jonah Rhodes. Chicago-based actors filled the other roles.[64] Durham felt that Ward wasn't right for the part, but the decision was out of his hands.[65] Two black directors, Roy Inman and Harold Johnson, alternated with WTTW's two white staff directors, Peter Strand and Louis Abraham, and black trainees or assistants joined the show's technical crew.

Durham also dipped into Chicago's talent-rich musicians' pool. He asked pianist/composer Muhal Richard Abrams to write the show's theme song.[66] Abrams headed the city's avant-garde black collective known as the Association for the Advancement of Creative Musicians (AACM). Formed in 1965 to "cultivate young musicians and to create music of a high artistic level for the general public," the AACM spawned such internationally acclaimed groups as the Art Ensemble of Chicago, Air, and the Ethnic Heritage Ensemble.[67] Drummer Steve McCall, saxophonist Anthony Braxton, and pianist/vocalist Amina Claudine Myers were just a few of the AACM's many talented members.

Once Abrams composed *Bird*'s theme, Durham collaborated with his son on the song's lyrics.[68] By this time, twenty-year-old Mark was developing into a fine musician. He had taken music appreciation classes when he was eight, and his music-loving parents later escorted him to piano lessons. Clarice laughed, remembering that Mark's piano teacher advised: "You know, not everybody has to be a pianist."[69] Instead, Mark gravitated to the clarinet and saxophone. Mark could not remember how many of the lyrics he'd written for *Bird*'s theme song his father kept. But, he said, "I know he liked the line I had, 'bird of midnight blue song.'"[70] Durham recruited Oscar Brown Jr. to sing the song, and its repeated opening lines reflected Durham's dedication to freedom:

> Birds that trail
> Slave ships at sea
> Seeds of freedom
> Planted in me[71]

Bird of the Iron Feather generated lots of prelaunch media buzz. The black press was especially excited. In early August and again in late October 1969, the *Chicago Defender* announced that *Bird* was on its way.[72] *Jet*, a popular, black-owned, pocket-sized magazine, profiled Durham under the headline "Black Muslim Editor, Chief Writer for Soul Drama."

The mainstream *Chicago Tribune* and *Chicago Sun-Times* newspapers also announced the show's birth, and WTTW-Channel 11 ramped up its promotional

FIGURE 12. Richard Durham speaks to reporters about *Bird*.
Courtesy of Clarice Durham.

efforts. Actress Louise Pruitt Dumetz Hodges remembered seeing "big signs
all over the South Side" promoting the show. WTTW probably advertised *Bird*
"extensively," Dumetz speculated, because the noncommercial station "wasn't as
popular with the average black person as maybe some of the other stations."[73]

Yet a couple of weeks before the series' debut, Durham lay flat on his back,
felled by pneumonia.[74] Durham had worn his body down by working on the show,
searching for a new home, and packing for the move. In early January 1970, Dick
and Clarice moved into a townhouse community several blocks north of their
soon-to-be-demolished Sixtieth Street and South Harper Avenue home. The
newly built, red-brick Stuart Townhomes sat about seven blocks west of Lake
Michigan's shores, twenty-six blocks south of the Loop's skyscrapers, and across
the street from Mercy Hospital. The Durhams' unit included a lower-level family

FIGURE 13. Clarice and Richard Durham pose in the living room of their new South Side townhome. Ben Burns Papers, Harsh Research Collection, Chicago Public Library.

room that led out to a small patio, an airy main floor living room, dining room and kitchen, and a top floor with three bedrooms and two baths.

Durham could barely appreciate his new home as he tried to get well. However, he ignored Clarice's pleas to stay in bed as *Bird*'s launch party approached.[75] He joined the show's cast and crew and celebrated, however briefly, its Monday, January 19, 1970, broadcast debut.

• • •

Reaction to *Bird of the Iron Feather* was swift—and mixed.

"Whatever else the series may be," *Chicago Tribune* reviewer Clarence Petersen wrote, "it is a noble experiment, capable of arousing new compassions in all of us." He noted that by the show's fifth episode, the series becomes "sufficiently complex to satisfy the most demanding devotee of serial drama." But Peterson determined that *Bird*'s first episode was "a bore."[76]

Bird's debut show, "Prescription for Pallbearers," was a prescription for dramatic disaster. Detective Jonah Rhodes's colleagues talked, with little physical action, about Rhodes impending funeral, their relationships with him, and the diary he left in his locker.[77] "As close to a dud as anything I have seen on television," *Chicago Daily News* reviewer Norman Mark wrote. But Mark optimistically claimed that the series "appears to improve as [it] goes along. The question is: Will viewers stick with the program through the early shows when the acting is wooden, and the writing is talky, until the entire production gets more professional in later episodes?"[78]

To be fair, many new TV dramas begin their broadcast lives on wobbly legs. Some strengthen their standing and survive as the writers, directors, and actors become more comfortable with the characters and fine-tune the show's storylines. Given *Bird*'s status as the first TV series of its kind, the show generated widespread interest—and skepticism. "Virtually everyone will find something wrong with *Bird*," WTTW program director Edward Morris told local and national reporters. "Black militants will claim it's not militant enough, the black middle class will say conditions aren't like that, white liberals will cringe at what they see and white conservatives will say we're helping blacks to overthrow the government," Morris said. He predicted, however, that people would watch *Bird* "in angry fascination."[79]

Morris's prediction prevailed. Despite the show's mixed reviews, including references to its sometimes "amateurish acting" and "simplistic plots," *Bird of the Iron Feather* attracted a large audience. By mid-February 1970, national newsmagazines *Time* and *Newsweek* reported that *Bird*'s half-million viewers made it the highest rated local production in WTTW's history.[80]

Bird earned this distinction in part because of Durham's insistence on dealing with issues TV often avoided. "In the soap operas of the old days, you couldn't write about all the social conflicts," Durham told a reporter. "You'd have to deal with personality and very little else. The thing I resent most about television, especially daytime television, is the refusal to take material from real life."[81] Durham certainly bucked that trend. For example, Durham used a health crisis that Detective Rhodes's deaf relatives suffered through to question the treatment of handicapped people on welfare.[82] Durham also brought the Vietnam War into play in his script, "The Sermon." According to a young minister character named Ragland:

> The last time I saw Jonah [Rhodes] alive, he was in my father's church and I had been drafted for Vietnam. I asked Jonah what he thought of the war, and he shook his head and said, "Oh what a tragedy to be born in the slums, raised in the ghetto and before you reach 21, be sent to die in the jungles 10,000 miles from home."[83]

Reflecting the real-life activism of the Afro-American Patrolmen's League, Durham's Ragland claims that when Rhodes brought black cops together to instill "a new sense of service and identity with the plight of their people," certain white officers "tried to bust him down, space him out." "Why," Ragland rhetorically asks, "do white people hate to see black people get themselves together?"[84]

Durham sought to make *Bird*'s dialogue as realistic as possible. In the episode "Speaking of Dreams," Rhodes's nemesis, a black police sergeant named Henry Vines, calls Jonah "an obstinate, hell-bent nigger."[85] Not only was the N-word used freely, but some characters used language that FCC regulations still prohibit on noncommercial and commercial television (excluding cable).[86] WTTW's switchboard lit up as viewers objected to *Bird*'s dialogue. In response, Channel 11 moved the series to a 9:30 P.M. program slot and added an "adult viewing" disclaimer.[87]

In a lighter moment in one episode, Jonah Rhodes reminisced about how his wife teased him each day as he headed to work. She'd shout, "J-O O-N-N-A-AH . . . Watch out for the whales!"[88] She was referencing the biblical tale of the prophet Jonah, who, after angering God, was swallowed by a whale and then survived three days and nights in the whale's stomach before the mammal "vomited out Jonah upon the dry land."[89] Durham symbolically put his Jonah in the belly of Chicago's law enforcement beast.

It is fascinating that Durham chose this biblical reference since he was skeptical about religious concepts and organized religion. "He always told me, man created God in his own image," Mark Durham said about his father. He told Mark that when you read about God, other sacred figures, or events in the *Bible* and other religious texts, "somebody wrote it down. Where did they get it from? Who did it benefit?"[90] Perhaps Durham reasoned that some viewers might better connect with *Bird*'s characters if he employed subtle sacred overtones.

One of Durham's more dynamic scripts, "The Target," dramatized an actual case involving the Chicago branch of the Black Panther Party for Self Defense. College students and Black Panther leaders Fred Hampton and Mark Clark lost their lives on December 4, 1969, after CPD officers rushed into Hampton's apartment, guns blazing, in a predawn raid.[91] The raid was not an aberration. Sociologist Todd Gitlin noted that between 1968 and 1969, local police officers and FBI agents raided thirty-one Black Panther offices across eleven different states.[92]

Determined to defend black people from oppression—including police brutality—Oakland, California, natives Huey Newton and Bobby Seale established the Black Panther Party in 1966. Dressed in leather jackets with berets on their bulging Afros, Black Panthers openly flaunted their legal right to own handguns or rifles—and to use them, if needed, to protect the oppressed and poor masses.[93] The Black Panthers' militancy provoked the ire of law enforcement agencies nationwide. Yet the Black Panthers also earned respect in black communities for creating free breakfast programs for poor school children, along with healthcare and other support programs.[94]

In "The Target," Durham's Jonah Rhodes and a handful of his colleagues accept a top-secret assignment. The officers are trained by "a real sharp sonofabitch," a no-nonsense instructor of military bearing who shows them how to effectively hit their "target."[95] The officers will attack the headquarters of a group called the Black Protectors, Durham's stand-in for the Black Panthers. However, Detective Rhodes wonders: "Is this the next step in the evolution of policemen? The way it was in Nazi Germany, Fascist Spain . . . police as executioners?"

Shortly thereafter, Rhodes is dropped from the mission. He believes it is because "certain people didn't want me sniffing about. I think it's cold-blooded murder."[96] By placing these words in Rhodes's mouth, Durham reveals the opinions of some black Chicagoans about the actual raid on the Hampton and Clark apartment.

Durham's Fred Hampton–like character, Julian, and one of his friends in the Black Protectors die in the subsequent police raid. The drama's police officers claim that they had a shoot-out with the men. In the real Hampton/Clark case, Renault Robinson and several other Afro-American Patrolmen's League officers rushed to the scene immediately after the raid and conducted their own impromptu investigation. "All the bullet holes in [the apartment's back] door were going in," Robinson recalled. "So we called a press conference to point out that the State's Attorney and his folks lied about the shoot-out."[97] Months later a report released by a federal grand jury found that of the more than eighty bullets identified in the apartment, only one might have come from a Black Panther member's gun.[98] The AAPL labeled the raid a "shoot-in," and Durham's well-written script reflected that viewpoint.[99]

But WTTW rejected it. "We worked on the script very hard and very long and we thought it was going to be a part of the series," Durham told historian J. Fred MacDonald.[100] Station officials probably considered the episode too incendiary for broadcast, especially coming only a few months after the actual Hampton and Clark killings.

As it turned out, WTTW's rejection of "The Target" script foreshadowed what would soon happen to the series. The station, in its own ironic parlance, "terminated" *Bird of the Iron Feather* in early March 1970.[101] WTTW essentially blamed the black community for the show's demise. Station officials told the *Chicago Tribune* that the Coalition for United Community Action's demands "helped drive up costs of the series and put it out of business after 21 episodes instead of the 100 originally planned." Program Director Edward Morris claimed that in order for WTTW to achieve the Coalition's objectives, "the cost of the series skyrocketed from the projected $6,000 to nearly $30,000 an episode."[102]

Not true, Durham countered. He told a *Chicago Defender* reporter that *Bird*'s cost per episode was actually around $7,000.[103] The same article reported that *Bird* cost about $21,500 per show. Despite such conflicting claims, the question remained: how did the series run out of money so quickly? Edward Morris said that in addition to the show's rising production costs, 20 percent of *Bird*'s Ford Foundation grant went to station overhead—a grant requirement.[104]

Certainly, other factors contributed to the show's demise after only seven weeks on the air. Durham had argued with station management over the series' concluding storyline. "The true ending was [supposed to be] a police assassination; police assassinating other police officers," Durham told J. Fred MacDonald. Durham admitted that he had agreed to change the storyline, since the depiction of cops killing cops was taboo at that time. "This was before [the movie] *Serpico* came out. I was always a little bit too ahead of the situation," Durham said. When the time came for him to change the series closer, "I didn't feel like doing it," Durham admitted.[105] His stubborn streak kicked in. Durham's decision no doubt angered WTTW officials.

Former CPD officer Renault Robinson said that Chicago's iron-fisted mayor, Richard J. Daley, "didn't like the show at all and he put pressure to get it off the air." Robinson attributed Daley's actions to "racism" and the assumption "that this show was going to show all of the negative sides of the [CPD]." Robinson smiled, conceding, "We had plenty of material."[106]

Durham often told his friend Abena Joan Brown, "What we're doing is very dangerous." She agreed. "That's why it [was] important to do," Brown said. She believed that Richard "understood and appreciated our historical experience within the context of these Americas. He was conscious. He had integrity. And," Brown concluded, "he wrote not only for himself but he wrote for us so that we could better understand what this journey is all about."[107] *Bird of the Iron Feather* may have been an example of the more thoughtful programming that WTTW board chairman and former FCC commissioner Newton Minow had championed during the early 1960s. But such inventiveness did not necessarily guarantee long-term financial support.

Representatives from the Coalition for United Community Action urged WTTW managers to seek additional funds from the Ford Foundation or elsewhere.[108] Yet in a March 9, 1970, press release, the station indicated that the series had run its course. Officials said they were pleased with *Bird* "as an experiment" and that they would "proudly make [the programs] available for network distribution, which we hope will be approved by the Public Broadcast Service."[109] Given his activist history, Durham could have mounted a vigorous campaign to save his series.

Instead, another writing opportunity had already stirred his soul.

He had joined forces with the self-proclaimed "greatest" boxer in the world, agreeing to write Muhammad Ali's autobiography. By channeling "the spirit of *Destination Freedom*," Mark Durham said his father could promote positive images of black people through the tale of this American hero—a black man who asserted his right to freedom of speech and religion regardless of the consequences.[110]

Richard was ready for this new journey.

CHAPTER 11

Globetrotting with The Greatest

The Induction

The room is still and the lieutenant looks at me intently. He knows that his general, his mayor and everybody in the Houston Induction Center is waiting for this moment. He draws himself up straight and tall . . .

But who is this white man, no older than me, appointed by another white man, all the way down from the white man in the White House? Who is he to tell me to go to Asia, Africa or anywhere else in the world to fight people who never threw a rock at me, or America? . . .

I'm looking straight into his eyes. There's a ripple of movement as some of the people in the room edge closer in anticipation.

"Cassius Clay—Army!"

The room is silent. I stand straight, unmoving . . .

"Mr. Cassius Clay," he begins again, "will you please step forward and be inducted in to the United States Army."

Again I don't move.[1]

—Muhammad Ali with Richard Durham,
The Greatest: My Own Story, 1975

Richard Durham relished the idea of chronicling the life of a man who had mastered his favorite sport, and who had become an internationally known, if controversial, cultural icon. Muhammad Ali and his manager Herbert Muhammad chose Durham as the book's credited ghostwriter because "Dick was somebody they felt they could have some trust in," Clarice Durham said. "They wanted a writer who was going to portray Muhammad in [the] positive light he deserved, so they asked Dick if he would do it."[2]

During his seven years as editor for *Muhammad Speaks*, Durham had interacted often with Ali and genuinely liked him. Durham told a reporter years later: "I remember what the training was like [for boxing], what getting hit was like and getting up off the floor after you've been hit, to hit back and win."[3]

Winning. Ali seemed to do that best, both as a young amateur and as a professional. Born Cassius Marcellus Clay Jr. on January 17, 1942, Clay boxed his way to local stardom in his segregated Louisville, Kentucky, hometown by the end of the 1950s. He earned a spot on America's 1960 Olympic team and headed to the Summer Games in Rome.[4] With his charming, high-octane personality, Clay emerged as one of the most popular athletes in the Olympic Village.[5] Later, the eighteen-year-old boxer returned home with a gold medal dangling from his neck.

Sportswriter Dick Schaap described a post-Olympics Cassius Clay as "an imposing sight," with his "developing light-heavyweight build" supporting "180 pounds spread like silk over a 6 foot 2 frame."[6] A flat-topped, bushy Afro framed Clay's handsome, light brown face, and he'd shout to whomever would listen:

I'm the World's Prettiest Fighter!
I'm the World's Strongest Fighter!
I'm the World's Fastest Fighter![7]

Clay also crowned himself "The Greatest" boxer in the world and set out to prove his loud and proud claims. Clay designed his prefight antics to rattle opponents and pump himself up. "Every time I go into the ring I'm scared to death," he later revealed to Durham in his autobiography. "After all that poppin' off, all that predicting, all those people wanting to see me get whipped, I know I'm in trouble. If I lose they'll be ready to run me out of the country. I'm out on a limb and I know I gotta win."[8]

Clay joined boxing's professional ranks in fall 1960. During the next three years he scored fifteen knockouts, four decision wins, and no losses.[9] He glided around the boxing ring, light on the balls of his feet—a graceful if lethal dancer. Clay became known as much for his fancy footwork and quicksilver punching skills as for his verbal hijinks. He offered poetic predictions about the specific round his opponents would fall, even if those rhyming projections caused some people to call Clay a braggart or a conman.[10]

Durham saw through Clay's outsized boasts. "It's impossible for a person to really conceal himself from another person who's attentive," Durham told a reporter. "You don't have to be a psychiatrist. If you like the person . . . you become very sensitive to him and see all the dips and dives. He doesn't really put on a con job, by the way. That's just one part of him. All of us perform somewhat when there are others around," Durham said, adding, "Ali just performs more. He does just about everything more!"[11]

By 1964 Cassius Clay was gunning for the world heavyweight boxing championship title, held at the time by Charles "Sonny" Liston, a slugger known for his shotgun-blast-style jabs.[12]

Clay taunted Liston, as he would do with subsequent opponents, calling Liston a "big, ugly bear" and a "chump" rather than a champ.[13] Clay caused such a screaming, wild-eyed ruckus at the Liston-Clay prefight weigh-in that journalist David Remnick observed: "Clay's performance seemed to be the sweaty rantings of a nut" and "the frightened rant" of a terrified kid.[14]

On February 25, 1964, the 210-pound Cassius Clay and the 218-pound Sonny Liston touched gloves at the start of their championship match in Miami Beach, Florida. Most people believed that the older, more experienced champion would quickly flatten the loud-mouthed upstart.[15] Instead, Clay danced around Liston, bobbing and weaving out of Liston's firing range. Liston's dangerous jabs, uppercuts, and hooks often missed Clay or did little damage when they connected. Clay's long, muscled arms pounded Liston's body and head, bloodying his nose and opening a nasty cut under Liston's left eye. With his stamina shot, his face and ego battered, Liston did not leave his corner for the seventh round.[16]

Against long odds, twenty-two-year-old Cassius Clay Jr. emerged as the heavyweight boxing championship of the world!

Shortly thereafter the new champ threw another revelatory punch. Before his fight with Liston, the rumor mill churned with speculation about why Clay had been associating with the Nation of Islam's top spokesman, Minister Malcolm X. Clay silenced the rumors when he identified the Honorable Elijah Muhammad as his spiritual leader and the Nation of Islam as his religious home.[17] And Clay had a new name: Muhammad Ali.[18] Ali's announcement further alienated some sportswriters and others who condemned Ali for his allegiance to this perceived radical religious sect.[19] But the Champ's commitment to his new faith was strong, as was his determination to demonstrate his boxing prowess.

Richard Durham believed that Ali wanted "to go down [in history] with a reputation of never refusing anybody a fight. That's why," Durham said, Ali became "the first fighter to really go around the world," trading punches and combinations with champions from countries like Great Britain, Germany, and Canada.

FIGURE 14. Muhammad Ali, then known by his birth name Cassius Clay, jokes with fans in St. Louis in 1962 as a smiling Malcolm X (with glasses) looks on. Courtesy of the Robert A. Sengstacke Archives.

Ali beat them all, along with his American opponents. In Durham's eyes, Ali used his grace and bruising power, his prefight antics and his rhyming predictions to establish his global boxing dominance.[20]

Underneath his brash exterior, Ali was a "sensitive, very humble, yet shrewd man—with as much untapped mental energy as he has physical power," Malcolm X told sportswriter George Plimpton.[21] Before Malcolm X left the Nation of Islam, Ali and the NOI's top minister had been very close. "Not many people know the quality of the mind [Ali's] got in there," Malcolm X said. "He fools them. One forgets that though a clown never imitates a wise man, the wise man can imitate the clown."[22]

Richard Durham agreed. "Ali has an amazing mind, and as a result [he] can concentrate harder on some things than almost anyone else. A lot of people think it's just roadwork, speed and his personality that got Ali to the top. But if you lived with him you'd see how much more it is," Durham explained. "He studies everything, doesn't miss anything, puts himself in every possible situation with his opponent countless times before it ever happens in the ring."[23]

Durham also could see that the Champ was hurting. Between spring 1967 and fall 1970, Muhammad Ali could not buy, rap, or fight his way into a ring. On April 28, 1967, just an hour after he refused to be inducted into the U.S. Army, the New York State Athletic Commission suspended Ali's boxing license. Other states quickly followed, effectively ending the Champ's reign. Two months later, a Houston, Texas, jury found Ali guilty of draft evasion. He received the maximum sentence: five years in prison and a $10,000 fine.[24] Ali stayed out of jail while he pursued a long, costly legal appeals process.

Ali had earned slightly more than $2 million during his first three years as a professional boxer.[25] Yet with his banishment from the sport he loved and his mounting legal fees, Ali scrambled to stay afloat. The dethroned champion, then age twenty-five, embarked on a college lecture tour and searched for other income sources. He certainly hoped to be well compensated for writing his autobiography, and Dick Durham played an integral role in the book negotiation process.

One day in January 1970, Durham received a phone call from Charles F. Harris, a black senior editor with Random House, the prestigious New York City–based publisher. Harris asked Durham whether rumors about Ali's plans to write an autobiography were true. Dick confirmed the rumors. But he also was upset. Durham told Harris that in a couple of days he and Ali were scheduled to meet with another New York–based publisher, Simon and Schuster. Yet Durham could not find a place to stay.[26]

Harris came to the rescue and booked the necessary hotel reservations. Our ultimate goal," Charles Harris said, "was to get Durham to bring the Champ to our offices before they went to Simon and Schuster." Durham flew to New York and met with Harris and Random House editor-in-chief James Silberman, assuring them that Ali would meet with them the next day. Sure enough, Ali strolled into Random House's midtown Manhattan offices with NOI representatives and Durham by his side. Ali lit up the room with his presence, and he was impressed that Random House had a black editor on staff.[27]

As book contract talks got underway, Durham ran interference, repeatedly calling Simon and Schuster to delay their prescheduled meeting. After hours of back and forth negotiations, Ali, Silberman, and Harris finally settled on an advance of more than two hundred thousand to be "split 50–50 between Ali and myself," Durham later reported.[28]

Durham wanted to write about the totality of Ali's multilayered character. "Some people have two personalities, Muhammad has five," Durham once told a *Chicago Defender* reporter. "When he is alone he is brilliant, when he is with a companion he is meditative, in the boxing ring he concentrates and for the press he is a clown."[29] In addition, Durham told his brother Earl that Ali "took the Muslim faith, as he understood it, seriously. He really considered himself a spokesperson for Islam." On the other hand, Earl Durham called Ali an "outstanding womanizer!" But Dick knew that the Nation of Islam would resist his efforts to focus on that trait. Still, Durham pressed on, intent on understanding and writing about as many of the elements in Ali's DNA as he could.[30]

Durham noticed, for example, that Ali had a "real and unadulterated" love for children. Ali essentially saw himself in every child. Durham believed that this attitude grew out of Ali's childhood, where he was buoyed by the support of his parents, Odessa and Cassius Clay Sr., his younger brother Rudolph, and extended family members.[31] Sports columnist Robert Lipsyte more bluntly described Ali as a "pampered first-born in an active, accomplished Louisville family."[32]

Richard Durham shadowed Muhammad Ali with his tape recorder and microphone, regularly recording the fighter's reflections and interactions. He even captured Ali talking in his sleep, sometimes speaking, as Durham laughingly described, "in lucid sentences."[33] Durham certainly loved traveling with Ali, since the Champ often enjoyed great accommodations and adoring fans. Ali "is the best known person in the world," Durham declared. "People know Ali who wouldn't know the president of any country!"[34]

A few months into the Ali-Durham book collaboration, however, Richard suffered a major loss. His mother, ninety-year-old Chanie Tillman Durham, died of natural causes on June 10, 1970.[35] With outward calm masking great sadness, Richard and his siblings buried the woman who had loved and nurtured them all.[36]

Even as Chanie passed on her passion for knowledge to her children, she never relinquished her own educational dreams. Chanie had returned to school in 1938, determined to earn the high school diploma that eluded her as a teenager. Feisty as ever, Chanie excelled in Wendell Phillips High's Adult Evening School, becoming the top student in her class.

In Chanie's June 1944 graduation speech, the sixty-four-year-old valedictorian recalled how "some six years ago we stopped procrastinating and started working toward a definite goal." Acknowledging the naysayers who asked why she and her fellow students returned to high school at such an advanced age, Chanie said: "We have been working to acquire what [Catholic Cardinal] John Henry Newman once described as a 'habit of mind.'" Durham's mother identified the attributes of this "habit" as calmness, moderation, wisdom—and perhaps most important, freedom.[37]

FIGURE 15. Chanie Durham receives a portrait painted in her honor from an unidentified Phillips High Adult Evening School official in 1944. Courtesy of Clarice Durham.

Freedom. Did Chanie inspire her second son's fixation on this concept? Did her writer son influence her? Could it have been a little bit of both?

Following their mother's funeral, Richard and his siblings agreed that their oldest brother, Curtis George Jr., should inherit their childhood Chicago home.[38] CG's family has lived there ever since.

After resuming his travels with Muhammad Ali, Durham found out that some fans and former cast members still hoped to revive *Bird of the Iron Feather*. In September 1970, Coalition for United Community Action members picketed in front of WTTW's North Side studios. The protesters demanded that WTTW's license be withheld because of the dearth of black programs on the station and the belief that Channel 11 blocked the national airplay of *Bird* episodes.[39] The latter claim was particularly potent because *Bird* had received one of television's highest honors a few months earlier. On May 25, 1970, *Bird* won an Emmy Award for "outstanding achievement for a local series."[40] In light of this significant recognition and the coalition's protest, WTTW asked for and received $17,000 from the

Ford Foundation to support *Bird*'s airing on Public Broadcasting Service (PBS) stations. PBS fed thirteen *Bird of the Iron Feather* episodes to member stations in September 1971.[41]

Yet the re-airing of portions of this series must have been bittersweet for Durham. Given the controversy that plagued the show from its inception, there was little hope that WTTW or another station would raise the hundreds of thousands of dollars necessary for the production of new *Bird* programs.

· · ·

As the actual writer of *The Greatest*, Durham first worked with Random House editor Charles F. Harris. But Harris eventually left Random House to head the newly formed Howard University Press in Washington, D.C.[42] Durham's new senior editor was a Howard graduate and writer named Toni Morrison. In later years, Morrison would secure prestigious awards like the Pulitzer Prize, the Presidential Medal of Freedom, and the Nobel Prize in Literature—the first African American woman so honored.[43] However, Toni Morrison recalled that in 1970, Durham "was a little wary at first" about working with her. "He'd been in the business forever as a journalist and editor," Morrison said. "I had published this one book which I don't think he liked much—*The Bluest Eye*."[44] Morrison's bite-sized novel about a young black girl's struggle with identity, race, and abuse had debuted to good reviews. Yet if Durham was "tentative" about Morrison's qualifications, "that didn't last more than a day or two," she said. "Otherwise, our relationship was very, very warm and very professional."[45]

Toni Morrison also really liked Muhammad Ali. "Ali was sort of flirtatious, like a boy almost. When I first met him he said, you know we can have three wives," Morrison laughed, recalling her reaction. "Please!" she said, laughing even more. "I'm old enough to be your mama!" Still, Morrison saw Ali as "an absolute delight, and that delightful quality Richard was able to catch. He was a very, very good writer."[46]

But with so many people vying for "a piece of Ali's time," Durham worried that he "wouldn't be able to get through to Ali." Also, "the Muslims had final say on the book if we ever did get it written," Durham noted.[47] In an attempt to move the writing process along, Ali and Durham outlined their recommendations for each section of the book. Shortly thereafter, however, Ali found out that he might be able to fight again. Through some clever political maneuvering, a black Georgia Senator named Leroy Johnson arranged for an October 26, 1970, match in Atlanta between Ali and white challenger Jerry Quarry.[48] Ali and Durham realized that their book might now need to focus more on Ali's reentry into the boxing world rather than his exile from it.

Yet as the fight date approached, Georgia Governor Lester Maddox almost succeeded in stopping the match, and Ali received threatening mail. One particularly vicious package contained a black Chihuahua, its head severed from its bloody body, with the message: "We know how to handle black draft-dodging dogs in Georgia."[49] Then, according to the account in *The Greatest*, during the dark, predawn hours on the morning of the fight Ali stepped off the porch of his rented lakeside cottage to limber up. Suddenly, gunfire zipped through the leaves of the trees around him. Ali dropped to the ground and crawled back into the cottage. Three angry voices screamed obscenities as more shots rang out. Atlanta police officers eventually arrived and escorted Ali and his crew to safety.[50]

During the five years he worked on *The Greatest*, Durham said that he rarely missed a fight.[51] So Durham may have been in that Atlanta cottage when the shooting incident occurred. Even if Durham had to rely on what he called Ali's "phenomenal memory" for details, Durham made sure that the story's potency resonated on the printed page.[52] And Durham's editor wasn't surprised. Toni Morrison said that Durham had "a theatrical eye," enabling him to determine "what to throw out and what to include . . . what was interesting and what was not and how to make a scene," Morrison explained. "So I found working with him very exciting."[53]

By the end of his first fight in three-and-a-half years, Ali again tasted the sweetness of victory after only three rounds. "But near the end I was tired," Ali revealed in *The Greatest*. "My jab was off target. My uppercuts were off. I saw openings I couldn't cash in on. . . . I wondered what would have happened if [Quarry] could have lasted 10 rounds."[54] Muhammad Ali and Richard Durham would soon find out about the former Champ's staying power.

• • •

Meanwhile, the professional boxing world had moved on during Ali's absence from the ring. By February 1970 Joe Frazier had become the sport's new champion, and according to sports columnist Robert Lipsyte, Frazier was characterized as "a human bulldozer, relentless, impervious to pain, ruthless in his determination."[55] In *The Greatest*, Durham included a lengthy, often rambling, verbatim conversation between Ali and Frazier. Durham had recorded these athletes—and adversaries—as they shared a two-hour car ride from Philadelphia to New York in August 1970. Their conversation bounced between serious reflections about their sport to jive-talk. Ali nicknamed Frazier "the Turtle." Frazier detailed how he'd whip Ali if the two ever fought.[56]

Ali knew that he *had* to fight Frazier to recapture the championship title. Still, he did not want "just to be in the ring with Frazier tearing away at each other." Durham reported that Ali had a "nightmarish image" of himself and Frazier as two "big, black slaves fighting, almost on the verge of annihilating each other" while white masters urged them on. Durham's own voice sneaked in, as it did throughout *The Greatest*, as Ali mused, "I wanted to be known as a freedom fighter, but I still wanted comrades—close friends who did the same work as I did, felt the same way I did . . . who would fight alongside me for blacks. I wanted a buddy like Joe." However, because of the high stakes rivalry between these boxers, Ali realized that he and Frazier would never be close friends.[57]

After Ali won a hard-fought battle against South American champ Oscar Bonavena in December, Frazier agreed to fight Ali the next year. For the March 8, 1971, match, each boxer was guaranteed a $2.5 million paycheck. Ali biographer Thomas Hauser noted that this fight would be the first time "two undefeated heavyweights, each with a legitimate claim to the title," would meet for a championship bout.[58] Ali predicted Frazier's defeat in round six. Instead, the fight lasted a grueling fifteen rounds. This intense contest of wills finally ended when Frazier knocked Ali to the boxing ring's mat in the last round.[59]

Ali told Durham about what he had long called the "half-dream room." It was the place where a fighter goes, metaphorically speaking, after a punch floors him. In that room, Ali said, boxers feel like they're "half awake and half dreaming." With poetic panache, Durham wrote in *The Greatest*:

A heavy blow takes you to the door of this room. It opens and you see neon orange and green lights blinking. You see bats blowing trumpets, alligators play trombones, and snakes are screaming. Weird masks and actor's clothes hang on the wall. . . . The blow makes your mind vibrate like a tuning fork."[60]

And in that half-dream space, Ali revealed that time seems to stretch and slow down, making it difficult for a boxer to determine just how fast seconds zip by. Joe Frazier sent Muhammad Ali to that half-dream room in round 15, and Ali lost his championship bid.

Three months later, however, Ali scored a victory outside the boxing ring. On June 28, the U.S. Supreme Court threw out Ali's draft evasion conviction.[61] However, the ruling did not restore Ali's championship status. So the former Champ spent the rest of 1971 and all of 1972 fighting—and winning—against contenders like Floyd Patterson and, once again, Jerry Quarry.[62]

In the meantime, Random House executives were getting antsy. They had advanced a substantial sum of money to Ali and Durham and they needed the men to produce a completed manuscript. Along with the pressure Ali and Durham faced from Random House executives, Durham and editor Toni Morrison had to deal with restrictions the Nation of Islam imposed. "Durham warned me that there would be some problems of censorship," Morrison said. She found Ali's manager, Herbert Muhammad, to be "very controlling. I did feel a little intimi-

FIGURE 16. Richard Durham and Muhammad Ali confer with each other about Ali's autobiography during the mid-1970s. Ben Burns Papers, Vivian G. Harsh Research Collection, Chicago Public Library.

dated . . . all of which I defied, by the way." Morrison explained that there was "a locker room language in the fight world, and [Richard] would use it in dialog. It was authentic." Herbert Muhammad insisted that such language be deleted.[63] But Ali's manager could not override the Champ's insistence that a conversation with his first wife appear uncensored in his book.[64]

Durham devoted a chapter to Muhammad Ali and Sonji Roi's discussion about how they met, fell in love, and then married in June 1964. Pretty and petite, Roi loved the fashions of the day, gravitating toward miniskirts and dresses that accented her curves. Muslim dress was much more conservative, almost puritanical. Ali argued with and even hit Sonji on several occasions when she wore more revealing clothes, including dresses that Ali bought for her. In *The Greatest*, Ali honestly acknowledged the role he played in the disintegration of his marriage to "the first woman I had loved and who had put my religious faith and creed to the final test."[65]

At one point Sonji referred to Ali's refusal to question his religious beliefs with the sentence: "You World Heavyweight Champion Motherfucker!"[66] Herbert Muhammad wanted the quote eliminated. Toni Morrison refused. "I just couldn't do it. So I just used the initials . . . M.F.," Morrison said with a smile. "And the person who soothed things for the most part was Richard."[67]

. . .

By the end of March 1973, America had withdrawn its last remaining troops from Vietnam.[68] But Ali literally could not talk about this milestone in a war that had uniquely touched his life as well as the lives of so many Americans and Southeast Asians. Ali's mouth was wired shut. A little known fighter named Ken Norton had broken Ali's jaw in their March 31 bout. Durham believed that Ali had not taken the fight seriously enough. "If he's fighting someone like a Frazier he will train, and [train] hard," Durham said. By underestimating Norton, Ali lost a fight for the first time since the Ali-Frazier battle two years earlier.[69]

After this embarrassing defeat, Durham said that people thought Ali should retire.[70] But retirement was the furthest thing from Ali's mind when Durham talked with the former champ in his hospital room the next day. "I think that was the first time I felt he really trusted me," Durham recalled. Perhaps sensing Durham's real concern for him, Ali confided in Durham even more, telling Dick how "a long line of victories weakens you."[71] According to Durham, Ali believed that a defeated fighter may occasionally be stronger than the boxer who has never lost because the loser knows what defeat looks and feels like, inspiring him to work harder to avoid future losses.[72]

"I think I was able to identify with Ali at the deepest point of what makes him tick," Durham told a reporter. "When's he's in that ring . . . his trainers, and handlers and managers can't do a thing for him. He's alone. And it's the same for a writer," Durham said. "No one else can help you while you're doing it. A boxer is all alone in the ring, and a writer is all alone at the typewriter."[73]

Ali soon headed back to his Louisville hometown with his second wife, Belinda, their daughters, and his training crew. Media headlines screamed:

Muhammad is Finished! End of an Era!
Ali Beaten by a Nobody! Big Mouth Shut for All Time![74]

Durham used this low point in Ali's career as the starting point for *The Greatest*. In the first chapter, Durham revealed that Ali returned to Louisville after his defeat "to remember who I am, where I came from and where I want to go."[75]

But by early 1974 Durham still had not delivered a completed manuscript to Random House. Editor Toni Morrison implored Durham to "just give me the book!" She laughed, remembering that Richard "would say 'yeah,'" yet he continued "stringing us along a little bit. But everything that he actually delivered was so good," Morrison said. "So he would keep me at arms length when he didn't have it or didn't want to turn it in . . . for whatever reasons."[76]

Durham likely had gotten distracted. Globetrotting with Ali to fights or exhibition matches in Indonesia, Ireland, parts of North and Southern Africa, as well as across America undoubtedly kept Durham from engaging in writing's solitary, cerebral demands. In addition, longtime friend Bennett Johnson said that Dick served as a kind of deputy manager to Ali.[77] Fiercely protective of the former champ who was twenty-five years his junior, Durham once heatedly argued with a film director over what Durham believed were questionable compensation arrangements for Ali. And with Herbert Muhammad, Durham helped to negotiate some of Ali's business contracts.[78] In this capacity, Durham met a whirlwind of a man whose hair always seemed to be caught in an invisible updraft.

That man was Don King.

During the mid-1960s, Don King had promoted an exhibition fight with Muhammad Ali, designed to raise money for a hospital in King's Cleveland, Ohio, hometown. Thereafter, King lobbied for the right to promote Ali's fights; Herbert Muhammad rejected King's requests.[79] Yet Don King found an ally in Richard Durham. Durham probably saw King as a kind of kindred spirit—someone who, like himself, knew how to work with, if not manipulate, others to get things done.

Dick Durham arranged for Don King to meet with NOI leader Elijah Muhammad. By supporting King in this way "my father took a real chance on his job," Mark Durham said, since Herbert Muhammad, one of Elijah Muhammad's sons, managed Ali's career.[80] To test King's business and financial acumen, Nation of Islam officials required him to establish a substantial line of credit.[81] Don King pulled the money together, and the NOI eventually agreed to let him promote a bout destined to become a historic sports event.

In late September 1974, Muhammad Ali and George Foreman, the new heavyweight champion, were scheduled to fight in the central African nation of Zaire—formerly the Belgian Congo. Each boxer would pocket $5 million, twice the amount Ali received for his first battle with Joe Frazier, and, as Ali biographer Thomas Hauser noted, more than boxing champions Joe Louis, Jack Dempsey, and Rocky Marciano earned during their entire careers.[82]

FIGURE 17. Richard Durham takes notes in Zaire, sitting near (from left to right) Ali's trainer Angelo Dundee, businessman Clyde Brooks (C.B.) Atkins, CPD officer Pat Patterson, an unidentified Zairian assistant, and Muhammad Ali. © Roy Lewis Archives 1974.

Ali flew to Kinshasa, Zaire's capital, several weeks before the September 25 match. Ali's entourage included Richard, Clarice, and Mark Durham.[83] Richard had hired his son to help him shape what would be the final chapters of *The Greatest*. Having authored articles for *Downbeat* magazine and the *Chicago Tribune*, Mark was a fine writer. "Basically," Mark said, "I would go around and write about what [Zaire] looked like, what it smelled like, what people were saying."[84]

The Ali camp stayed in a presidential compound about forty miles from Kinshasa.[85]

The compound's distance from the capital and the stadium where the fight would be held allowed Durham to see more of the country. He recorded some of his observations on tape. Traversing the Congo River one day in an old tugboat, Durham marveled at the river's expanse, "almost as wide as a lake at certain points," with pretty floating plants containing lilac blooms.[86]

Yet the country's stark contradictions troubled him. Durham knew that President Mobutu Sese Seko was one of the wealthiest men in the world because of

Zaire's rich cache of valuable raw minerals. However, Durham observed that far too many Zairians suffered in poverty, living "in hovels, shacks, less than shacks; an existence in which one would know that any disease, any sickness, any contagion could flourish." And he was struck by how much Zaire's citizens resembled African Americans. "Every face you see here, you've seen it on an American street in a black community," Durham asserted.[87]

Along with his daily training sessions, Ali held a press conference almost every day. "My job would be to stick a tape recorder up there with the rest of the recorders and get what he [said]," Mark Durham explained.[88] In one press conference, Ali alluded to President Richard Nixon's August 9, 1974, resignation. Nixon walked away from the White House, under threat of impeachment, because of the scandal known as Watergate. This Republican president had sanctioned and tried to cover up an illegal, 1972 break-in attempt at the Democratic National Party's offices at the Watergate complex in Washington, D.C.[89] Muhammad Ali rhymed:

> You think the world was shocked when Nixon resigned?
> Wait till I whup George Foreman's behind.
> Float like a butterfly, sting like a bee
> His hands can't hit what his eyes can't see.[90]

Meanwhile, Durham and his son combed through the material they had gathered. "He would talk to me about what he wanted a certain chapter to do, what he wanted a certain character to do, and then he would ask me to draft it," Mark explained. "He'd read it and say, 'Okay, now I need more drama. I need more emotion.' So I would deal with that and some dialogue."[91] As he had done during his tenure as editor at *Muhammad Speaks*, Durham crafted new pieces out of the drafts his son wrote. Mark then rushed his father's polished writing to an American airline. A courier carried the documents to Random House as soon as the plane landed in New York.[92]

Then, eight days before this highly anticipated match, George Foreman's sparring partner accidentally slammed an elbow into his boss's face, opening up a huge cut above Foreman's right eye. Rumor and speculation swirled. Was the fight off permanently? Might Zaire's government place the boxers under house arrest to keep them in the country?

"Whether President Mobutu actually gave any orders preventing us from leaving, I'll never know," Ali said in *The Greatest*.[93] But both boxers stayed in Zaire while Foreman healed. Durham told Rose Jennings, who was in Zaire as a press liaison, that *The Greatest* "had to end when Ali won his title back." Both Durham and Jennings were confident that Ali would win. Ali "was in the best shape of his life and Foreman was not," Jennings asserted.[94]

Yet most boxing fans considered George Foreman unbeatable. The twenty-four-year-old champion's forty-fight record included thirty-seven knockouts and no losses—even against Joe Frazier and Ken Norton. Columnist Dave Anderson claimed that with his sledgehammer-like punches, "George Foreman might be the heaviest puncher in the history of the heavyweight division."[95] A thirty-two-year-old Muhammad Ali acknowledged: "I'm fighting the youngest, most powerful opponent I've ever faced, and one with the highest knockout percentage in history."[96]

. . .

The Foreman-Ali match was rescheduled for the predawn hours of October 30.[97] Richard Durham vividly recounted the fight in *The Greatest*, letting Ali take readers inside the ring.

In round 1, Ali danced over to Foreman and delivered stinging jabs. By the second half of the three-minute round, however, Foreman forced Ali to move six steps to Foreman's two, "doing it better than anyone I've been up against," Ali said.[98] Ali resumed dancing and jabbing in the ring's center as round 2 began. But about thirty seconds later, Ali changed strategies. "For the first time in all my fights, I decide not to wait until I'm tired to play the ropes, but take to the corners while I'm fresh and still strong, to gamble on the ropes all the way."[99]

Ali stayed on the ropes for the next few rounds, later calling it his rope-a-dope strategy.[100] Durham said that Ali had practiced this tactic of leaning against the ropes "hour after hour, day after day. And everyone was screaming at him not to do it. But he kept right on."[101] In *The Greatest*, Ali explained: "I like to test a heavyweight when he's throwing his best shots wide open, to find out how long he can keep it up. I need to know because I'll have to wear down an opponent stronger than me."[102]

By the seventh round, Ali knew that Foreman was tiring. Ali summoned his remaining strength in round 8 and hit Foreman squarely on his chin. With a dazed look, Foreman slowly fell. Ali said that Foreman had entered "the room of the half-dream for the first time in his life."[103] Foreman stayed in that room too long, rising from the boxing ring's mat after the referee finished the mandatory knockout count.

The Kinshasa stadium exploded in celebration. Muhammad Ali was once again the heavyweight champion of the world—regaining the title that had been stripped from him seven years earlier.

Durham ended *The Greatest* with a brief postscript summarizing Ali's exhausting September 1975 battle against Joe Frazier. "The next thing to death," Ali called this fight. After Ali's fifteenth-round win, the Champ knew that the crowd wanted him to comment, to rhyme, to talk. "But I'm too tired," Ali admitted. "Besides, I already told them. And I already told you. Didn't you hear me? I said I was The Greatest."[104]

· · ·

In mid-November 1975, columnist Dave Anderson predicted that *The Greatest*'s "readable style" might make it "the most successful sports book in history." Reporting that Random House had printed 175,000 copies and ordered paper for 50,000 more, Anderson said that the book "will be translated into at least a dozen languages with foreign rights having produced $500,000 so far, with $200,000 from Germany alone."[105]

Author Ishmael Reed called Ali and Durham's 415-page tome "a bone-crushing, quality thriller that belongs in the same class as autobiographies written by Booker T. Washington, Frederick Douglass and James Weldon Johnson." Reed appreciated Durham's "very professional job in getting the Champ's style and tone down on paper, though one gets the impression that a considerable amount of the book is un-ghosted," an obvious reference to the verbatim conversations Durham included in *The Greatest*.[106]

Chicago Tribune reviewer Phillip E. Borries was pleased that Durham spared readers "the monotonous chronological style that is the keystone of so many celebrity autobiographies."[107] But David Shaw of the *Los Angeles Times* was disappointed that the Champ's gentle warmth, playfulness, and sincerity "rarely emerge in his book." Shaw wondered why Ali "does not explain why he writes poetry and all but ignores charges that he indulges in reverse racism"—a likely reference to Nation of Islam philosophies. "The man-child that is Muhammad Ali is too often obscured by the swirling sands of etiolated rhetoric and self-serving revisionism," Shaw concluded.[108]

Durham's ability to write captivating scenes was evident throughout *The Greatest*. But his proclivity for dramatic flourishes also undermined the book's credibility in a few instances. A prime example was *The Greatest*'s Olympic gold medal story.

In Durham's telling, after the teenaged Olympic gold medalist—then known as Cassius Clay—triumphantly returned from Rome, he tried to buy a hamburger in a downtown Louisville restaurant. The restaurant's white owner refused to serve Cassius and his best friend Ronnie because of their race.[109] Outside the restaurant, members of a white motorcycle gang harassed Clay, demanding that he hand over the Olympic gold medal Cassius wore everywhere. Fighting words flew between Clay and the gang members, and Durham's fast-paced, well-written chase sequence was intriguing.[110]

The gang chased Cassius and Ronnie to the Jefferson County Bridge, a dividing line between Kentucky and Indiana. Cassius and Ronnie ultimately got the upper hand in a fight that convinced the gang members to retreat. Shortly thereafter, as Durham described, Cassius Clay snatched the gold medal from his neck and angrily pitched it "into the black water" of the Ohio River.[111] "There was, however, never any white motorcycle gang incident and Clay did not throw away his medal, he lost it," journalist David Remnick reported. "Like the autobiographies of [boxing champs] Joe Louis and Jack Johnson, *The Greatest* mixes fact and folklore—in this case folklore in the service of Elijah Muhammad's agenda," an agenda that encouraged black self-determination without the need for white validation. In Remnick's opinion, "Durham made Ali out to be a champion fueled almost solely by anger and racial injustice."[112]

Ali denied that the Olympic medal tale "was true when the book came out," Toni Morrison told Remnick. "He also said he hadn't read the book. So [Ali], in a sense, discredited the book in a way that was unfair to the stories he had told Richard in the first place, or to the stories Richard may have invented to make a point."[113]

Richard Durham wrote gripping, often brilliant passages about dedication and sacrifice, love and loss, and injustice and freedom in *The Greatest: My Own Story*. But it was an uneven book. Apparently, the tensions between the Nation of Islam's restrictions, Random House's deadlines, as well as Ali and Durham's storytelling choices kept the book from being a cohesive whole.

Coinciding with the book's fall 1975 release, Columbia Pictures announced that Muhammad Ali would play himself in a forthcoming film based on the book.[114] The film, "The Greatest," showed up in American movie theaters on May 20, 1977. Durham did not write the script, and he disliked scriptwriter Ring Lardner Jr.'s interpretation of Ali's life.[115] The movie generated mixed reviews, although most critics enjoyed Ali's performance.[116]

Columbia Pictures paid Durham $150,000 for his share of the book rights, and he benefited from whatever royalty agreement he and Ali arranged with Random House.[117] Richard was now free to pursue new creative challenges.

And he did.

CHAPTER 12

Black Political Power

Inaugural Address of Mayor Harold Washington

This is a very serious vow that I've just taken before God and man, to do everything in my power to protect this City and every person who lives in it.

I do not take this duty lightly. I was up late last night thinking about this moment—it went through my head hundreds of times—and the words I was reading put me in a reflective and a somber mood.

On my right hand last night was a Bible, which is a very good book for a new Mayor to pay attention to. In front of me was a report of the city's finances, which my transition team had prepared, and it did not contain very good news. To my left there was no book, because the one I wanted the most doesn't exist. It's the one I wish had been written by my tribesman, Jean Baptiste DuSable, who settled Chicago over 200 years ago. What I wish he had written was a book about how to be mayor of a vast city like ours, a repository of wisdom to be handed down from mayor to mayor for all these years.[1]

—Harold Washington, April 29, 1983
   (with input from Richard Durham)

Creative options. Richard Durham now had plenty of them.

For years, all types of project ideas had floated in his head. Many remained undeveloped as Durham pursued income-producing writing jobs. But with the completion of *The Greatest* book and movie, he now had a sizable savings account. "The money lets you catch up on the things you've been putting off, [to] finally do what you want to do," Durham told a reporter.[2]

Durham had long talked about writing a book about Aesop—the man whose morality tales known as fables carry his name.[3] "Aesop was an important historical figure," Durham said. "He's universally known because of the fables, but few people know anything about Aesop the man, that he was black, for example, and that he was put to death for his beliefs."[4] Based on accounts by Greek writer Planudes and other research, Durham believed that Aesop was an Ethiopian who had been brought to Greece as a slave during the sixth century B.C.[5] Durham eventually gained access to plays about Aesop that consistently depicted him as a black, "very homely man, the same way we talk about Abraham Lincoln's homeliness," Durham said. But Aesop used his extraordinary wit "as a method of getting his point across," Durham noted, adding that Aesop essentially was a diplomat who moved between nations, making agreements.[6]

Durham's excitement about this relatively unknown man was infectious. Oscar Brown Jr. floated on "cloud nine" after Durham revealed that he planned to turn his proposed book about Aesop into a film featuring Oscar in the lead role. "Hot damn, I'm Aesop!" Brown said. "Here we go!"[7] But when Brown pressed Durham about the project's progress, little materialized except excuses.

Another historical figure who had long tugged on Durham's creative heartstrings was a man named Hannibal Barca, sometimes called Hannibal the Great or Hannibal the Conqueror.[8] Considered to be a third-century B.C. military genius, Hannibal was born in Carthage—now a suburb of Tunis, the capital of the North African nation of Tunisia. Hannibal's army rode elephants over the snow-capped Alps mountain range and won battles against the Roman Empire that are still studied in military academies worldwide.[9]

Durham believed that Hannibal was black "with woolly hair," based on descriptions of the Carthaginian people by Greek historian Herodotus and Greek poet Homer. "Homer is generally accepted as being correct in almost everything," Durham claimed.[10] But Durham's brother-in-law, Charles A. Davis, wasn't so sure about Hannibal's race. "We had some heated arguments over that," Davis recalled. "My own sense of the need for history to be accurate led me to challenge that. So we argued and it was inconclusive."[11]

Once again, Durham picked Oscar Brown Jr. to play the lead in the play or movie he planned to write. "Oscar, you are Hannibal," Durham said. "Ah, damn!" Oscar excitedly replied.[12] Durham told his friend that he had found backers in the Middle East for this project, but each time Brown asked about it, Durham talked about delays. He must have made similar promises, and excuses, to former *Destination Freedom* cast regular Fred Pinkard. "I remember at one point," Brown recalled, "Fred said, you know, the guy just lies to you like that, you don't want to even talk to him."[13]

In June 1980 Durham told historian J. Fred MacDonald that he had signed a contract to write a screenplay about Ida B. Wells, one of his favorite *Destination Freedom* personalities. But Durham first wanted to finish his Hannibal project. He claimed that England's Granada Press was set to publish his book about Hannibal in February 1981.[14] However, neither the Aesop nor the Hannibal book nor any movie plans materialized.

Durham could have been worn out. He had just spent five intense years working on, and missing deadlines for, *The Greatest*. Good intentions aside, Durham may not have had the energy to work consistently on his Aesop and Hannibal projects. In addition, no proof exists that Granada Press published a book by Durham. This publishing deal could have fallen through, Durham might have exaggerated his publishing claims, or he might have been an uncredited ghostwriter. After all, Durham did have a history of writing without credit.

In fact, Durham and his good friend Bennett Johnson said that celebrated Mexican American actor Anthony Quinn's autobiography, *The Original Sin*, was, in part, Dick Durham's handiwork. Durham even showed Johnson the check he received for his ghostwriting effort.[15] Quinn's account of self-discovery and redemption definitely contains recognizable traces of Durham's dramatic flair. But it appears that Durham did not complete the other book projects he talked about in part because of his continuing association with Herbert Muhammad, the man who still managed Muhammad Ali.

"Painful." That's how Clarice Durham described this period of their lives. She believed that her husband tied himself to projects unrelated to his craft, making questionable choices in the process. "He was looking for ways to better his [economic] situation, and really got kind of sidetracked on that," Clarice said.[16]

Durham surely would have objected to Clarice's assessment. He might have described this period as a time in which he could indulge in his fascination with economics and finance, subjects that first captivated him during his high school years.

Hoping to make money through a series of international business deals, Herbert Muhammad established a company called Herbert Muhammad Enterprises. Along with Bennett Johnson and others, Durham invested in several of the company's proposed ventures, including shipbuilding and selling in the Bahamas and the acquisition of precious minerals from Africa for sale in the United States.[17] At one point, Bennett Johnson recalled, Herbert Muhammad sent Durham to buy gold and diamonds in the West African nation of Liberia. "Durham doesn't take me; he goes by himself," Johnson explained. "Big mistake."[18]

After landing in Monrovia, Liberia's capital, Durham met a man from the nearby country of Ghana who claimed that with about $50,000 and his help, Durham could walk away with three times the amount of diamonds and gold he could purchase in Liberia. Although Liberia was one of the African continent's hot spots for the mining and exportation of precious minerals, "most of the stuff they had was stolen one way or another, or some of it wasn't mined right there in Liberia," Bennett Johnson said. "Therefore, [gold and diamonds] did have a higher price in Liberia."[19]

Durham gave his Ghanaian contact the requested sum—and never saw that man, the promised diamonds and gold, or Herbert Muhammad Enterprise's money again.

Clarice thought that this incident proved that her husband needed to return to what he did best—writing.[20] However, Durham continued working with his business associates on projects they hoped would yield great returns. One intriguing proposition came from a wealthy, former Europe-based opera singer named Rukmini Sukarno—the oldest and reportedly "favored" daughter of former Indonesian President Achmed Sukarno.[21] Rukmini Sukarno and her American husband, actor Franklin Latimore Kline, wanted to broker lucrative international deals with support from Herbert Muhammad and the Nation of Islam.

Based as she was in New York City, Sukarno (Johnson and Durham believed) was "perfect for international transactions" that included the buying and selling of commodities like dyes, rice, and coffee beans.[22] But Sukarno was an inexperienced businesswoman. Clarice called her an "enigma" and a bit odd.[23] Sukarno described herself as "a prima donna" who approached her business projects with "forte" energy. She bankrolled her lavish lifestyle with money she acquired from her father, royalties from her opera records, and the income her husband earned as an actor.[24] Once Sukarno found out about Durham's literary talents, she enlisted him to write her autobiography.

With his attention focused on global business deals and another ghostwriting possibility, Durham was barely involved in Chicago's vibrant black arts movement of the 1970s. However, he did serve as an advisory board member for nonprofit organizations that supported black artists and their communities.[25] And by the late 1970s, Durham knew that the seeds of a growing black political movement were sprouting in his hometown. The fact that Durham's longtime friend, Illinois congressman Harold Washington, eventually became the first black mayor in one of the most segregated and politically contentious cities in America was nothing short of revolutionary.

. . .

Harold Washington's ascent to Chicago's top elected position could be attributed, in part, to demographics. During Washington's 1922 birth year, blacks made up just 4 percent of the city's population. That percentage skyrocketed to nearly 40 percent of the three million people who called Chicago home by the beginning of the 1980s.[26]

In the city's fifty wards, essentially electoral districts, aldermen represented residents on the Chicago City Council. Also, so-called committeemen—Democratic Party officials in each ward—"rationed out patronage jobs, delivered favors, and turned out the vote," journalist Gary Rivlin explained.[27] All of these politicians were beholden to the city's supreme leader—a burly, Irish American and Eleventh Ward–native named Richard J. Daley. Mayor Daley did not create Chicago's so-called Democratic "machine" structure; former mayor Anton Cermak earned that credit. But Daley, mayor since 1955, "perfected" the city's machine, Gary Rivlin asserted.[28]

Attempts by black Chicago to make the city's formidable, predominately white political machine respond to its needs met with various levels of avoidance or tepid response. But blacks kept pushing. In just one example, Richard Durham, Bennett Johnson, Gus Savage, and several other like-minded souls organized the League of Negro Voters during the late 1950s. Independent of the machine, the league ran black candidates "for various and sundry city offices," Earl Durham recalled. In one election, the league supported black attorney Lemuel Bentley's run for city clerk—the third most powerful position after the mayor and city treasurer.[29] Bentley did not win, but urban-studies scholar Conrad Worrill said that Durham and the league "worked tenaciously at independent politics to try to upset the balance of political power in the city." [30]

Durham sporadically offered his speechwriting skills to prominent black Chicago politicians like Third Ward Alderman Ralph Metcalfe and William Dawson, former machine committeeman and U.S. congressional representative. Conrad Worrill, another person Durham mentored, believed that Durham's philosophical base dictated his actions. "I never asked him, but he must have been a Leninist," Worrill speculated. "Lenin wrote this kind of organizer's manual called *What Is to Be Done*."[31] Lenin's organizing blueprint called for "getting inside structures and boring from within to exert influence on organizations and their members to embrace communism," Worrill explained. "Richard Durham personified the classic strategies of boring from within. His approach was to link up with activists and organizers in an attempt to influence their work."[32]

In the years leading up to Mayor Daley's death in 1976, black Chicagoans increasingly defied the Democratic machine's ubiquitous power. One of the best examples of this defiance involved the incident Durham had tried to dramatize in *Bird of the Iron Feather*. Black Chicagoans blamed the CPD and State's Attorney Edward Hanrahan for the deaths of young Black Panthers Fred Hampton and Mark Clark.[33] Hanrahan, a Daley protégé and heir apparent to the mayoral throne, green-lighted and oversaw the deadly 1969 law enforcement raid on the apartment where Hampton and Clark died. In retaliation, blacks voted Hanrahan out of office in 1972, effectively ending his political career.[34] Gary Rivlin called this the "first citywide anti-machine insurrection"—exactly the type of political action Durham would have championed and helped organize. Instead, he was consumed by his travels and work with Muhammad Ali on *The Greatest*.

In 1975 Bennett Johnson, Gus Savage, and a few other influential Chicagoans formed the Committee for a Black Mayor.[35] Committee members were serious about fielding a black candidate for Chicago's most powerful elected office. Harold Washington became a viable choice. At the time, Washington was a state senator with an independent streak that sometimes enabled him to buck Chicago's machine.[36] Washington had long cultivated his political skills, running his late father's law practice, succeeding his father as the city's assistant corporate counsel, and working for Alderman Ralph Metcalfe. Starting in 1965 Harold Washington spent five terms in the Illinois State House of Representatives. He became a state senator in 1976.[37]

When he decided to run for mayor the next year, Senator Washington selected Gus Savage as his campaign manager.[38] Richard Durham should have been involved as well. But in 1977, the year he turned sixty, Durham's involvement with international business deals monopolized his time.

Washington's first mayoral campaign was poorly financed and disorganized; he would win only 11 percent of the general vote. Still, Renault Robinson said that organizers learned "how to structure a citywide campaign," and the campaign energized black middle-class voters in the five South Side wards that Washington won.[39]

Meanwhile, Michael Bilandic, Mayor Richard J. Daley's weak successor, struggled to manage the city.[40] During the harsh winter of 1979, eighty-seven inches of white flakes—more than twice the city's average snowfall—blanketed Chicago. Bilandic's missteps during these snowstorms upset residents. But his actions after one particular storm outraged black citizens. Mayor Bilandic decreed that rush hour metro trains would run nonstop from the Loop to South Ninety-Fifth Street—bypassing ten stops that serviced black South Side communities.[41]

In the Democratic primaries held shortly thereafter, Jane Byrne, head of Chicago's Consumer Sales Commission, ran as an independent reform candidate, pledging to eliminate the abuses of machine fat cats. Byrne won the primary, even though most white voters backed Bilandic. Blacks overwhelmingly voted for Byrne and the reforms she promised. Candidate Byrne went on to win the 1979 general election, becoming the city's first Madam Mayor.[42]

State Senator Harold Washington was on his own upward political trajectory as well. Washington headed to Washington, D.C., as a United States Congressman in 1980—the same year that former California Governor, conservative Republican Ronald Reagan, became president in a landslide victory.[43] Durham watched all these developments while courting business deals. But he was not as active as he could have been. He was dealing with a more pressing issue at the time: his health.

One day in June 1980 as Dick and Clarice sat at home, he complained of sudden weakness and pain in his chest. Clarice immediately took him across the street to Mercy Hospital. Durham was admitted. He'd had a mild heart attack—a sobering diagnosis since his father had died of a heart attack. Durham decided not to tell people about his medical condition because "he didn't want people worrying about him," Clarice said.[44] But Durham was still overweight, as he had been during much of his adult life. He had high blood pressure. His diet wasn't the best. Like his "incorrigible" phase as a teenage thief, Richard, according to his brother Earl, was "incorrigible" about the dietary restrictions his doctors imposed. He did not always comply. "I remember Clarice hiding the salt and stuff like that," Earl said.[45] Yet Dick knew he needed to change. He started walking in the mornings and tried eating healthier.[46]

· · ·

Newly elected Mayor Jane Byrne thanked black Chicagoans for their support by appointing blacks to key positions in the city's transit authority and police department. She also appointed African American and Latino members to the Board of Education and Chicago Housing Authority (CHA). Durham's friend Renault Robinson became one such CHA board appointee.[47] But midway through Byrne's term, it suddenly seemed "as if a new mayor more hostile to black Chicago took over," reporter Gary Rivlin observed.[48] Mayor Byrne started courting the same Democratic machine cronies she had disparaged earlier, and journalist Salim Muwakkil reported that Byrne "flip-flopped" on a busing desegregation plan she previously supported. In an especially controversial move, Mayor Byrne replaced black appointees to the Chicago Board of Education and Chicago Housing Authority with whites.[49]

Reflecting the growing discontent in black Chicago, influential journalist and radio personality Lu Palmer coined the phrase, "We shall see in '83." Palmer used the slogan to spark discussions about the possible election of a black mayor.[50] Richard Durham definitely supported the man most black Chicagoans could see as mayor: Harold Washington.[51] Yet Congressman Washington "was very leery,"

Renault Robinson revealed. Washington "didn't even want to get in the [mayoral] race because he had just become congressman and he liked that." Washington's reluctance to mount another mayoral campaign angered Lu Palmer and other supporters. They pressured the congressman to commit. He resisted.[52]

Washington finally relented—with conditions. He said he would consider another mayoral run only if organizers registered fifty thousand new voters and raised about $250,000 for the campaign. The organizers' "Come Alive on October 5" campaign was so successful that before the October deadline, "we registered close to 100,000 new voters," Renault Robinson said. "Because of that success, money started trickling in."[53] In early November 1982, Washington announced his intention to run in the Democratic primary race against Mayor Byrne and Cook County State's Attorney, Richard M. Daley, the eldest son of the late Mayor Richard J. Daley.[54]

In short order, "we had a few meetings to try to get the show on the road," Earl Durham remembered. "At one of these meetings, Harold was present, and someone said to the congressman, 'You need somebody very close to you who kind of knows the ropes . . . and can put your position out and write your stuff.'" Earl noted that everyone in this group of about thirty to forty people looked at his brother Dick. "We looked at Harold, and asked, 'Is that all right?' Harold said, 'Sure, you're giving me the Guru. You're damn right, it's all right!'"[55]

Richard Durham agreed to work with Harold Washington and his campaign organizers, including his buddy Renault Robinson, Jewish activist Sid Ordower, and members of a newly formed organization, the Task Force for Black Political Empowerment. Northeastern Illinois University professors Conrad Worrill and Robert Starks helped create this group, and Starks said that he and his colleagues wanted to turn Harold into a revolutionary. "He was far from a revolutionary, believe me," a smiling Starks said. "But he was revolutionary in comparison to other politicians that we had seen, and he understood our revolutionary rhetoric."[56]

Durham understood their rhetoric as well. Yet Dick "didn't want Harold to come off like [militant African leader] Patrice Lumumba because that wasn't going to work. Harold would frighten everybody," Renault Robinson said. Durham preferred that Washington be the statesman he was, talking about the issues of the day "without invoking," Robinson added, "the stereotype of a black guy with a hatchet running through the white community."[57]

Durham planned to write a book about Washington's campaign, so he "asked Harold if he could ride in the car with him, to advise him as well as take notes," Robert Starks recalled. "Harold said, 'Fine, come on Dick. Do it.'"[58]

Most mornings on the campaign trail, Washington and his driver picked up Durham from his home and together they headed to various campaign events.[59] Essentially, the car became Washington and Durham's mobile command center.

FIGURE 18. Chicago mayoral candidate Harold Washington greets supporters from his car in 1983. © Brent Jones

"Certain people would ride, from here to there, maybe for an hour and then they'd go," Renault Robinson explained. Others would then ride along to offer advice or campaign updates. Robinson believed that this arrangement worked "because Harold was so smart that he knew how to listen to people, and he could read between the lines."[60]

So could Durham. Both Durham and Washington had grown up in Bronzeville with their heads in books, enriching their minds and their vocabulary.[61] And both men were stubborn, street-smart warriors. As teenagers, Washington and Durham channeled their fighting spirits into running track and boxing, respectively. As adults, they used their intellect and verbal agility to fight for the causes that moved them. Yet while Durham shunned the spotlight, Washington basked in it. Washington was a charismatic, articulate public speaker who "sent the press corps here to the dictionary every single day of their lives," writer Rose Jennings said, only half joking.[62]

Richard Durham and Robert Starks talked several times every day, with Durham offering "very valuable advice on every aspect of the campaign," Starks said. One of the many issues the men discussed concerned how they might ease the tension between Washington and another magnetic black Chicago leader, Reverend Jesse Jackson, who had founded and led the social justice organization Operation PUSH (People United to Serve Humanity).[63] Durham said that with Washington and Jackson you had two "giant egos operating, and you have two camps of people around both of them who are trying to push one the other way," Starks remembered. Dick suggested: "Let's not magnify [their] differences because in the end, they'll probably come together while the groups [of people around them] are still fighting."[64]

In the meantime, the Democratic mayoral candidates agreed to participate in four televised debates starting in late January 1983.[65] Thinking about how Washington might approach those debates, Robert Starks, Conrad Worrill, and their colleagues came up with a line they believed Washington should use to tap into black voters' anger over Mayor Byrne's reversals. Starks and Worrill ran the line past Durham. "Richard thought it was a great idea because, he said, older [blacks] will understand it explicitly," Starks said.[66]

In the first debate, Washington peppered his "grand speech with all these statistics and everything was going fine," Starks recalled. "But then he said, 'Jane Byrne you've been hiding figures, you've been deceiving people, but you know what? You can run, but you can't hide.'"[67] During his reign as the heavyweight boxing champion, Joe Louis had used a variation of that phrase. Before Louis's victorious matches against Bob Paster in 1939 and Billy Conn in 1946, the popular champion, affectionately nicknamed "The Brown Bomber," predicted: "He can run, but he can't hide."[68] Harold Washington's similar declaration "was his symbolic knock-out blow to Jane Byrne," Robert Starks claimed. Washington "balled up his fist" as he delivered the line and "that did it!" Starks added.[69] Black viewers screamed with delight—whether they knew the context of those words or just appreciated the gesture.

"One of Richard Durham's constant pleas to us was how do you position this man to speak to the masses, to all the people, but at the same time not lose sight of the fact that you've got to make sure that black people come out and vote, and vote in large numbers for Harold," Robert Starks explained. Polling data indicated that after the debates, black support pushed Harold Washington into second place behind a still strongly polling Mayor Byrne.[70] Richard M. Daley's poor debate performances dropped him into third place.

About two weeks before the primary's mid-February election day, the Washington campaign held its last major rally in a twelve-thousand-seat pavilion on the University of Illinois-Chicago campus.[71] Campaign strategists worried about filling the cavernous space. They shouldn't have. The rally drew a standing-room-only, predominately black crowd. "Being inside the pavilion that Sunday afternoon was like being inside a living thing," scholar William Grimshaw reported. "It rocked and pulsated in a way that touched all the senses."[72] After almost three hours of music and speeches by a rainbow of performers and politicians, Washington entered the hall.

While planning for this rally, campaign organizers thought, "Why don't we have [Harold] go to the podium and say my first act as mayor would be to fire Brezeczek," Robert Starks said.[73] As the city's youngest top cop, CPD Superintendent Richard J. Brezeczek was the public face of a police force that black residents resented because of its brutality, racial discrimination, and overall lack of respect.[74]

Starks and his colleagues presented their idea to Durham, who agreed. Harold Washington delivered the line and audience members enthusiastically chanted, "Fire Brezeczek!" over and over again. It took several minutes to quiet the crowd.[75] In the afterglow of this rally, "an exhilarating air of impending victory swept across the black community. The impossible suddenly seemed within reach," scholar William Grimshaw asserted.[76]

On February 22, 1983, Harold Washington sprinted to the finish line. He won Chicago's Democratic primary with 36 percent of the more than one million votes cast. Byrne came in second with 34 percent; Daley had 30 percent. Washington earned 85 percent of the black vote and benefited from the fact that Jane Byrne and Richard M. Daley split the white vote. "We just barely squeezed out the victory," Robert Starks said, adding that Richard Durham "was very instrumental in helping us work that out."[77]

Black Chicagoans were elated with Washington's primary win; their white counterparts were stunned. As white residents considered their options for the April 12 general election, some became instant Republicans. Certain lifelong Democrats refused to accept Washington's candidacy either because of his race, his reformist agenda, or both. This attitude paved the way for Bernard Epton, the little known Republican candidate, to become a "white folk hero virtually overnight," journalist Gary Rivlin wrote.[78] If this had been a normal election cycle in this overwhelmingly Democratic city, Epton would have had as much chance of winning a mayoral election "as a capitalist in [communist] Russia," Robert Starks joked.[79] But with Washington's primary victory, Epton became the rallying cry for many in the city's white communities.

In mid-March, Jane Byrne entered the race as a write-in candidate, implying that a black mayor would tear the city apart. But Byrne's campaign lasted barely a couple of weeks. White voters and the Democratic machine faithful overwhelmingly supported Bernard Epton.[80] With Byrne's departure, Epton extended Byrne's racially coded message. His campaign slogan, "Epton—Before It's Too Late," touched all of the old boogeyman buttons about blacks. The slogan echoed earlier scare tactics that had encouraged white flight as blacks moved to Chicago from

FIGURE 19. Harold Washington consults with campaign staffers, including Richard Durham (writing on a notepad behind Washington), on Chicago's Democratic mayoral primary election day in February 1983. ©Marc PoKempner from *Harold!*

the South, or as black Chicagoans moved out of their overcrowded, decaying communities into white neighborhoods.

Washington biographer Dempsey Travis determined that Epton's "venomous campaign style was unrelenting."[81] Epton ripped into Washington for his failure to file tax returns for four years; Washington had spent forty days in jail as a result. And Epton revealed that Washington's law license had been suspended briefly in the early 1970s for "failure to render adequate service to a client." In journalist Salim Muwakkil's opinion, "the cultural linkage of 'blackness' and crime was an ever-present subtext" in Epton's campaign against Washington.[82]

Durham advised Washington to continue concentrating on getting out the black vote, and he pressed Washington to hammer home his reform message. He wanted Harold to emphasize "that Chicago is one city, made up of many ethnic groups, but we need to bring harmony to the whole city by having everybody get their fair share," Robert Starks remembered.[83] On Election Day, April 12, 1983, Durham started writing Washington's acceptance speech. "Richard and I talked the night before, and we had no doubt in our hearts, down to our toes that [Washington] was going to win," Robert Starks recalled. "Other people might have doubted it, but we were the true believers."[84]

Indeed, Harold Washington accomplished the seemingly impossible. He became the city's first black leader after winning 51 percent of the slightly more than one million votes cast. Washington walked into Chicago's, if not the nation's, history books with 82 percent of the Latino vote, about 12 percent of the white vote, and nearly 100 percent of the black turnout.[85]

In his acceptance speech, Mayor-elect Washington said he wanted to seek economic and social healing for Chicagoans by reaching "out my hand in friendship and fellowship to every living soul in this city."[86] Richard Durham stood on the sidelines, taking it all in—the jubilance of a remarkable achievement, the emotional rollercoaster of an ugly campaign, the historical significance of it all. Durham, the king maker, had helped bring about this momentous day.

Seventeen days later, April 29, 1983, Harold Washington delivered his inauguration speech. Once again, Durham wrote the speech he thought the new mayor should give. Washington's mention of Jean Baptiste Point Du Sable, the black man credited with settling Chicago, came from Durham. Durham's speech also cast, in broad strokes, a vision of the inclusive path Washington planned to follow as the mayor for all Chicagoans.[87]

But Harold did not deliver the speech Dick wrote. Instead, Washington's inauguration speech "was part accusation and condemnation of the outgoing administration," Durham's brother-in-law Charles A. Davis recalled.[88] Mayor Washington talked about the millions of dollars in shortfalls that Chicago's public schools, the city's general fund, and its transportation system faced, as well as the hundreds of new jobs the Byrne administration had handed out.[89]

"The shock!" Davis said. "I was present and I could see this lady's face. [Byrne] didn't expect to be criticized." Davis believed that Washington's speech and the fact that he used so little of Durham's material was a major disappointment for his brother-in-law. "But if you have written speeches for clients you know that this happens sometimes to your best work," Davis reasoned.[90]

After the inauguration celebrations ended, Durham chose not to join his friend's historic administration. He did not want to be in the sizzling spotlight under which Washington's regime would be scrutinized and ferociously challenged. Yet Durham continued to be one of Mayor Washington's trusted, unofficial advisors. Harold would often call or stop by Dick and Clarice's home to talk and get a dose of Dick's wisdom.[91]

• • •

During the next year, Durham worked with Bennett Johnson and Herbert Muhammad on business deals. He remained in touch with Rukmini Sukarno, consulting with her about business opportunities as well as the autobiography she wanted him to write.[92] Durham also served on the election campaign of labor union leader Charles Hayes, who successfully won the U.S. Congressional seat vacated by Harold Washington when he became mayor.

On Friday, April 27, 1984, Durham was in New York City meeting with Sukarno. After the meeting, Durham and Sukarno's husband, Franklin Kline, took in a movie. As the two men left a Manhattan theater, Durham suddenly felt a stabbing pain in his chest. The pain was so intense it knocked him to the ground.[93] Kline frantically hailed a cab and they rushed to the nearest hospital, St. Luke's-Roosevelt Hospital Center on Fifty-Ninth Street and Tenth Avenue.[94]

Meanwhile back in Chicago, Clarice was getting ready for a dinner-dance where her son's band would perform.[95]

In New York, hospital staff members quickly wheeled Durham into an Emergency Room. He was in cardiac arrest, his heart barely beating.

As she prepared to put on the finishing touches for the evening's festivities, Clarice's phone rang. She picked up the receiver and Dr. Aaron Wells identified himself. As gently as he could, the physician told Clarice that St. Luke's-Roosevelt Hospital's emergency team had done everything they could.[96] But her husband, the man she had loved for forty-three years, had just died of a massive heart attack.

Clarice was speechless.

Dr. Wells asked Clarice if she was alone. She was. He suggested that she ask family members to come over.[97]

As soon as she could coordinate her hands and her mind, Clarice called her son's home. When Mark heard the news from his wife Octavia, he couldn't believe it. His father? Dead? Mark told his mother that he'd be right over. But in a time long before cell phones or instant text messages, Mark knew that his bandmates were already in transit. So he jumped in his car and drove to the venue. He told his band members what happened and then headed to his parents' home.[98]

When Mark arrived, Harold Washington was already there, embracing his mother as she sobbed in the mayor's arms. Earl Durham arrived shortly thereafter, devastated by the news.[99]

In New York, Durham's body was moved to the hospital morgue. He had died of an acute coronary thrombosis. A blood clot had blocked one of the main arteries leading to Dick's heart.[100]

Gradually, a small crowd converged on the Durham home. Clarice's sister Marguerite and brother Charles, Dick's sister Winifred, and a host of other family members and friends tried to console Clarice and each other.

The next morning, Clarice, Earl, and Mark flew to New York to identify Dick's body. Rukmini Sukarno and Franklin Kline accompanied Durham's family members to the hospital. Clarice said Sukarno regretted not knowing that Dick used nitroglycerin, a medication for patients with heart problems. Had she known, Sukarno said, she would have made sure that Dick had the medication with him. But Clarice wasn't sure that the nitroglycerin would have saved her husband.[101]

Once she landed back in Chicago, Clarice asked A. A. Rayner and Sons to handle her husband's funeral arrangements. She planned to have Dick cremated, and to inter his ashes in the city's Burr Oak Cemetery. Clarice also asked Rayner's to schedule her husband's memorial service for May 2. The funeral director later told Clarice that he wished she had waited a bit longer so that they could have secured a larger place to hold the service.

"But you don't always think wisely in situations like that," Clarice said.[102]

She was still dealing with the unbelievable reality that her husband would never smile at her, rail against an injustice, or write a lyrically powerful sentence again.

Isadore Richard Durham was sixty-six years old.

And he was gone.

Epilogue

In the years following her husband's death, Clarice Durham, in her own dignified way, quietly mounted a campaign to keep Dick's legacy alive.

In 1987 Clarice allowed three radio producers in Washington, D.C.—artist Lyn Dyson and Howard University communications professors William Barlow and Judi Moore Latta—to revive four of Durham's original *Destination Freedom* scripts. The producers also asked Oscar Brown Jr. to narrate Durham's scripts about Harriet Tubman, W. E. B. Du Bois, Denmark Vesey, and Frederick Douglass.[1] These dramas reached a new generation of listeners via National Public Radio (NPR) member stations.

And Clarice permitted the publication of fifteen of her husband's original scripts in historian J. Fred MacDonald's 1989 book, *Richard Durham's Destination Freedom: Scripts from Black Radio Days, 1948–1950.*[2] In addition, from the late 1990s through the early years of the present century, Clarice allowed producer Donnie L. Betts to dramatize several *Destination Freedom* scripts.[3] In 2000, Betts brought Oscar Brown Jr., Fred Pinkard, and Studs Terkel to his Denver, Colorado, radio studios to perform Durham's script about Gwendolyn Brooks. It was the first time these original *Destination Freedom* cast members had performed together in more than fifty years.[4]

On November 3, 2007, shortly before her eighty-eighth birthday, Clarice sat beaming with her son Mark at a black-tie reception and dinner in Chicago's Renaissance Hotel. She and other well-wishers, including myself, celebrated Durham's induction into the Museum of Broadcast Communications' National Radio Hall of Fame.[5] Clarice graciously accepted her husband's posthumous honor; fellow Hall of Fame inductees that year included President Franklin D. Roosevelt for his radio "fireside chats," pianist Marian McPartland for her *Piano Jazz* NPR series, and Jimmy Durante, one of radio's hottest stars during the 1940s.[6]

Today, via online archives, Internet users may listen to forty-two original broadcasts of Durham's *Destination Freedom* episodes. Web users may also hear Durham's *CBS Radio Workshop* dramas and view the only two programs known to have survived from *Bird of the Iron Feather*.[7] Additionally, *Destination Freedom* episodes are available for on-site listening in the Chicago Public Library's Vivian G. Harsh Research Collection, and in the Moving Image and Recorded Sound Collection of the New York Public Library's Schomburg Center for Research in Black Culture. Interviews with Durham by historians J. Fred MacDonald and John Dunning are housed in the Harsh Collection and available online as well.[8]

• • •

Richard Durham deserved the many accolades and awards he received during his lifetime. Yet promotional materials and obituaries indicating that Durham received the George Foster Peabody Award—one of the most prestigious honors recognizing outstanding achievement in the electronic media—puzzled me.[9] The award's official list of winners does *not* include Richard Durham's name, nor does it include the shows he is credited with authoring.

After careful study, however, I came up with a likely explanation. In 1948, Peabody judges honored CBS with an institutional award for the network's "work in the promotion of international understanding."[10] *Democracy USA* aired on CBS affiliate, WBBM, during this awards period. Because of the special citation this series received from President Truman for its attempts to strengthen "the bonds of interracial harmony," the show probably fell under the "special programs" category of the Peabody award to CBS that year.[11] Therefore, the Peabody Award claims for Richard Durham appear to be valid.

• • •

Given the sudden, unexpected nature of his death, many of Richard Durham's creative dreams went unfulfilled. What kept him from finishing the biographies, plays, and autobiographies Durham claimed were either completed or on their way to completion? And why didn't Richard write the great American novel that family members and friends felt was in him?

Durham created some of his best work while tackling tight, almost impossible deadlines—including the weekly research and writing grind that shows like *Destination Freedom* and *Democracy USA* demanded, or the intense pressures he labored under to write *The Greatest*. Without such tension, Durham tended to flounder. Perhaps he could not muster the energy to finish pet projects since, as he once told his sister Clotilde, writing was never easy for him. Or maybe he became overwhelmed by the many projects he juggled to support his family. Additionally, the health challenges Richard faced during his last years may have adversely affected his ability to complete projects.

Still, Durham left behind a powerful legacy. Before Vernon Jarrett and Oscar Brown Jr. died in 2004 and 2005, respectively, Dick's buddies told me that they sometimes reached for the phone to call for advice before remembering that their friend/mentor was gone.[12] Several other people I interviewed echoed those feelings, remembering Durham as a sage, inspiring change agent. And Mark Durham remembered how much his father enjoyed playing his favorite musicians' records over and over again. Durham's love affair with music clearly rubbed off on his only child.

One of the discussions that stuck with Durham's brother-in-law Charles Davis, years after it occurred, took place the day Dr. Martin Luther King Jr. was killed. "I called the house to talk," Davis recalled, "and I happened to say I hope black people don't riot. Vern, as we called him, said 'I hope they do.'" Davis believed that Frederick Douglass, the nineteenth-century orator Durham admired, influenced his thinking.[13] In August 1857 Douglass had stated:

> If there is no struggle, there is no progress. Those who profess to favor freedom, and yet depreciate agitation, are men who want crops without plowing up the ground. They want rain without thunder and lightning. They want the ocean without the awful roar of its many waters.
>
> This struggle may be a moral one; or it may be a physical one; or it may be both moral and physical; but it must be a struggle. Power concedes nothing without a demand. It never did and it never will.[14]

"I think that was what he had in mind," Charles Davis said. "Blacks had to strike a blow for freedom and the rioting would be such a blow, or a manifest. I guess my view was that rioting would bring repercussions that we could not control. Was he more right than I was?" Davis asked. "Has enough time passed to truly assess the results of those riots—those spasms of violence in the cities, whose scars have yet to be healed?"[15]

Durham would probably have asked those same questions, and then found some creative means to present his conclusions. He wasn't always right, but he was a pragmatic optimist who analyzed the dilemmas of the day, searched for ways to bring about positive social change, and inspired others to do the same.

Throughout his life Richard Durham remained a dedicated warrior who used his wordsmith skills like a weapon. He fervently fought for freedom, justice, and equality for African Americans and other oppressed people, changing only the method of his pioneering artistic assault—poetry or print reporting here, broadcast drama or political speechmaking there. "In the best sense of the word, he was a vigorous propagandist," Charles Davis said, "and that sometimes makes for powerful journalism, powerful radio writing, powerful drama—and he was good at it."[16]

Good enough to touch the lives of millions of media consumers, young and old, of this generation and the next, who may yet learn from the fiery eloquence of Richard Durham's writing and his life's journey toward freedom.

Appendix

Destination Freedom Radio Log, 1948–1950

1948

June 27	The Knock-Kneed Man (Crispus Attucks)
July 4	Railway to Freedom (Harriet Tubman)
July 11	Dark Explorers (Black explorers accompanying Spanish Conquistadores)
July 18	Denmark Vesey
July 25	The Making of a Man (Frederick Douglass/Part I)
August 1	The Key to Freedom (Frederick Douglass/Part II)
August 8	The Heart of George Cotton (Ulysses Grant Dailey and Daniel Hale Williams)
August 15	Truth Goes to Washington (Sojourner Truth)
August 22	Arctic Biography (Matthew Henson)
August 29	The Story of 1875 (Charles Caldwell)
September 5	Poet of Pine Mill (James Weldon Johnson)
September 12	The Father of the Blues (W. C. Handy)
September 19	Boy with a Dream (J. Ernest Wilkins Jr.)
September 26	Shakespeare of Harlem (Langston Hughes)
October 3	Citizen Toussaint (Toussaint L'Ouverture)
October 10	Little David (Joe Louis)
October 17	The Boy Who Was Traded for a Horse (George Washington Carver)
October 31	The Heart of George Cotton (repeat performance)
November 7	Echoes of Harlem (Duke Ellington)
November 14	One Out of Seventeen (Mary McLeod Bethune)
November 21	The Rime of the Ancient Dodger (Jackie Robinson)
November 28	Investigator for Democracy (Walter White)
December 5	Autobiography of a Hero (Dorie Miller)
December 12	The Pied Piper Vs. Paul Revere (Albert Merritt)
December 19	Choir Girl from Philadelphia (Marian Anderson)
December 26	Mike Rex (Willard Motley)

1949

January 2	Maiden Speech (Oscar DePriest)
January 9	The Boy Who Beat the Bus (William H. Hastie)
January 16	The Chopin Murder Case (Hazel Scott)
January 23	World's Fastest Human (Jesse Owens)
January 30	Last Letter Home (332nd Fighter Group)
February 6	Searcher for History (W. E. B. Du Bois)
February 13	The Death of Aesop
February 20	Peace Mediator (Ralph Bunche)
February 27	The Houses that Paul Built (Paul Williams)
March 6	Do Something! Be Somebody! (Canada Lee)
March 13	Up from Slavery (Booker T. Washington)
March 20	Black Boy (Richard Wright)
March 27	Transfusion (Charles R. Drew)
April 3	Pagan Poet (Countee Cullen)
April 10	Woman with a Mission (Ida B. Wells)
April 17	Before I Sleep (Paul Lawrence Dunbar)
April 24	Apostle of Freedom (Richard Allen)
May 1	Help the Blind (Josh White)
May 15	The Ballad of Satchel Paige
May 22	The Secretary of Peace (Benjamin Banneker)
May 29	The Saga of Melody Jackson (Henry Armstrong)
June 5	Anatomy of an Ordinance (Archibald Carey)
June 12	Negro Cinderella (Lena Horne)
June 19	Ghost Editor (Roscoe Dungee)
June 26	Harriet's Children (first anniversary program)
July 3	Norfolk Miracle (Dorothy Maynor)
July 17	Tales of Stackalee
July 24	The John Henry Story
July 31	The Trumpet Talks (Louis Armstrong)
August 7	The Long Road (Mary Church Terrell)
August 14	Black Hamlet/Part I (Henri Christophe)
August 21	Black Hamlet/Part II (Henri Christophe)
August 28	Segregation, Incorporated (Report of the Committee against Segregation in the Nation's Capital)
September 4	The Saga of Blanche K. Bruce
September 11	The Tiger Hunt (761st Tank Batallion)
September 18	Poet in Bronzeville (Gwendolyn Brooks)
September 25	A Garage in Gainesville (Prejudice series/Part I)
October 2	Execution Awaited (Prejudice series/Part II)
October 9	Father to Son (Adam Clayton Powell, Senior and Junior)
October 16	Of Blood and the Boogie (Albert Ammons)
October 23	Diary of a Nurse (Jane Edna Hunter)

October 30	Keeper of the Dream (Hugh Mulzac)
November 6	The Man Who Owned Chicago (Jean-Baptiste Point Du Sable)
November 13	Blind Alley Symphony (Dean Dixon)
November 20	The Tale of the Tobacco Auctioneer (Kenneth R. Williams)
November 27	The Death of Aesop (repeat performance)
December 4	Joe Rainey vs. The Status Quo (Joseph Homer Rainey)

1950

January 15	The Birth of the League (the Urban League)
January 22	Lawyer of Liberty (William Henry Huff)
January 29	Portrait of Bill Robinson
February 5	Housing: Chicago
February 12	Recorder of History (Carter G. Woodson)
February 19	Brotherhood Week Begins at Home (Brotherhood Week)
February 26	The Umfundisi of Ndotsheni (Todd Duncan)
March 5	The Atlanta Thesis (E. Franklin Frazier)
March 12	Premonition of the Panther ("Sugar" Ray Robinson)
March 19	The Making of a Balladeer (Lonnie Johnson)
March 26	The Liberators/Part I (William Lloyd Garrison)
April 2	The Liberators/Part II (Wendell Phillips)
April 9	The Buddy Young Story
April 16	Crime Fighter (Kinzie Bleuitt)
April 23	Dance Anthropologist (Katherine Dunham)
May 7	The Case of Samuel Johnson (Jane Bolin)
May 14	The Sorrow Songs (Spirituals)
May 21	John Hope, Educator
June 4	The Grave Diggers' Handicap (Isaac Murphy)
June 11	The Shy Boy (Thomas "Fats" Waller)
June 18	The Case of the Congressman's Train Ride (Richard Westbrooks)
June 25	The Angel of Federal Street (Ruth Blue Turnquist)
July 2	Kansas City Phone Call (Nat King Cole)
July 9	Mr. Jericho Adjusts a Claim (William Nickerson Jr.)
July 16	Test by Fire (Charlotte Hawkins)
July 23	Sing a Song for Children (Pruth McFarlin)
July 30	repeat performance of The Knock-Kneed Man
August 6	repeat performance of Peace Mediator
August 13	repeat performance of Last Letter Home

Notes

Prologue

Hugh Cordier, "A History and Analysis of Destination Freedom," Summer 1949, Richard Durham Papers, Vivian G. Harsh Research Collection of Afro-American History and Literature, Chicago Public Library, box 6, folder 4, 24–25 (hereinafter Durham Papers).

1. Richard Durham, *Destination Freedom*: Free Download and Streaming, Internet Archive, accessed July 15, 2013, http://archive.org/details/DestinationFreedom.

2. Michael Kernan, "Around the Mall and Beyond," *Smithsonian Magazine*, April 1996, accessed December 18, 2014, http://www.smithsonianmag.com/people-places/around-the-mall-amp-beyond-10-112965819.

3. Timuel D. Black Fellowship, Vivian G. Harsh Society, accessed June 21, 2013, http://harshsociety.org/timuel-d-black-fellowship.

4. Vivian G. Harsh Research Collection of Afro-American History and Literature, Chicago Public Library, accessed April 21, 2014, http://www.chipublib.org/vivian-g-harsh-research-collection (hereinafter Harsh Research Collection).

Chapter 1. Remembering

1. Charles S. Childs Jr. interview; Earl Durham interview, 2000; Clarice Durham interview, 2001.

2. "Weather Report," *Chicago Tribune*, May 2, 1984.

3. Mark Durham interview, 2010.

4. Charles S. Childs Jr. interview; Green, *Selling the Race*, 196–97, 201.

5. Clarice Durham interview, 2001; "Program, Memorial Services for Richard Isadore Durham: September 6, 1917–April 27, 1984," Wednesday, May 2, 1984, Clarice Durham personal files, 3.

6. Mark Durham interview, 2010.

7. Earl Durham interview, 2000.

8. Mark Durham interview, 2010.

9. Clarice Durham interview, 2001.

10. Caldwell Durham interview, 2010.

11. Clarice Durham interview, 2001.

12. Ibid.

13. Ibid.

14. Louis "Studs" Terkel interview, 2001.

15. Ibid.

16. Ibid.

17. Margaret Burroughs, Memorial Service Address, May 2, 1984, Clarice Durham personal files, 1.

18. Ibid., 2–3.

19. Ibid.

20. "Memorial Services," program, 3; Mark Durham interview; Clarice Durham interview, 2001.

21. Clarice Durham interview, 2001; Mark Durham interview, 2010.

22. "Memorial Services," program, 3; Mark Durham interview, 2010.

23. Oscar Brown Jr. interview, 2000.

24. Ibid.

25. Clarice Durham interview, 2001.

26. Jone Johnson Lewis, "*Battle Hymn of the Republic:* History and Words [First Version]," accessed July 19, 2013, http://womenshistory.about.com/library/etext/bl_howe_battle_hymn.htm.

27. "Memorial Services," program, 3; Earl Durham interview, 2000.

28. Clarice Durham interview, 2001.

29. Earl Durham interview, 2000.

30. Mark Durham interview, 2010.

31. "Harold Washington for Chicago, Campaign Directory," March 14, 1983, in Harold Washington Archives and Collections, Special Collections Department, Harold Washington Library Center, Chicago Public Library (hereinafter Washington Archives).

32. Mark Durham interview, 2010.

33. Ibid.

34. Ibid.

35. Earl Durham interview, 2000.

36. Ibid.

37. Ibid.

Chapter 2. Rural Wanderings

1. Isadore Richard Durham, "Poetry by Richard," in Durham Papers, box 6, folder 12.

2. Clotilde Durham Smith interview.

3. Ibid.

4. Ibid.; Caldwell Durham interview.

5. Chanie Durham, "Narrative of the Life of Chanie Durham, Founder of the Wendell

Phillips Evening School Alumni, Recorded by Herself, Edited by Claudia M. Durham, Daughter," n.d., Clotilde Durham Smith personal files, 12.

6. Ibid.

7. Ibid.; Wharton, *Negro in Mississippi*, 61–62; Bureau of the Census, *Negro Population 1790–1915* (Washington: GPO, 1918), 470.

8. Clotilde Durham Smith interview.

9. Chanie Durham, "Narrative," 12.

10. Wilson, *Education for Negroes*, 40.

11. Chanie Durham, "Narrative," 12.

12. Ibid.

13. Bundles, *On Her Own Ground*, 21, 179.

14. Ibid., 277.

15. Rebecca Blackwell Drake, "Kaleidoscope of History: History of Raymond, Mississippi," accessed June 12, 2013, http://www.raymondhistory.org; Arthell Kelley, "The Geography," McLemore, in *History of Mississippi*, 1:8–9, 12–13.

16. Rowland, *History of Hinds County*, 16; William Scarborough, "Slavery in Mississippi," in Miller and Smith, *Dictionary of Afro-American Slavery*, 483.

17. Scarborough, "Heartland of the Cotton Kingdom," in McLemore, *History of Mississippi*, 1:310.

18. Chanie Durham, "Narrative," 11; Caldwell Durham, "My Tour of Duty," unpublished manuscript, 2005, 13.

19. Sydnor, *Slavery in Mississippi*, 66.

20. Durham, "My Tour of Duty," 13.

21. Earl Durham interview, 2000.

22. Du Bois, *Black Reconstruction*, 432.

23. James G. Revels, "Redeemers, Rednecks, and Racial Integrity," in McLemore, *History of Mississippi*, 1:608.

24. Caldwell Durham interview.

25. Durham, "My Tour of Duty," 14.

26. Caldwell Durham interview.

27. Chanie Durham, "Narrative," 11.

28. Ibid.

29. Ibid., 2.

30. Ibid., 2.

31. Wharton, *Negro in Mississippi*, 70–72.

32. Woodruff, *American Congo*, 32–33; McMillen, *Dark Journey*, 124–29; Powdermaker, *After Freedom*, 86–87.

33. Chanie Durham, "Narrative," 3.

34. Ibid., 4.

35. Ibid.

36. Ibid., 7.

37. "About Alcorn: Brief History," 2014, accessed December 19, 2014, http://www

.alcorn.edu/discover-alcorn/history/index.aspx; Wharton, *Negro in Mississippi*, 253–54; Williams and Ashley, *I'll Find a Way*, 31; Wilson, *Education for Negroes*, 476.

38. Wilson, *Education for Negroes*, 53–73.

39. Ibid., 315; McMillen, *Dark Journey*, 103–6.

40. Chanie Durham, "Narrative," 11.

41. Ibid.

42. Ibid., 11–12; Clotilde Durham Smith interview; Caldwell Durham interview.

43. Caldwell Durham interview.

44. Clotilde Durham Smith interview.

45. Anderson, *Education of Blacks*, 204.

46. McMillen, *Dark Journey*, 73.

47. Ibid., 83.

48. Chanie Durham, "Narrative," 13.

49. Wharton, *Negro in Mississippi*, 251; McMillen, *Dark Journey*, 96; Wilson, *Education for Negroes*, 471–73.

50. Chanie Durham, "Narrative," 13.

51. Ibid.

52. Ibid.

53. Ibid.; "M-112: *St. Louis Globe-Democrat* Collection," University of Missouri-St. Louis, accessed June 15, 2013, http://www.umsl.edu/mercantile/collections/mercantile-library-special-collections/special_collections/slma-112.html.

54. Chanie Durham, "Narrative," 13.

55. Clotilde Durham Smith interview.

56. Ibid.

57. Chanie Durham, "Narrative," 13.

Chapter 3. Chicago

1. Richard Durham, "Poetry by Richard," N.d. Durham Papers, box 6, folder 12.

2. Chanie Durham, "Narrative," 13.

3. Clotilde Durham Smith interview.

4. Ibid.; Chanie Durham, "Narrative," 14.

5. Clotilde Durham Smith interview.

6. Wilkerson, *Warmth of Other Suns*, 197.

7. Grossman, *Land of Hope*, 112–13, 100–101; Illinois Central Historical Society, "A Brief Historical Sketch of the Illinois Central Railroad," accessed August 2, 2013, http://icrrhistorical.org/history.html; ICHS Maps, http://icrrhistorical.org/maps.html.

8. Clotilde Durham Smith interview.

9. Grossman, *Land of Hope*, 116.

10. Durham, "My Tour of Duty," 29.

11. Chanie Durham, "Narrative," 14.

12. Ibid., 15.

13. Drake and Cayton, *Black Metropolis*, 61.

14. Chanie Durham, "Narrative," 13–14.

15. Travis J. Dempsey, "Bronzeville" in Grossman, Keating, and Reiff, *Encyclopedia of Chicago*, 357.

16. Ibid.

17. Drake and Cayton, *Black Metropolis*, 8; Campbell Gibson and Kay Jung, "Illinois—Race and by Hispanic Origin for Large Cities and Other Places: Earliest Census to 1990," table 14, in *Historical Census Statistics on Population Totals by Race, 1790–1990, and by Hispanic Origin, 1970–1990 for Large Cities and Other Urban Places in the U.S.*, population division, Working Paper 76 (Washington, D.C.: Census Bureau, 2005), accessed January 10, 2013, http://www.census.gov/population/www/documentation/twps0076/ILtab.pdf; Chicago Commission on Race, *Negro in Chicago*, 108–10.

18. Gibson and Jung, "Illinois," 152–54; Drake and Cayton, *Black Metropolis*, 61–62.

19. Paul Neimark, "The Man Who Knew Muhammad Ali Best," *Sepia*, May 1976, 25.

20. Wright, *12 Million Black Voices*, 104.

21. Ibid., 104–5.

22. Chanie Durham, "Narrative," 14.

23. Earl Durham interview, 2002.

24. Wallace Best, "Grand Boulevard," in Grossman, Keating, and Reiff, *Encyclopedia of Chicago*, 357–58.

25. Durham, "My Tour of Duty," 29.

26. Ibid.

27. Ibid., 31; Earl Durham interview, 2002.

28. Chanie Durham, "Narrative," 15.

29. Clotilde Durham Smith interview.

30. Richard Wright, *Ethnographical Aspects of Chicago's Black Belt*, in Illinois Writers Project/"Negro in Illinois" Papers, Harsh Research Collection, box 53, folder 53-1, p. 3–5; Chicago Commission on Race, *Negro in Chicago*, 135–36.

31. Clotilde Durham Smith interview.

32. Drake and Cayton, *Black Metropolis*, 178–79.

33. Homel, *Down from Equality*, 39.

34. Ibid; Edward T. Clayton, "Four Chicago Pioneers," *Negro Digest*, September 1950, 90–92.

35. Chanie Durham, "Narrative," 14; Clotilde Durham Smith interview.

36. Earl Durham interview, 2000; Durham, "My Tour of Duty," 30.

37. Ibid., 43.

38. Fenton Johnson, *Recreation Facilities in Chicago's Negro District*, n.d., in Negro Studies Project, Federal Writers Project, Library of Congress, box A 879, folder—Chicago Contemporary Culture Lifestyle General, p. 2–3 (hereinafter FWP/LOC); Richard Wright, *Amusements in Districts 38 and 40*, n.d., in Negro Studies Project, FWP/LOC, box A 879, Folder—Chicago Contemporary Culture Lifestyle—Richard Wright, p. 2–4.

39. Drake and Cayton, *Black Metropolis*, 379–80.

40. Clotilde Durham Smith interview.

41. Neimark, "Man Who Knows," 28.

42. Clarice Durham interview, 2010.

43. Sterling and Kittross, *Stay Tuned*, 91.

44. Watkins, *On the Real Side*, 272.

45. MacDonald, *Don't Touch That Dial*, 91; "DTTD!: The Great Escape—The Story of Radio Comedy," accessed July 29, 2013, http://jfredmacdonald.com/comedy.htm.

46. Judith Waller interview with Frank Ernest Hill, June 1, 1951, Judith Waller Papers, Wisconsin Historical Society, box MAD 4/14/SC 797, folder 1, transcript, p. 18; Elizabeth McLeod, *"Amos 'n' Andy"* in Sterling, *Encyclopedia of Radio*, 1:78–82.

47. Watkins, *On the Real Side*, 279.

48. Ibid.

49. Elizabeth McLeod *"Amos 'n' Andy"* in Sterling, *Encyclopedia of Radio, 80*.

50. Clotilde Durham Smith interview; Caldwell Durham interview.

51. Neimark, "Man Who Knows," 25.

52. John Cannon, "Richard I," *Oxford Companion to British History*, 2002, retrieved April 29, 2014, http://www.encyclopedia.com/topic/Richard_I.aspx

53. Earl Durham interview, 2000; Clotilde Durham Smith interview.

54. Clotilde Durham Smith interview.

55. Terkel, *Hard Times*, 306.

56. "The Key to Prosperity," *Pittsburgh Courier*, February 9, 1929, A8.

57. Carl R. Osthaus, "The Rise and Fall of Jesse Binga, Black Financier," in *Journal of Negro History* 58, no. 1 (January 1973): 50.

58. Tracey Deutsch, "Great Depression," in Grossman, Keating, and Reiff, *Encyclopedia of Chicago*, 360–61; Badger, *New Deal*, 25; Drake and Cayton, *Black Metropolis*, 512.

59. Clotilde Durham Smith interview.

60. Ibid.; Durham, "My Tour of Duty," 34; Provident Foundation, "History—Dr. Daniel Hale Williams," accessed May 12, 2013, http://www.providentfoundation.org/index.php/history/history-dr-daniel-hale-williams; Earl Durham interview, 2002.

61. Richard Durham, "The Savoy Athletic Club," November 22, 1938, Federal Writers Project, Lincoln Presidential Library, box 63, folder 2, p. 1 (hereinafter FWP/Lincoln Presidential Library).

62. Clotilde Durham Smith interview.

63. Earl Durham interview, 2002.

64. Durham, "Savoy Athletic Club," 2.

65. Ibid., 4.

66. Clarice Durham interview, 2001.

67. "Greatest Boxing Show to Open Tomorrow," *Chicago Tribune*, February 25, 1934.

68. Earl Durham interview; "Golden Gloves Results," *Chicago Tribune*, February 27, 1934; Caldwell Durham interview.

69. Dyja, *Third Coast*, 194; Kent, *Gwendolyn Brooks*, 102.

70. Kent, *Gwendolyn Brooks*, 24.

71. Earl Durham interviews, 2000, 2002.

72. Earl Durham interview, 2000; Clotilde Durham Smith interview.

73. Ibid; Durham, "My Tour of Duty," 45; Earl Durham interview, 2000.

74. Reagon, *We'll Understand*, 15.

75. Best, *Passionately Human*, 106; Michael W. Harris, "Conflict and Resolution in the Life of Thomas Andrew Dorsey," in Reagon *We'll Understand*, 181.

76. Harris, "Conflict and Resolution," 181.

77. Durham, "My Tour of Duty," 45; Clotilde Durham Smith interview; Earl Durham interview, 2002.

78. Watts, *God, Harlem, U.S.A.*, x, 4; Clotilde Durham Smith interview.

79. Clotilde Durham Smith interview.

80. Ibid.

81. "Crowds Jam Library on Opening Day," *Chicago Defender*, January 23, 1932, Harsh Research Collection, Hall Branch Program Files, box 3, folder—GC Hall Branch Library.

82. Michael Flug, "Harsh, Vivian Gordon," in Schultz and Hast, *Women Building Chicago*, 359–61.

83. Vivian G. Harsh Research Collection, accessed April 12, 2014, http://www.chipublib.org/vivian-g-harsh-research-collection.

84. Caldwell Durham interview.

85. Ibid.; Michael Flug, "George Cleveland Hall (1864–1930)," in VGH/HECW Research, 2001, Harsh Research Collection, folder—George Cleveland Hall Biographical Research.

86. Richard Durham interview with John Dunning, January 16, 1983, Durham Papers, box 19, AV 8.

87. Ibid.

88. Ibid.

89. Earl Durham interviews, 2000, 2002.

90. Du Bois, *Souls of Black Folk*, 1.

91. Clotilde Durham Smith interview.

92. Neimark, "Man Who Knew," 25.

93. Darryl Cowherd, author interview, August 20, 2009; Forrest, *Furious Voice*, 86; Rose Jennings author interview.

94. Earl Durham interview, 2000.

95. Walker, Richard Wright, 77; Bone and Courage, *Muse in Bronzeville*, 166–67.

96. Rowley, *Richard Wright*, 117.

97. Hook, *Understanding of Karl Marx*, [83], [81].

98. Wright, "Blueprint for Negro Writing," 167–70.

99. Bone, "Richard Wright," 448; Rowley, *Richard Wright*, 118; Hine and McCluskey, *Black Chicago Renaissance*, xv–xvi.

100. Richard Durham, "Hell's Kitchen," *New Masses*, April 1938; Durham, "Death in a Kitchenette," *Chicago Defender*, April 1938, in Durham Papers, box 6, folder 12.

101. Langston Hughes to Vern Durham, September 10, 1939, Durham Papers, box 6, folder 12.

102. Durham, "Death in a Kitchenette."

103. Hughes to Durham, September 10, 1939, Durham Papers, box 6, folder 12.

104. Ibid.

105. Ibid.

106. Neimark, "Man Who Knows," 24.

107. Ibid.

108. "Poetry by Richard," Durham Papers, box 6, folder 12.

109. Hughes to Durham, September 10, 1939, Durham Papers, box 6, folder 12.

110. "Poetry by Richard," Durham Papers, box 6, folder 12.

111. Earl Durham interview, 2002.

112. Clotilde Durham Smith interview.

113. "Four Black Leather Notebooks; Northwestern University School of Commerce General Psychology Syllabus," February 17, 1939, Durham Papers, box 8.

114. Clarice Durham interview, 2010.

Chapter 4. Radio Beckons

1. Richard Durham, "Dawn Patrol," in Bontemps, *Golden Slippers*, 134.

2. Richard Durham, "A Day at the Relief Station," n.d., Durham Papers, box 6, folder 2, p. 1.

3. Ibid.

4. Mangione, *Dream and the Deal*, 4, 29–30, 42; Penkower, *Federal Writers' Project*, 26–27.

5. Penkower, *Federal Writers' Project*, 70–74; Mangione, *Dream and the Deal*, 48–50; Taylor, *Soul of a People*, 12–13.

6. Durham, "Day at the Relief Station," 2.

7. Ibid., 2–3.

8. Ibid., 3.

9. Richard Durham, "Neighbors," *Chicago Defender*, June 1937; Richard Durham, "Mecca" and "Death in a Kitchenette," *Chicago Defender*, April 1938; Richard Durham, "Pool Addict" and "Sparrows at Dawn," *Youth*, March 1937; Richard Durham, "Hell's Kitchen," *New Masses*, April 1938, all in Durham Papers, box 6, folder 12.

10. Richard Durham, "Sounds at Night," *Pittsburgh Courier*, June 1, 1938; Richard Durham, "Review of How to Win Friends and Influence People," *Northwestern Review*, September 1, 1938, in Durham Papers, box 6, folder 2.

11. Durham, "Review," 1.

12. Ibid., 4.

13. Ibid.

14. Mangione, *Dream and the Deal*, 123–27; Taylor, *Soul of a People*, 44.

15. Arna Bontemps, "Famous WPA Writers," *Negro Digest*, June 1950, 45–46.

16. Ibid., 44–45.

17. Ibid., 45; Richard Wright, "Ethnographical Aspects of Chicago's Black Belt," December 11, 1935, Illinois Writers Project/*Negro in Illinois* Papers, Harsh Research Collection, box 53, folder 53-1-Richard Wright; Bontemps, "Famous WPA Writers," 44–45.

18. Federal Writers' Project, *WPA Guide to Illinois*, v; Penkower, *Federal Writers' Project*, 21–24; Taylor, *Soul of a People*, 11.

19. Mangione, *Dream and the Deal*, 359.

20. Ibid., 260; Penkower, *Federal Writers' Project*, 146; Dolinar, *Negro in Illinois*, ix–x.

21. Federal Writers' Project, "Outline and Program for The Negro Press in Chicago," FWP/Lincoln Presidential Library, box 200, Folder—Manual for the Study of the Negro Press in Chicago, p. 1–3.

22. Richard Durham, "Don't Spend Your Money Where You Can't Work," 1939, Illinois Writers Project, in *The Negro in Illinois* Papers, Harsh Research Collection, box 41, pp. 2, 7; Halpern, *Down on the Killing Floor*, 107.

23. Clarice Davis Durham interview, 1999.

24. "The Negro Press in Chicago: Questionnaire on the Negro Press in Chicago," February 20, 1939, FWP/Lincoln Presidential Library, box 200, folder 1—Negro Press in Chicago, pp. 1–9.

25. Ibid., March 1, 15, 25; April 1; May 4, 1939.

26. Durham, "Don't Spend Your Money," 1.

27. Ibid., 3, 5–6.

28. Ibid., 13, 17–18.

29. Ibid., 21–22.

30. Ibid., 24.

31. Clarice Durham interview, 2010.

32. Washington, *Other Blacklist*, 75–76.

33. Ibid., 24–25.

34. Ibid., 28–29.

35. Richard Durham, "Civil Liberties," May 11, 1940, FWP/Lincoln Presidential Library, box 205, Folder—Freedom of Speech; Richard Durham, "Civil Liberties," May 29, 1940, FWP/Lincoln Presidential Library, box 203, folder 1, Rights of Unemployed.

36. Taylor, *Soul of a People*, 53; Terkel, *Hard Times*, 9; Mangione, *Dream and the Deal*, 128.

37. Mangione, *Dream and the Deal*, 128.

38. Federal Writers' Project, "Works Progress Administration, Special Studies and Projects, Regional and National Files," FWP/LOC, boxes A862-A867, folders—Radio Scripts, Illinois.

39. Mangione, *Dream and the Deal*, 128.

40. Bontemps, "Famous WPA Writers," 46.

41. Richard Durham, "Mormon Miracle," *Legends of Illinois*, June 23, 1940, script in Durham Papers, box 5, folder 8.

42. See note 38.

43. Richard Durham, "The Story of Auguste Rodin," *Great Artists*, December 18, 1940, script in Durham Papers, box 5, folder 1; Richard Durham, "Benedict Arnold," *Great Artists*, January 14, 1941, script in FWP/Lincoln Presidential Library, box 299, folder— Great Artists Program; Richard Durham, "The Story of Winslow Homer," *Great Artists*,

August 8, 1941, script in Negro Studies Project/FWP/LOC, box A863, Folder—Richard Durham.

44. Richard Durham, "Goya: The Disasters of War," *Great Artists*, February 11, 1941, script in Durham Papers, box 5, folder 3, p. 1.

45. Ibid., 2–3.

46. Ibid., 3.

47. Ibid., 6.

48. Clarice Davis Durham and Marguerite Davis interview with author, March 19, 2001.

49. Solomon, *Cry Was Unity*, 303–4, 307.

50. Gellman, *Death Blow to Jim Crow*, 61, 158.

51. Clarice Durham interview, 2011.

52. Ibid.

53. Ibid.; Fenton Johnson, "Recreation Facilities in Chicago's Negro District," Negro Studies Project/FWP/LOC, box A879, folder—Chicago Contemporary Culture Lifestyle General, p. 2–3; Richard Wright, "*Amusements in Districts 38 and 40*," Negro Studies Project/FWP/LOC, box A879, Folder—Chicago Contemporary Culture Lifestyle—Richard Wright, pp. 2–4.

54. Clarice Durham interview, 2011.

55. Clarice Durham interview, 2011.

56. Mavigliano and Lawson, *Federal Art Project in Illinois*, 203; Rowley, *Richard Wright*, 108.

57. Penkower, *Federal Writer's Project*, 186.

58. Clarice Durham interview, 2011.

59. Ibid.

60. Richard Durham to Clotilde Durham, n.d., Durham Papers, box 6, folder 12.

61. Earl Durham interview, 2000.

62. Richard Durham to Clotilde Durham, n.d., Durham Papers, box 6, folder 12.

63. Ibid., 2.

64. Richard Durham, "A Matter of Technique," *Art for Our Sake*, January 16, 1943, script in Durham Papers, box 5, folder 7.

65. Richard Durham, *At the Foot of Adams Street*, February 6 and 27, March 20, April 10, 1943, scripts in Durham Papers, box 5, folder 7.

Chapter 5. Scripts and Scoops

1. Richard Durham, "Dr. Dailey and the Living Human Heart," *Democracy U.S.A.*, script in Durham Papers, box 7, folder 3, p. 1.

2. Neimark, "Man Who Knows," 25.

3. Rothel, *Who Was That Masked Man?* 88; B. R. Smith, "The Lone Ranger, Western Adventure Program," in Sterling, *Encyclopedia of Radio*, 878–79.

4. Neimark, "Man Who Knows," 28.

5. Braxton, *Collected Poetry*, 71.

6. Smith, "Striker, Fran," in Sterling, *Encyclopedia of Radio*, 1349–50.

7. Federal Bureau of Investigation, "Richard Isadore Durham File, #1150281-000-100-367649," February 14, 1950, section 1, p. 3; Neimark, "Man Who Knows," 28.

8. Richard Durham interview with J. Fred MacDonald, June 13, 1980.

9. Clarice Durham interview, 2010.

10. Ibid.

11. Ibid.

12. Ibid.

13. Albert Crews, "A Report of the Summer Radio Institute of Northwestern University in Collaboration with the National Broadcasting Company," Radio, Television and Film Department: Department and Administrative Records, series 20/30, Northwestern University Archives, Evanston, Ill., box 4, folder 4, p. 2; Waller, *Radio*, ix; Summer Radio Institute, certificate, July 31, 1943, Durham Papers, box 9, folder 3.

14. O'Dell, *Women Pioneers in Television*, 196.

15. Judith Waller, interview with Frank Ernest Hill, June 1, 1951, Judith Waller Papers, Wisconsin Historical Society, box MAD 4/14/SC 797, folder 1, transcript, p. 5.

16. Margot Hardenbergh, "Waller, Judith Cary (1889–1973)," in Godfrey and Leigh, *Historical Dictionary of American Radio*, 408–9.

17. Durham interview with MacDonald, 1980.

18. Durham interview with MacDonald, 1975.

19. Durham, Correspondence, n.d., in Durham Papers, box 6, folder 6.

20. Richard Durham to Andrew Paschal, n.d., Durham Papers, box 6, folder 6.

21. Brown, *Why Race Riots?*, 1; Savage, *Broadcasting Freedom*, 177.

22. Durham to Paschal, in Durham Papers, box 6, folder 6, p. 1.

23. Ibid.

24. Bunche, *Political Status of the Negro*, 611.

25. Durham to Paschal, in Durham Papers, box 6, folder, p. 1.

26. Ibid, 2.

27. Savage, *Broadcasting Freedom*, 91.

28. Durham to Pascal, in Durham Papers, box 6, folder 6, p. 2.

29. Savage, *Broadcasting Freedom*, 177–79.

30. Barnouw, *Radio Drama in Action*, 68.

31. Ibid., 75.

32. Durham interview with MacDonald, 1980.

33. Neimark, "Man Who Knows," 24.

34. Mullen, *Popular Fronts*, 54.

35. Burns, *Nitty Gritty*, 4.

36. Mullen, *Popular Fronts*, 47.

37. Rampersad, *Life of Langston Hughes*, 2:64.

38. Richard Durham to Langston Hughes, December 2, 1944, Langston Hughes Papers, James Weldon Johnson Collection, Yale Collection of American Literature, Beinecke Rare Book and Manuscript Library, box 57, folder 1089, p. 1 (hereinafter Hughes Papers).

39. Ibid., 2.

40. Neimark, "Man Who Knows," 28.

41. Burns, *Nitty Gritty*, 19.

42. Neimark, "Man Who Knows," 24.

43. Richard Durham to Hayward Kirkpatrick, April 25, 1944, Durham Papers, box 9, folder 6; Bunche, *Political Status of the Negro*, 496–97.

44. Bunche, *Political Status of the Negro*, 330, 337.

45. Durham to Kirkpatrick, Durham Papers, box 6, folder 6.

46. Richard Durham, "Crump Thinks Negroes Given Fair Treatment," *Chicago Defender*, April 8, 1944, 1.

47. Ibid.

48. Ibid.

49. Clarice Durham interview, 2011.

50. Burns, *Nitty Gritty*, 5; Kenan Heise, "Doc Lochard; 50 Years as Editor at *Defender*," February 3, 1984, in Ben Burns Papers, Harsh Research Collection (hereinafter Burns Papers), box 1, folder Defender—Metz Lochard; Henry Locke, "Farewell to 'Doc' Lochard," *Chicago Defender*, February 9, 1984, 4, 22; Waters, *American Diary*, 126.

51. Burns, *Nitty Gritty*, 20.

52. Ibid., 19.

53. Richard Durham, "Governor Dewey Sidesteps Queries," *Chicago Defender*, July 8, 1944, 1.

54. Richard Durham, "Vest Pocket Plank to Be Very Vague," *Chicago Defender*, July 22, 1944, 1.

55. Richard Durham, "Both Parties Assailed for Ignoring Negro," *Chicago Defender*, July 29, 1944, 1.

56. Mullen, *Popular Fronts*, 47.

57. Durham interview with MacDonald, 1980; Richard Durham, "Dewey Home Town Lily White—Mother Anti-Semetic," *Chicago Defender*, August 26, 1944.

58. Durham, "Dewey Home Town."

59. Ibid.

60. "Bias Laid to Dewey's Mother but She Denies Quotes on Negroes and Jews," *New York Post*, August 29, 1944; Durham, "Dewey Home Town," 4.

61. "Franklin D. Roosevelt, The White House," accessed July 11, 2013, http://www.whitehouse.gov/about/presidents/franklindroosevelt.

62. Allen, *Port Chicago Mutiny*, 22.

63. Ibid; 64; Buchanan, *Black Americans in World War II*, 87.

64. John Robert Badger, "50 Sailors Face Trial for Mutiny," *Chicago Defender*, September 23, 1944, 1, 4; "Names of Sailors Facing Trial for California Mutiny," *Chicago Defender*, October 7, 1944, 1; Langston Hughes, "Here to Yonder, Fifty Young Negroes," *Chicago Defender*, December 2, 1944, 12; Allen, *Port Chicago Mutiny*, 75–92.

65. "Navy Refuses to Review Trials of 50 Port Chicago Gobs," *Chicago Defender*, July 21, 1945, 1; Buchanan, *Black Americans in World War II*, 87; "Navy Frees 83 in Mutiny Cases, Port Chicago, Guam Sailors Win Clemency," *Chicago Defender*, January 12, 1946, 1, 6.

66. Clarice Durham interview, 2011; Toni Morrison interview, 2011.

67. Richard Durham, "Army Bucks Lily-Whites in Battle Over WACs," *Chicago Defender*, June 30, 1945, 1.

68. Richard Durham, "Four Seabees Flogged," *Chicago Defender*, April 14, 1945, 1.

69. Burns, *Nitty Gritty*, 20.

70. Richard Durham, "Millionaire Plots Tighter Noose on 'Black Ghetto,'" *Chicago Defender*, February 24, 1945, 10.

71. Ibid.

72. "All-Star Coverage at All-Nations Conference," *Chicago Defender*, April 28, 1945, 1.

73. Bennett, *International Organizations*, 48–52.

74. Richard Durham, "Delegates Juggle Colonial Question," *Chicago Defender*, May 5, 1945, 1.

75. Richard Durham, "Soviet Demand Wins Okay for Amendments, Right to Work Plan Rejected by US Delegation," *Chicago Defender*, May 12, 1945, 1; Richard Durham, "Anti-Negro Smuts Drafts Parley Equal Rights Plan," *Chicago Defender*, May 12, 1945, 4; Richard Durham, "Britain Stands Pat on Refusal to Quit Colonies," *Chicago Defender*, May 12, 1945, 4; Richard Durham, "Haiti Wins Wide Backing in Racial Equality Fight," *Chicago Defender*, May 12, 1945, 4; Richard Durham, "U.S. Knifes Colonial Freedom," *Chicago Defender*, May 26, 1945, 1; Richard Durham, "Full Independence Opposed by Parley, China, Russia Line Up for Colonial Liberty but Lose Fight," *Chicago Defender*, May 26, 1945, 1.

76. Mullen, *Popular Fronts*, 71.

77. Robert Davis to Langston Hughes, October 5, 1945, Hughes Papers, box 53, folder 984, p. 1.

78. Leab, *Union of Individuals*, 2, 4–6, 60.

79. Davis to Hughes, October 5, 1945, 1.

80. "Register of the Hollywood Studio Strike Collection, 1930s–1940s," Online Archive of California, Southern California Library for Social Studies and Research, Los Angeles, accessed April 12, 2014, http://www.oac.cdlib.org/findaid/ark:/13030/tf7g5005mn/admin/#did-1.7.1; Denning, *Cultural Front*, 89; Robert Davis to Langston Hughes, April 17, 1945, Hughes Papers, box 53, folder 984, p. 2.

81. Ibid.

82. Waters, *American Diary*, 126.

83. Homer Heck interview with J. Fred MacDonald, June 12, 1980; Durham interview with MacDonald, 1975.

84. Savage, *Broadcasting Freedom*, 249; Barnouw, *Radio Drama in Action*, 354–55.

85. Waters, *American Diary*, 237.

86. Hugh Cordier, "A History and Analysis of Destination Freedom," Summer 1949, Northwestern University Seminar Paper, in Durham Papers, box 6, folder 4, p. 6.

87. Ibid.

88. Durham interview with MacDonald, 1980.

89. Clarice Durham interview, 2011.

90. Burns, *Nitty Gritty*, 92.

91. Clarice Durham interview; Metz Lochard to Ben Burns, interoffice communication, March 28, 1946, Burns Papers, box 1, folder—Defender, Metz Lochard; Robert Lucas to Arna Bontemps, July 15, 1946, Arna Bontemps Papers, Special Collections Research Center, Syracuse University Library, box 7, folder—Durham, Richard (hereinafter Bontemps Papers).

92. Clarice Durham interview, 2011.

93. Richard Durham, "The Strange Case of Mary Green," *Chicago Star*, July 6, 1946, 1.

94. F.B.I., Richard Durham File, 1150281-000-100-367649, February 14, 1950, section 1, p. 3–4; FBI, Richard Durham File, "Activities and Affiliations," 1150281-000-100-367649, June 6, 1950, section 1, p. 3.

95. Masthead," *Chicago Star*, July 6, 1946, 1.

96. Richard Durham, "The Story of Harry Deas," *Democracy USA*, August 31, 1946, script in Durham Papers, box 7, folder 1.

97. Oscar Brown Jr. interview, 2000.

98. Richard Durham, "Dr. Dailey and the Living Human Heart," script in Durham Papers, box 7, folder 3; "Dr. Ulysses Grant Dailey Receives Distinguished Service Award for 1949," *Journal of the National Medical Association* 42, no. 1 (January 1960): 39–40.

99. Durham, "Dr. Dailey and the Living Human Heart," script in Durham Papers, box 7, folder 2-3.

100. Ibid., 8.

101. Ibid., 9–10.

102. Memorandum Agreement to *Democracy USA* Contract Signed with Richard Durham, December 27, 1946, Durham Papers, box 9, folder 1, p. 1; "Contract for Radio Show-*Democracy USA*," n.d., Durham Papers, box 9, folder 1, pp. 1–3.

Chapter 6. Rare Broadcasts

1. Richard Durham, "Colonel B. O. Davis, Commander of the 332nd Fighter Squadron," *Democracy USA*, December 22, 1946, script in Durham Papers, box 7, folder 5, pp. 5–6.

2. Durham interview with MacDonald, 1980.

3. Durham interview with MacDonald, 1975.

4. "Truman Cites Defender—WBBM for Program 'Democracy USA,'" *Chicago Defender*, March 8, 1947, 1; "National Fame, President's Award Mark 'Democracy USA's' First Year," *Chicago Defender*, May 10, 1947, 12.

5. Ibid.

6. Award Certificates, Durham Papers, box 9, folder 3.

7. "The Negro's Status in Radio," 1947, Papers of the National Negro Congress, part 1: Records and Correspondence, reel 34, series 2, NNC Records of the Executive Secretaries, 1943–1947, Harsh Research Collection, box 69, folder 0216, pp. 1–2.

8. Ibid.

9. Lenthall, *Radio's America*, 186, 188.

10. Clarice Durham interview, 2011.

11. Durham interview with MacDonald, 1980.

12. Durham interview with MacDonald, 1975.

13. Durham interview with MacDonald, 1980.

14. Richard Durham, "Albert W. Williams—President of the Unity Mutual Insurance Company," *Democracy USA*, January 12, 1947, script in Durham Papers, box 7, folder 6.

15. Ibid., 7–8.

16. Ibid., 9.

17. O'Dell, *Women Pioneers in Television*, 190; Marilyn J. Matelski, "Soap Opera: Daytime Radio Drama," in Sterling, *Encyclopedia of Radio*, 3:1286.

18. Jennifer Hyland Wang, "Phillips, Irna, 1901–1973: U.S. Creator of Radio Serial Dramas," in Sterling, *Encyclopedia of Radio* 3:1072.

19. Ibid., 1073; O'Dell, *Women Pioneers in Television*, 186.

20. Ohmart, *Don Ameche*, 211; Richard Durham interview with John Dunning, January 16, 1983.

21. Durham interview with Dunning.

22. Ibid.

23. O'Dell, *Women Pioneers in Television*, 186.

24. Ibid., 188.

25. Ibid., 184.

26. Wang, "Phillips, Irna," in Sterling, *Encyclopedia of Radio*, 3:1072; Irna Phillips to Lewis H. Titterton, September 17, 1951, Irna Phillips Papers, Wisconsin Historical Society, box 38, folder—New "Guiding Light" Correspondence, p. 2 (hereinafter Phillips Papers); Meg James, "CBS' Guiding Light to End in September," *Los Angeles Times*, April 2, 2009, accessed April 29, 2013, http://articles.latimes.com/2009/apr/02/entertainment /et-guiding-light2.

27. O'Dell, *Women Pioneers in Television*, 190–91.

28. "Irna Phillips Cited by American Legion for Fight Against Juvenile Delinquency," Press Release, September 27, 1944, Phillips Papers, box 62, folder—NBC Correspondence, 1933–1948; Matelski, "Soap Opera," in Sterling, *Encyclopedia of Radio*, 1288.

29. Durham interview with MacDonald, 1980.

30. Ibid.

31. Earl Durham interviews, 2000, 2002.

32. Lewis, *W. E. B. Du Bois*, 307–10.

33. Swati Pal, "Theater and Activism: The Agit Prop Theater Way," *Music and Arts in Action* 3, no. 1, (2010): 48, accessed December 14, 2014, http://www.musicandartsinaction .net/index.php/maia/article/view/agitprop/51; Clarice Durham interview, 1999.

34. Denning, *Cultural Front*, 115–16.

35. Eugene Perkins, "Chicago, Crisis in Black Theater," *Black World*, April 1973, 28; Oscar Brown Jr. interview.

36. Vernon Jarrett, author interview, March 20, 2002.

37. Earl Durham interview, 2002.

38. Ibid.

39. Ibid., Earl Durham interview, 2000.

40. Durham interview with Dunning, 1983.

41. Janice Kingslow, "I Refuse to Pass," *Negro Digest*, May 1950, 31.

42. Richard Durham, *Here Comes Tomorrow*, September 10, 1947, scripts in Clarice Durham personal files, p. 1.

43. Oscar Brown Jr. interview.

44. Durham, *Here Comes Tomorrow*, scripts in Clarice Durham personal files.

45. Robert E. Weems Jr., *Black Business*, xi, 57.

46. Ibid., 57; Mark Newman, "On the Air w/Jack L. Cooper: The Beginning of Black Appeal Radio," *Chicago History* 12 (Summer 1983): 51, 54–56.

47. "Launch First All-Negro Radio Commercial on WJJD Monday," *Chicago Defender*, September 6, 1947, in Durham Papers, box 9, folder 1, p. 1.

48. "Here Comes Tomorrow," September 24, 1947, *Billboard*, Durham Papers, box 9, folder 4, *Durham v. NBC* (4) 1947–1978.

49. Ibid.

50. Ibid.

51. Ulmer Turner, "Sun Dial: Negro Life Told in a Soap Opera," *Chicago Sun and Times*, November 9, 1947, Durham Papers, box 9, folder 4, *Durham v. NBC* (4) 1947–1978.

52. "Wednesday, October 15, 1947," *Variety*, Durham Papers, box 9, folder 4, *Durham v. NBC* (4) 1947–1978.

53. Ibid.

54. Ibid.

55. "Insurance Firm's Radio Drama Wins Nation Radio Honors," *Chicago Defender*, December 18, 1948, 18.

56. Clarice Durham interview, 1999.

57. Cordier, "History and Analysis," 6; Richard Durham, "The Story of Albert Merritt," *Democracy USA*, February 15, 1948, script in Durham Papers, box 7, folder 12.

58. Oscar Brown Jr. interview.

59. Vernon Jarrett interview.

60. Culver and Hyde, *American Dreamer*, 456–58, 486; Norman D. Markowitz, *Rise and Fall*, 27.

61. Clarice Durham interview, 2011; Earl Durham interview, 2002.

62. Cordier, "History and Analysis," 7; Richard Durham to Ira Marion, Radio Writers Guild, Grievance Committee and Attorneys Myers-Rothstien, memorandum, n.d., Durham Papers, box 9, folder 1, *Durham vs. NBC* 1946–56, 5; handwritten notes about *Destination Freedom*, n.d., Durham Papers, box 9, folder 5.

63. Cordier, "History and Analysis," 7.

64. Durham interview with MacDonald, 1980.

65. Cordier, "History and Analysis," 7.

66. Ibid.; Durham to Marion, memorandum, Durham Papers, box 9, folder 9-1, *Durham v. NBC* 1946–56, p. 5.

67. Ehrlich, *Radio Utopia*, 14.

68. Richard Durham, handwritten *Destination Freedom* notes, box 9, folder 5-1954–55.

69. Oscar Brown Jr. interview.

70. J. Fred MacDonald, "Radio's Black Heritage: Destination Freedom, 1948–1950," *Phylon* 39, no. 1 (March 1978): 67; Durham interview with MacDonald, 1975.

71. Cordier, "History and Analysis," 24.

72. Waller interview with Hill, 1951, pp. 17–19.

73. Durham interview with MacDonald, 1980.

74. Cordier, "History and Analysis," 7.

75. Oscar Brown Jr. interview.

76. Richard Durham, "The Knock-Kneed Man: Crispus Attucks," *Destination Freedom*, June 27, 1948, script in Durham Papers, box 1, folder 2, pp. 5, 9.

77. Ibid., 15.

78. Ibid., 5; Durham interview with MacDonald, 1980.

79. Durham, "Crispus Attucks," 17.

80. Ibid., 23.

81. Ibid., 26–27.

82. Durham interview with MacDonald, 1980.

83. Cordier, "History and Analysis," 7.

84. Ibid., 28; Richard Durham to Homer Heck, June 27, 1948, Durham Papers, box 6, folder 7, p. 1.

85. Durham to Heck; Cordier, "History and Analysis," 28.

86. Cordier, "History and Analysis," 28; Durham to Heck.

87. Durham to Heck, 2; Cordier, "History and Analysis," 30.

88. Cordier, "History and Analysis," 30; Durham to Heck, 3.

89. Homer Heck interview with J. Fred MacDonald, June 12, 1980.

90. Clarice Durham interview, 1999.

91. Cordier, "History and Analysis," 7–8.

92. Ibid., 8–9.

93. Ibid.

94. Denning, *Cultural Front*, 88; Matthew Nichter, May 3, 2013, email.

95. Denning, *Cultural Front*, 8–10.

96. Ibid., 11.

97. Ibid., 10–11.

98. Ibid., 12.

99. Oscar Brown Jr. interview.

100. Clarice Durham interview, 1999.

101. Earl Durham interview, 2002.

102. Ibid.; Caldwell Durham interview; Clotilde Durham Smith interview.

103. Clarice Durham interview, 2010.

Chapter 7. Freedom

1. Richard Durham, "Railway to Freedom: The Story of Harriet Tubman," *Destination Freedom*, July 4, 1948, script in Durham Papers, box 1, folder 3, p. 2.

2. "Hall Branch Program Files," n.d., Hall Branch Library Archives, Harsh Research Collection, box 3, folder—GC Hall Branch Library and Its Social Environment 1957, p. 1.

3. Cordier, "History and Analysis," 26.

4. Smith, *Visions of Belonging*, 208.

5. Durham interview with MacDonald, 1980.

6. Cordier, "History and Analysis," 25.

7. Ibid.

8. MacDonald, *Richard Durham's Destination Freedom*, 4.

9. Richard Durham, "Negro Cinderella: The Story of Lena Horne," *Destination Freedom*, June 12, 1949, script in Durham Papers, box 2, folder 23, pp. 22–23; MacDonald, "Radio's Black Heritage," 68; Durham, "The Long Road: The Story of Mary Church Terrell," *Destination Freedom*, August 7, 1949, script in Durham Papers, box 3, folder 1, pp. 23–24.

10. Heck interview with MacDonald, 1980.

11. Durham, "Railway to Freedom," 2.

12. Ibid., 5.

13. Ibid.; Larson, *Bound for the Promised Land*, xvi.

14. Durham, "Railway to Freedom," 15.

15. Franklin and Moss, *From Slavery to Freedom*, 204–9.

16. Larson, *Bound for the Promised Land*, xvii; Franklin and Moss, *From Slavery to Freedom*, 210.

17. Durham interview with MacDonald, 1980.

18. Ibid.

19. Franklin and Moss, *From Slavery to Freedom*, 164; MacDonald, *Richard Durham's Destination Freedom*, 47.

20. Durham interview with MacDonald, 1980.

21. Richard Durham, "Denmark Vesey," July 18, 1948, Script in Durham Papers, box 1, folder 5, p. 2.

22. Ibid., 4–26.

23. Ibid., 28–29.

24. MacDonald, *Richard Durham's Destination Freedom*, 47.

25. Oscar Brown Jr. interview; Heck interview with MacDonald.

26. Savage, *Broadcasting Freedom*, 246, 263.

27. Richard Durham, "Father of the Blues—W. C. Handy," *Destination Freedom*, September 9, 1948, script in Durham Papers, box 1, folder 13.

28. Ibid., 6.

29. Ibid.

30. Ibid., 17.

31. Ibid., 25.

32. Studs Terkel interview.

33. Richard Durham, "The Rime of the Ancient Dodger: The Story of Jackie Robinson," *Destination Freedom*, November 21, 1948, script in Durham Papers, box 1, folder 21, p. 4.

34. Navasky, *Naming Names*, 21.

35. Durham, "Rime of the Ancient Dodger," 3.

36. Studs Terkel interview.

37. Richard Durham, "The Story of Louis Armstrong, King of the Trumpeters," *Destination Freedom*, script in Durham Papers, July 31, 1949, box 2, folder 29; Richard Durham, "The Anatomy of an Ordinance: The Story of Reverend Archibald Carey," *Destination Freedom*, June 5, 1949, script in Durham Papers, box 2, folder 22.

38. Richard Durham, "The Story of 1875: The Life and Death of Senator Charles Caldwell," *Destination Freedom*, August 29, 1948, script in Durham Papers, box 1, folder 11.

39. Richard Durham, "The Heart of George Cotton: The Story of Dr. U. G. Dailey and Dr. Daniel Williams," *Destination Freedom*, August 8, 1948, script in Durham Papers, box 1, folder 8; Richard Durham, "Boy with a Dream: The Story of Dr. J. Ernest Wilkins," *Destination Freedom*, September 19, 1948, script in Durham Papers, box 1, folder 14; Richard Durham, "Investigator for Democracy: The Story of Walter White," *Destination Freedom*, November 28, 1948, script in Durham Papers, box 1, folder 22.

40. Richard Durham, "Shakespeare of Harlem: The Story of Langston Hughes," *Destination Freedom*, September 26, 1948, script in Durham Papers, box 1, folder 15; Langston Hughes, *Shakespeare in Harlem*.

41. Richard Durham to Langston Hughes, Western Union message, September 20, 1948, Hughes Papers, box 57, folder 1089.

42. Langston Hughes to Richard V. Durham, October 1, 1948, Hughes Papers, box 57, folder 1089.

43. Ibid.

44. Cordier, "History and Analysis," 13.

45. Clarice Durham interview, 1999.

46. Oscar Brown Jr. interview with J. Fred MacDonald, February 1975; Savage, *Broadcasting Freedom*, 263; Cordier, "History and Analysis," 15.

47. Ibid., 14.

48. Ibid., 15.

49. Ibid., 18.

50. Ibid., 19; Richard Durham, "Echoes of Harlem: The Story of Duke Ellington," *Destination Freedom*, November 7, 1948, script in Durham Papers, box 1, folder 19.

51. Cordier, "History and Analysis," 19.

52. Clarice Durham interview, 2011.

53. Ibid.

54. Oscar Brown Jr. interview, 2000.

55. Oscar Brown Jr. interview.

56. Ibid.

57. Studs Terkel interview.

58. Dunning, *On the Air*, 197.

59. Ibid.

60. Personal/handwritten notes, Durham Papers, box 9, folder 9-5, *Durham vs. NBC* 1954–55.

61. Oscar Brown Jr. interview.

62. Durham interview with MacDonald, 1980.

63. Durham interview with Dunning, 1983.

64. Cordier, "History and Analysis," 19–20; "NBC Chicago Trade News," February 9, 1949, Durham Papers, box 9, folder 3, p. 6.

65. *Education on the Air: Nineteenth Yearbook of the Institute for Education By Radio*, Joe Olson, ed., (Columbus: Ohio State University, 1949), 412; Cordier, "History and Analysis," 21.

66. Durham interview with MacDonald, 1980.

67. Clarice Durham interview, 2011.

68. Ibid.

69. Richard Durham to Langston Hughes, November 17, 1949, Hughes Papers, box 57, folder 1089, p. 2.

70. Clarice Durham interview, 2011.

71. Ibid.

72. Richard Durham, "Harriet's Children: The Story of the Negro in American History," *Destination Freedom*, June 26, 1948, script in Durham Papers, box 2, folder 25.

73. MacDonald, *Richard Durham's Destination Freedom*, 10; "The Friends of the Negro Writer Brunch Invitation," Durham Papers, box 9, folder 9-1, *Durham vs. NBC* (1) 1946–56.

74. Commission on Human Relations, December 19, 1949, Negro Museum, February 10, 1950; Conference of Christians and Jews, March 1, 1950, all in Durham Papers, box 9, folder 9-2, *Durham vs. NBC*, 1948–57.

75. Richard Durham, "The John Henry Story: The Legend of the Famous Steel Driver," *Destination Freedom*, July 24, 1949, script in Durham Papers, box 2, folder 28; Richard Durham, "Tales of Stackalee: The Story of the Negro Paul Bunyan," *Destination Freedom*, July 17, 1949, script in Durham Papers, box 2, folder 27.

76. Oscar Brown Jr. interview.

77. Durham interview with MacDonald, 1980.

78. Ibid.; Richard Durham, "Woman with a Mission: The Story of Ida B. Wells," *Destination Freedom*, April 10, 1949, script in Durham Papers, box 2, folder 12, pp. 2, 16, 28.

79. Durham with MacDonald, 1975; Richard Durham, "Truth Goes to Washington: The Story of Sojourner Truth," *Destination Freedom*, August 15, 1948, script in Durham Papers, box 1, folder 9; Richard Durham, "Peace Mediator: The Story of Dr. Ralph Bunche," *Destination Freedom*, February 20, 1949, Durham Papers, box 2, folder 8; Richard Durham, "Father to Son: The Story of Adam Clayton Powell, Senior and Junior," *Destination Freedom*, October 9, 1949, script in Durham Papers, box 3, folder 10.

80. Durham with MacDonald, 1980; Richard Durham, "Dark Explorers," *Destination Freedom*, July, 11 1948, script in Durham Papers, box 1, folder 4.

81. Durham interview with Dunning, 1983; Richard Durham, "Brotherhood Begins at Home," *Destination Freedom*, February 19, 1950, script in Durham Papers, box 3, folder 24.

82. Richard Durham, "Poet in Bronzeville: The Story of Gwendolyn Brooks," *Destination Freedom*, September 1, 1949, script in Durham Papers, box 3, folder 7; Kent, *A Life: Gwendolyn Brooks*, 87.

83. Kent, *A Life: Gwendolyn Brooks*, 87.

84. Durham interview with MacDonald, 1980.

85. Richard Durham to Ira Marion, memorandum, n.d., Durham Papers, box 9, folder 9-1, *Durham vs. NBC* 1946–56, p. 6.

86. James L. Hill, "Frank Yerby," in *Writers of the Black Chicago Renaissance*, 394–96; Durham to Hughes, November 17, 1949, 2.

87. MacDonald, *Richard Durham's Destination Freedom*, 6; Savage, *Broadcasting Freedom*, 267.

88. Durham with MacDonald, 1975; Durham interview with Dunning, 1983.

89. MacDonald, *Richard Durham's Destination Freedom*, 6.

90. Durham interview with MacDonald, 1975.

91. Durham to Hughes, November 17, 1949, 1.

92. Richard Durham, "The Long Road: The Story of Mary Church Terrell," *Destination Freedom*, August 7, 1949, script in Durham Papers, box 3, folder 1, p. 21; Durham to Hughes, November 17, 1949, 1; Richard Durham, "Blind Alley Symphony: The Story of Dean Dixon," *Destination Freedom*, November 13, 1949, script in Durham Papers, box 3, folder 15.

93. Richard Durham, "Segregation, Incorporated," *Destination Freedom*, August 18, 1949, script in Durham Papers, box 3, folder 4, p. 20; Richard Durham, "Investigator for Democracy: The Story of Walter White," *Destination Freedom*, November 28, 1948, script in Durham Papers, box 1, folder 22, p. 20.

94. Richard Durham, "Woman on a Mission: The Story of Ida B. Wells," *Destination Freedom*, April 10, 1949, script in Durham Papers, box 2, folder 15, p. 25.

95. MacDonald, *Richard Durham's Destination Freedom*, 9.

96. Durham to Hughes, November 17, 1949, 1.

97. Ibid., 2.

98. Cordier, "History and Analysis," 21.

99. Richard Durham to Ira Marion, Radio Writers Guild, Memorandum, Durham Papers, box 9, Folder 9-1, *Durham v. NBC* 1946–56.

100. Personal/handwritten notes, Durham Papers, box 9, folder 9-5, *Durham v. NBC* 1954–55.

101. Ibid.

102. Durham interview with MacDonald, 1975.

103. Durham interview with Dunning, 1983.

Chapter 8. Moving On

1. Richard Durham to Robert Weaver, March 23, 1951, Durham Papers, box 6, folder 8, p. 2.

2. Ibid., 9; Richard Durham Fellowship Application, February 20, 1950, John Hay Whitney Foundation Records Manuscripts and Archives, Yale University Library, box 32, folder 5, p. 4 (hereinafter Whitney Papers).

3. Raushenbush, *John Hay Whitney Foundation*, 1:xv, 63, 70–71, 125; Kahn, *Jock*, 178–79.

4. Recommendations, March 13, 1950, Whitney Papers box 32, folder 5; Robert Charles F. Jones, "The Opportunity Fellowships Program 1949–1960," June 12, 1961, Whitney Papers, box 93, folder 16, p. 23; Raushenbush, *John Hay Whitney Foundation*, Appendix A, 184–90.

5. Durham to Weaver, March 23, 1951, p. 7.

6. Richard Durham to Louis Friedman, February 25, 1951, Durham Papers, box 9, folder 1, p. 1.

7. Sterling and Kittross, *Stay Tuned*, 84, 89.

8. "Destination Freedom," description, Durham Papers, box 9, folder 7, *Durham v. NBC*, p. 1.

9. Richard Durham to Ira Marion, Radio Writer's Guild, Memorandum, n.d., Durham Papers, box 9, folder 1, *Durham vs. NBC*, p. 2.

10. "Destination Freedom Series Returns to Air: To Point Up Dangers to American Democracy," press release, October 11, 1950, Durham Papers, box 9, folder 3—*Durham vs. NBC*, 1943–1978.

11. Richard Durham to Ira Marion, Radio Writer's Guild, memorandum, n.d., Durham Papers, box 9, folder 1, *Durham vs. NBC*, p. 8.

12. Allan G. Harris to Richard Durham, February 19, 1951, Durham Papers, box 9, folder 2, p. 1.

13. Durham to Friedman, February 25, 1951, Durham Papers, box 9, folder 1, p. 3.

14. Ibid.

15. Ibid., 4.

16. Durham to Marion, memorandum, n.d., Durham Papers, box 9, folder 1, p. 8.

17. Ibid., 9.

18. Ibid.

19. Ibid., 10; United States Office of Copyright, Richard Durham, *Destination Freedom: Crispus Attucks*, #DP15554—June 27, 1948, and *Destination Freedom: Harriet Tubman*, #DP15555—July 4, 1948, Library of Congress; Durham to Marion, memorandum, 10.

20. Durham to Marion, n.d., Durham Papers, 9.

21. Vernon Jarrett interview; G. K. McCorkle to Metz P. Lochard, December 11, 1950, Metz T. P. Lochard Papers, Howard University, Moorland-Spingarn Research Center, Manuscript Department, box 137–1, folder 18; Burns, *Nitty Gritty*, 210.

22. Allen G. Harris to Richard Durham, February 19, 1951, Durham Papers, box 9, folder 2, *Durham v. NBC* (2), 1948–57.

23. Durham to Friedman, February 25, 1951, 1.

24. Ibid., 2.

25. Vernon Jarrett interview.

26. American Business Consultants, *Red Channels*, 2–3, Index of Names 9-160; Dyja, *Third Coast*, 200.

27. Bearden and Henderson, *History of African-American Artists*, 412.

28. Durham to Weaver, March 23, 1951, 10–11.

29. Robert Weaver to Richard Durham, April 25, 1951, Durham Papers, box 6, folder 8.

30. Richard Durham to Langston Hughes, October 8, 1951, Hughes Papers box 57, folder 1089; Clarice Durham interview, 2010.

31. Vernon Jarrett interview.

32. Roger Horowitz, "The Limits of Social Democratic Unionism in Midwestern Meatpacking Communities," in Stromquist and Berman, *Unionizing the Jungles*, 142.

33. Ibid.

34. Russell Lasley to Bookkeeping Department, memorandum, January 7, 1952, United Packinghouse, Food and Allied Workers of America Papers, Wisconsin Historical Society box 346, folder 16 (hereinafter the UPWA Papers).

35. Halpern, *Down on the Killing Floor*, 8.

36. Jablonsky, *Pride in the Jungle*, 10–11; Herbst, *Negro*, 3.

37. Herbst, *Negro*, 4.

38. Leslie F. Orear interview, 2009; Jablonsky, *Pride in the Jungle*, 16.

39. "Number of Workers and Number of Establishments in Industries under UPWA Jurisdiction by County," March 15, 1953, UPWA Papers, MSS 118, box 373, folder 10.

40. Halpern, *Down on the Killing Floor*, 21–23, 28; Horowitz, *Negro and White*, 23–24, 61–64.

41. Horowitz, *Negro and White*, 4.

42. Addie Wyatt interview, 2001; Horowitz, *Negro and White*, 165.

43. Halpern, *Down on the Killing Floor*, 16–17, 21, 23.

44. Horowitz, *Negro and White*, 24, 94.

45. Rosie Simpson interview, 2007; Horowitz, *Negro and White*, 94.

46. Horowitz, *Negro and White*, 124–26.

47. Leslie F. Orear interview, 2009.

48. Horowitz, *Negro and White*, 171; Robinson, *Marching with Dr. King*, 68–69.

49. Halpern, *Down on the Killing Floor*, 237–38; "Survey and Analysis of UPWA Human Relations Survey—Kansas City Area, conducted by Fisk University," UPWA Papers, box 350, folder 10; Robinson, *Marching with Dr. King*, 79.

50. "Supreme Court of the State of New York, County of New York, Richard Durham, Plaintiff against National Broadcasting Company, Defendant, June 2, 1952, Durham Papers, box 9, folder 3.

51. Clarice Durham interview, 2011; Oscar Brown Jr. interview.

52. Earl Durham interview, 2000; Oscar Brown Jr. interview.

53. Richard Durham, *Action against Jim Crow*, n.d., UPWA Papers box 347, folder 13, p. 1.

54. Horowitz, *Negro and White*, 12.

55. Durham, *Action against Jim Crow*, 2–3.

56. Ibid., 4.

57. Ibid., 6, 10.

58. Leslie F. Orear interview; Oscar Brown Jr. interview.

59. "Call to the First National A-D Conference," n.d., UPWA Papers box 454, folder 7; UPWA Anti-Discrimination Department 1952–1954: Report of Vice President Lasley, n.d., UPWA Papers box 342, folder 11; "Packinghouse Conference Tackles Plant Discrimination," *Federated Press*, November 2, 1953, UPWA Papers box 454, folder 7, p. 1.

60. Ralph Helstein to Russell R. Lasley, Memorandum, August 30, 1952, UPWA Papers, box 346, folder 16; Robinson, *Marching with Dr. King*, 84–85.

61. Russell Lasley to Ralph Helstein, October 9, 1952, UPWA Papers, box 346, folder 16; Robinson, *Marching with Dr. King*, 85.

62. Richard Durham to Ralph Helstein, memorandum, February 25, 1954, UPWA Papers box 350 folder 18.

63. Russell Lasley to Hathaway and Uchihara, memorandum, March 31, 1953, UPWA Papers box 351, folder 13.

64. Ibid.; Clarice Durham interview, 2010.

65. Ibid.

66. Ibid.

67. Clarice Durham and Marguerite Davis interview, 2010.

68. Leslie F. Orear interview.

69. Gilyard, *John Oliver Killens*, 110–11; Richard Durham to John Oliver Killens, October 12, 1954, Manuscripts, Archives and Rare Books Library, Emory University; John Oliver Killens Papers box 2, folder 8.

70. Leslie F. Orear interview.

71. Richard Durham to Harold H. Lasley, November 30, 1953, UPWA Papers box 350, folder 19.

72. Leslie F. Orear interview.

73. Richard Durham to Ralph Helstein, memorandum, November 19, 1954, UPWA Papers box 367, folder 20.

74. Leslie F. Orear interview.

75. Richard Durham to Ralph Helstein (re: Jomo Kenyatta), memorandum, August 21, 1953, UPWA Papers, box 351, folder 1; Durham to Earl B. Dickerson, August 12, 1953, UPWA Papers box 350, folder 8; Durham to Studs Terkel, April 30, 1953, UPWA Papers box 351, folder 1; Durham to Mordecai Johnson, UPWA Papers box 350, folder 8.

76. Addie Wyatt interview.

77. Green, *Selling the Race*, 196; "Summary Fact Sheet of the Emmett Till Lynch Case," n.d., UPWA Papers, box 369, folder 7, 1.

78. Rosie Simpson interview.

79. Press release from Delegation of Women of the UPWA-CIO, Louisiana, September 23, 1955, UPWA Papers box 369, folder 7; Summary Fact Sheet of the Emmett Till Lynch Case, n.d., UPWA Papers box 369, folder 7, p. 2.

80. John "Jack" Telfer to Richard Durham, September 21, 1955, UPWA Papers box 369 folder 7, p. 1; Telfer to Mr. Richard Durham, September 23, 1955, UPWA Papers box 369 folder 7, p. 1.

81. Press Release, September 23, 1955, from Delegation of Women of the UPWA-CIO, Louisiana, UPWA Papers box 369, folder 7.

82. Richard Durham to Mrs. Lillian Pittman, October 22, 1955, UPWA Papers box 369, folder 7; Durham to Mrs. Alvin Vicknair, October 22, 1955, UPWA Papers box 369, folder 7.

83. Green, *Selling the Race*, 181.

84. Report to the Membership on Political Action, Education, Anti-Discrimination, Women's Activities and Farm-Labor, n.d., UPWA Papers, box 347, folder 13—Proceedings, p. 11.

85. Branch, *Parting the Waters*, 128–29.

86. Proceedings: The Montgomery, Ala. Bus Boycott Conference, February 13, 1956, UPWA Papers box 366, folder 3, p. 1.

87. Branch, *Parting the Waters*, 139–41.

88. Proceedings, February 13, 1956, 1.

89. Ibid.; Branch, *Parting the Waters*, 146.

90. Proceedings, February 13, 1956, 1; Halberstam, *Children*, 325; Belafonte and Shnayerson, *My Song*, 171–72.

91. Proceedings, February 13, 1956, 2.

92. Ibid., 2

93. Matthew Nichter, August 23, 2013, email, Sanford University, Martin Luther King Jr. Papers Project, December 8, 1955, accessed March 10, 2014, http://mlk-kpp01.stanford.edu/primarydocuments/Vol3/8-Dec-1955_ToNationalCityLines.pdf.

94. Report to the Membership on Political Action, Education, Anti-Discrimination, Women's Activities and Farm-Labor, n.d., UPWA Papers box 347, folder 13—Proceedings, p. 11.

95. Addie Wyatt interview.

96. Report to the Membership, UPWA Papers, box 347, folder 13, p. 193.

97. William Rossmoore to David Rothstein, Esq., Durham Papers, box 9, folder 9-1, *Durham vs. NBC* (1) 1946–56; press release "Negro Writer Sues NBC for $250,000," Durham Papers, box 9, folder 1, *Durham vs. NBC* (3) 1943–1978, p. 1.

98. William Rossmoore to Richard Durham, March 21, 1955, Durham Papers, box 9, folder 9-2.

99. Richard Durham to William Rossmoore, March 30, 1955, Richard Durham Papers, box 9, folder 9.

100. Clarice Durham interview, 2011.

101. Ibid.; Mark Durham interview, 2010.

102. Oscar Brown Jr. interview.

103. Horowitz, *Negro and White*, 235–36.

104. Oscar Brown Jr. interview.

105. Horowitz, *Negro and White*, 235.

106. Leslie F. Orear interview.

107. Earl Durham interview, 2002.

108. Leslie F. Orear interview; Oscar Brown Jr. interview.

109. Russell Lasley to Richard Durham, memorandum, March 11, 1957, UPWA Papers, box 38, folder 6.

Chapter 9. Empowerment

1. Richard Durham, "Sweet Cherries in Charleston," *CBS Radio Workshop*, August 25, 1957, audio CD in Durham Papers, box 19, AV 2; Richard Durham, "Sweet Cherries in Charleston," *CBS Radio Workshop*, Free Download and Streaming: Internet Archive, accessed December 18, 2014, https://ia600400.us.archive.org/32/items/CBSRadio Workshop/CBSrw_57-08-25_ep82-Sweet_Cherries_in_Charleston.mp3.

2. Rose Simpson interview; Oscar Brown Jr. interview; Clotilde Smith interview; Richard Durham, "On the Death of Union Officials in the 'Movement,'" Notes on the Union Conflicts and Characters, Durham Papers, box 6, folder 10.

3. Robert Davis to Langston Hughes, April 11, 1957, Hughes Papers, JWJ MSS 26, box 53, folder 985.

4. Oscar Brown Jr. interview.

5. Frank Chorba, "Columbia Workshop," in Godfrey and Leigh, *Historical Dictionary of American Radio*, 86; Dunning, *On the Air*, 144.

6. Richard Durham, "The Heart of a Man," *CBS Radio Workshop*, August 4, 1957, audio CD in Durham Papers, box 19, AV 1; Durham, "Sweet Cherries in Charleston."

7. Richard Durham, "The Heart of the Man," show credits, *CBS Radio Workshop*, accessed December 18, 2014, https://ia600400.us.archive.org/32/items/CBSRadioWorkshop/CBSrw_57-08-04_ep79-The_Heart_of_the_Man.mp3; Durham Papers, box 19, AV 1.

8. Durham, "Sweet Cherries in Charleston," show credits, *CBS Radio Workshop*, accessed December 18, 2014, https://ia600400.us.archive.org/32/items/CBSRadioWorkshop/CBSrw_57-08-25_ep82-Sweet_Cherries_in_Charleston.mp3; Durham Papers, box 19, AV 2.

9. Durham with MacDonald, 1980.

10. Clarice Durham interview, 2011; Robert Davis to Langston Hughes, August 6, 1958, Hughes Papers box 53, folder 985, Davis 1957–58, p. 3.

11. "On the Novel *A la the Union*, Notes on the Union Conflicts and Characters," n.d., Durham Papers, box 6, folder 10, p. 1.

12. "Of the Inner Union Conflict," Notes on the Union, n.d., Durham Papers, box 6, folder 10, p. 1.

13. Timuel Black interview, 2002.

14. Richard Durham to Clotilde Durham, n.d., Durham Papers, box 6, folder 6.

15. Halberstam, *Children*, 83; Branch, *Parting the Waters*, 271.

16. Ibid., 275; Williams, *Eyes on the Prize*, 127.

17. Halberstam, *Children*, 260–62.

18. Branch, *Parting the Waters*, 779; Williams, *Eyes on the Prize*, 190–91.

19. Williams, *Eyes on the Prize*, last page (unnumbered).

20. Elijah Muhammad, "What the Black Muslims Believe," *Negro Digest*, November 1963, 3; "A Historic Look at the Most Honorable Elijah Muhammad," Nation of Islam, 2014, accessed December 17, 2014, http://www.noi.org/about_the_honorable_elijah_muhammad.shtml.

21. Elijah Muhammad, "The Coming and Presence of the Son of Man," *Pittsburgh Courier*, November 16, 1957; Clegg, *Original Man*, 45.

22. Clegg, *Original Man*, 159; Kimberly Stanley, "Dan Burley," in Tracy, *Writers*, 147.

23. Brenetta Howell Barrett interview, 2007; Earl Durham interviews, 2000, 2002.

24. Earl Durham interviews, 2000, 2002; Clotilde Durham Smith interview.

25. Muhammad, "What the Black Muslims Believe," 5.

26. Clegg, *Original Man*, 6, 20–23.

27. Ernest Allen Jr., "Religious Heterodoxy and Nationalist Tradition: The Continuing Evolution of the Nation of Islam," *Black Scholar* 26, no. 3–4 (Fall 1996/Winter 1997): 2.

28. Clegg, *Original Man*, 114–15.

29. Katherine Dunham, "Revolt in Green Pastures," April 24, 1939, United States Works Projects Administration Records, Negro Studies Project, FWP/LOC, box A 879, folder—Chicago Contemporary Culture, Social and Benevolent Organizations, p. 4.

30. Elijah Muhammad, "Mr. Muhammad Speaks: 'Who is the Original Man?'" *Pittsburgh Courier*, July 28, 1956; Muhammad, "What the Black Muslims Believe," 4; "The Muslim Program (Wants and Beliefs)," *Nation of Islam*, 2014, accessed December 14, 2014, http://www.noi.org/about_beliefs_and_wants.shtml; Clegg, *Original Man*, 45–46.

31. Clegg, *Original Man*, 49–51.

32. Dunham, "Revolt in Green Pastures," 4.

33. Lincoln, *Black Muslims in America*, 2.

34. Darryl Cowherd interview.

35. *Muhammad Speaks*, December 1961, front page.

36. Maureen Smith, "Muhammad Speaks and Muhammad Ali: Intersections of the Nation of Islam and Sport in the 1960s," *International Sports Studies 1999–2000* 22, no. 1, p. 64.

37. Earl Durham interview, 2002.

38. Ibid.

39. Brenetta Howell Barrett interview.

40. Lincoln, *Black Muslims in America*, 124; Evanzz, *Messenger*, 221; Elijah Muhammad, "Mr. Muhammad Speaks," *Pittsburgh Courier*, July 7, 1956.

41. Askia Muhammad interview; Evanzz, *Messenger*, 173.

42. Clegg, *Original Man*, 27.

43. Ghayth Nur Kashif interview; *Mr. Muhammad Speaks* 1, no. 1 (May 1960): 1–11; Clegg, *Original Man*, 116;

44. Askia Muhammad interview.

45. Clarice Durham interviews, 1999, 2011; John Woodford, "Testing America's Promise of Free Speech: Muhammad Speaks in the 1960s; A Memoir," *Voices of the African Diaspora: the CAAS Research Review* 7 (Fall 1991): 9.

46. Brenetta Howell Barrett interview; "Savage, Gus: U.S. House of Representatives, History, Art and Archives," accessed December 18, 2014, http://history.house.gov/People/Detail/21235?ret=True.

47. Brenetta Howell Barrett interview.

48. John Woodford interview.

49. Brenetta Howell Barrett interview.

50. Darryl Cowherd interview.

51. Ibid.

52. Brenetta Howell Barrett interview.

53. Forrest, *Furious Voice for Freedom*, 87.

54. John Woodford interview.

55. Forrest, *Furious Voice for Freedom*, 88.

56. John Ali to Richard Durham, April 15, 1963, Clarice Durham personal files, 1.

57. Elijah Muhammad to Richard Durham, April 19, 1963, Clarice Durham personal files, 1.

58. Inside COINTELPRO, "COINTELPRO: The U.S. Government's War Against Dissent" Nation of Islam's official Web site, accessed December 18, 2014, http://www.noi.org/cointelpro.

59. Caldwell Durham interview.

60. Clegg, *Original Man*, 258–59.

61. Brenetta Howell Barrett interview.

62. Joseph, *Dark Days, Bright Nights*, 54; Smith, "Muhammad Speaks and Muhammad Ali," 64; Askia Muhammad interview.

63. Askia Muhammad interview.

64. Ali with Durham, *The Greatest*, 206.

65. Muhammad, *Muhammad Speaks*, October 15, 1962, 9; Smith, "Muhammad Speaks and Muhammad Ali," 56–57.

66. Earl Durham interview, 2000; Allen, "Religious Heterodoxy," 15.

67. "John F. Kennedy," The White House, accessed July 18, 2013, http://www.whitehouse.gov/about/presidents/johnfkennedy.

68. Muhammad, "Muhammad on President Kennedy, Nation Still Mourns Death," *Muhammad Speaks*, December 20, 1963, 1; Marable, *Malcolm X*, 312; Clegg, *Original Man*, 200; "Blast Kennedy on Bias in America, North and South," *Muhammad Speaks*, April 15, 1963, 20.

69. Marable, *Malcolm X*, 315–16; Clegg, *Original Man*, 200.

70. Ibid., 202; Muhammad, "Mr. Muhammad's Statement on the President's Death," *Muhammad Speaks*, December 20, 1963, 3.

71. Earl Durham interview, 2002.

72. Minister Philbert, "Malcolm Exposed by His Brother," *Muhammad Speaks*, April 10, 1964, 3; Minister Lewis, "Minister Who Knew Him Best, Rips Malcolm's Treachery, Defection," *Muhammad Speaks*, May 8, 1964, 13; Brother Jeremiah X and Brother Joseph X, "Biography of a Hypocrite by Two Muslim Brothers Who Knew Him Best," *Muhammad Speaks*, September 25, 1964, 16; Muhammad, "Beware of False Prophets," *Muhammad Speaks*, July 31, 1964, 1, 3.

73. "Sees Upsurge in Black Population of Chicago," *Muhammad Speaks*, July 31, 1964, 4; Charles P. Howard Sr., "What You Can't Do as a Black African in South Rhodesia," *Muhammad Speaks*, August 1, 1963, 24; "A Strike for Freedom on the High Seas," *Muhammad Speaks*, February 14, 1964, 15.

74. Muhammad to Durham, September 18, 1964, Clarice Durham personal files, 1.

75. Minister Louis X, "Boston Minister Tells of Malcolm—Muhammad's Biggest Hypocrite," *Muhammad Speaks*, December 4, 1964, 11–15.

76. Earl Durham interview, 2000.

77. Clarice Durham interview, 2011.

78. Elijah Muhammad to Richard Durham, May 4, 1965, Clarice Durham personal files.

79. Langston Hughes, "Simple Solution to Viet Nam War: Draft All Older White Men First," *Muhammad Speaks*, August 20, 1965, Hughes Papers, JWJ MSS 26, box 423, folder 9297, p. 17.

80. Karnow, *Vietnam*, 26.

81. Gitlin, *Sixties*, 242.

82. "American Adventure in Viet Nam a Desperate and Despicable Act," *Muhammad Speaks*, March 17, 1967, 5; "Negroes Beginning to Ask: Why Should Blacks be Cannon Fodder in Devil's Unholy Viet War?" *Muhammad Speaks*, April 14, 1967, 7.

83. Mark Durham interview, 2002; "250 Top Students Awarded 4-Year College Scholarships," *Chicago Defender*, February 8, 1966, 21; "Scholarships Announced," *Chicago Defender*, February 19, 1966, 36.

84. Durham interview with MacDonald, 1975.

85. Muhammad to Durham, September 18, 1964, Clarice Durham personal files.

86. Edward "Buzz" Palmer, author interview, December 15, 2007; Forrest, *Furious Voice for Freedom*, 90.

87. Forrest, *Furious Voice for Freedom*, 90.

88. John Woodford interview; Lawson, *Theory and Technique*; Plekhanov, *Role of the Individual*, preface, 5, 23.

89. John Woodford interview.

90. Darryl Cowherd interview; Edward "Buzz" Palmer interview.

91. Forrest, *Furious Voice for Freedom*, 86–87.

92. Darryl Cowherd interview.

93. "On the Death of John Coltrane," *Muhammad Speaks*, April 28, 1967, 21.

94. Rampersad, *Life of Langston Hughes*, 2:423.

95. Neimark, "Man Who Knew," 24.

96. Caldwell Durham interview.

97. John Woodford interview.

98. Rose Jennings interview.

99. Robert Sengstacke interview.

100. John Woodford interview.

101. Darryl Cowherd interview.

102. John Woodford interview.

103. Darryl Cowherd interview.

104. Rose Jennings interview.

105. Ibid.; John Woodford interview; Ghayth Nur Kashif interview; Rose Jennings interview.

106. Von Eschen, *Race against Empire*, 174.

107. Muhammad to Durham, September 18, 1964, 1.

108. Smethurst, *Black Arts Movement*, 181.

109. Ghayth Nur Kashif interview.

110. Lonnie 2X, "Sterilization Clinics Built for the Murder of the Black Unborn," *Muhammad Speaks*, October 13, 1967, 5–6, 22; "Birth Control," *Muhammad Speaks*, January 24, 1969, July 4, 1969, August 29, 1969.

111. John Woodford interview.

112. Gitlin, *Sixties*, 298; Karnow, *Vietnam*, 528–30.

113. Branch, *At Canaan's Edge*, 767.

114. "To the Family of Dr. Martin Luther King, Jr.," *Muhammad Speaks*, April 12 and 19, 1968, 3.

115. Alex Carruthers, "Dr. Martin L. King on Dixie Hot Seat, Denies Switch to New Ideology," *Muhammad Speaks*, February 1962, 10.

116. Earl Durham interview, 2002; "Martin Luther King Jr.: King Writes of Reasons Triggering Big City Riots," *Muhammad Speaks*, October 9, 1964, 12; "Muhammad, King Meet on Eve of Savior's Day," *Muhammad Speaks*, March 4, 1966, 3.

117. Witcover, *Year the Dream Died*, 253–59.

118. Ibid., 327–28.

119. Ibid., 187–90.

120. Clotilde Durham Smith interview; Mark Durham interview, 2010.

121. Woodford, "Testing America's Promise," 9.

122. Ibid.

Chapter 10. Struggling to Fly

1. Richard Durham," Jonah and the Whales," *Bird of the Iron Feather*, n.d., script in Durham Papers, box 10, folder 2, pp. 11–13.

2. "WTTW/Channel 11 News," press release, July 30, 1969, Ford Foundation records, Public Broadcasting, FA687, Television Grant Files, Series I, box 1, folder "Illinois, Chicago WTTW, 1968," Rockefeller Archives Center, 1 (hereinafter Rockefeller Archives Center).

3. Durham interview with MacDonald, 1975; Earl Durham interview, 2002.

4. Abena Joan Brown interview, 2002.

5. Barnouw, *Tube of Plenty*, 300; MacDonald, *Blacks and White TV*, 84.

6. "Bird(s) of the Iron Feather," Newton N. Minow interview segment, Archive of American Television, Emmy TV Legends, accessed July 15, 2013, http://www.emmytvlegends .org/interviews/shows/birds-of-the-iron-feather.

7. Gibson, *30 Billion Dollar Negro*, 24–25.

8. Bogle, *Prime Time Blues*, 93.

9. Williams, *Eyes on the Prize*, 285.

10. MacDonald, *Blacks and White TV*, 119–21; Bogle, *Prime Time Blues*, 115, 125.

11. Bogle, *Prime Time Blues*, 119–20.

12. Ibid., 126–29, 130–36.

13. Ibid., 141, 144–46; Donald Bogle, *Brown Sugar*, 150.

14. MacDonald, *Blacks and White TV*, 117, 124; Bogle, *Prime Time Blues*, 141, 144–46.

15. Robert Cross, "Proud Bird with a Black, Blunt Tale," *Chicago Tribune Magazine*, March 1, 1970.

16. Chicago Educational Television Association (CETA) to the Ford Foundation, "Project for New Television Programming, Program Proposal," category 1, October 1968, Rockefeller Archives Center, 1.

17. Howard R. Dressner to McGeorge Bundy, memorandum, March 21, 1969, Rockefeller Archives Center, 2.

18. CETA, "Project for New Television Programming, Program Proposal," Rockefeller Archives Center, 1.

19. Judith Michaelson, "Latinos Take Exception to KCET Hiring," September 24, 1989, *Los Angeles Times*, accessed December 17, 2014, http://articles.latimes.com/1989-09-24/entertainment/ca-411_1_latino-community; Dressner to Bundy, memorandum, 2–3; Trevino, *Eyewitness*, 116.

20. CETA, "Project for New Television Programming," Attachment A, October 1968, Rockefeller Archives Center, 1.

21. "Bird of the Iron Feather: A Report to the Ford Foundation," n.d., Rockefeller Archives Center, 1.

22. Ibid.

23. WTTW/Channel 11 *News*, for immediate release, July 30, 1969, Rockefeller Archives Center, 1.

24. Ibid.; Richard Durham, *Bird of the Iron Feather*, United States Office of Copyright, #EU154749, December 29, 1969.

25. WTTW/Channel 11 *News*, Rockefeller Archives Center, 1.

26. Witcover, *Year the Dream Died*, 276.

27. Ibid., 472.

28. Mark Durham interview, 2002; Edward "Buzz" Palmer interview; Renault Robinson interview.

29. Renault Robinson interview.

30. "Biographical/Historical Note in African American Police League, Chicago, Ill.," AAPL Records, Chicago History Museum, 2005; "Power, Politics and Pride: Afro-American Patrolmen's League," *DuSable to Obama: Chicago's Black Metropolis*—WTTW, accessed January 10, 2013, http://www.wttw.com/main.taf?p=76,3.

31. Renault Robinson interview.

32. Edward "Buzz" Palmer, "Precinct/District Life," part 3, chapter 4, Alice and Edward Palmer Papers, Vivian G. Harsh Research Collection, Chicago Public Library, box 1, untitled folder, 3.

33. Renault Robinson interview.

34. "Bird of the Iron Feather Character List and Description of Characters," n.d., Durham Papers, box 7, folder 15, pp. 1–4.

35. "Bird of the Iron Feather," section 1-A, n. d., Durham Papers, box 7, folder 16, p. 1.

36. Ibid., 2–12.

37. Edward "Buzz" Palmer interview; Renault Robinson interview.

38. Cross, "Proud Bird"; "Bird of the Iron Feather: A Report to the Ford Foundation," 1.

39. "Bird of the Iron Feather: A Report to the Ford Foundation," 1.

40. Harold C. Johnson interview.

41. Ibid.; Committee on Communications Media, Member List, Ford Foundation Archives, 1; Edward L. Morris to David M. Davis, November 7, 1969, Rockefeller Archives Center, 3.

42. United States Commission on Civil Rights, "Window Dressing on the Set: Women and Minorities in Television; A Report of the United States Commission on Civil Rights" (Washington, D.C.: University of California Libraries reprint, 1977), 115–16, 126–30.

43. Ira Rogers interview.

44. Ibid.

45. Harold Johnson interview.

46. Ibid.

47. Agreement for "More from My Life, WTTW-Channel 11/WXXW-Channel 20, Chicago Educational Television Association, Rockefeller Archives Center, 2–3; Morris to Davis, November 7, 1969, 1.

48. Harold Johnson interview.

49. John Woodford interview.

50. Ira Rogers interview.

51. Harold Lee Rush Jr. interview.

52. Statement of Edward L. Morris to Black Coalition Sub-Committee, October 27, 1969, Ford Foundation Archives, 1–2; Morris to Davis, November 7, 1969, 3; "Statement from the Management of the Chicago Educational Television Association Regarding 'Bird of the Iron Feather,'" March 9, 1970, Rockefeller Archives Center, 2.

53. Harold Johnson interview.

54. Cross, "Proud Bird."

55. Statement of Edward L. Morris to Black Coalition Sub-Committee, 1.

56. John Woodford interview.

57. Elijah Muhammad to Richard Durham, September 23, 1969, Durham Papers, box 6, folder 5.

58. Ibid.

59. John Woodford interview.

60. Ibid.

61. "In Television Today Everything Is White," *Life*, n.d., accessed January 15, 2013, http://whgbetc.com/iron/lifemag2.html; Clarice Durham interview, 2011.

62. Edward L. Morris to Davis M. Davis, November 7, 1969, Rockefeller Archives Center, 3; William H. Nims, Assistant Secretary, Ford Foundation, to Dr. John W. Taylor, Executive Director, Chicago Educational TV Association, November 25, 1969, Rockefeller Archives Center.

63. "Bird of the Iron Feather: A Report to the Ford Foundation," 1–2.

64. Cross, "Proud Bird."

65. Clarice Durham interview, 1999.

66. Mark Durham interview, 2002.

67. Lewis, *Power Stronger than Itself*, 170.

68. Mark Durham interview, 2002.

69. Clarice Durham interview, 2001.

70. Mark Durham interview, 2002.

71. *Bird of the Iron Feather*, show credits, January 14 and 29, 1970, Richard Durham's Destination Freedom: Home, Additional A-V Materials, accessed June 30, 2013, http://www.jfredmacdonald.com/rddf/index.htm.

72. "TV Highlight: Richard Durham to Pen TV Series," *Chicago Defender*, August 5, 1969, 10; Faith Christmas, "Television Black Bird Is Ready to Fly," *Chicago Defender*, October 22, 1969, 27.

73. Clarence Petersen, "TV Today: Paar, Lions Entertain in Special," *Chicago Tribune*, September 9, 1969; "Black Serial Getting Ready for Takeoff," *Chicago Sun-Times*, December 9, 1960; Louise Pruitt Dumetz Hodges interview.

74. Clarice Durham interview, 2011.

75. Ibid.

76. Peterson, "TV Today: New Series Is Soap with a Difference," *Chicago Tribune*, January 19, 1970.

77. Richard Durham, *Bird of the Iron Feather*, "Chapter 1: Prescription for Pallbearers," n.d., script in Durham Papers, box 10, folder 3.

78. Norman Mark, "Birth of the Bird New Soap Opera Will Be Blacker and More Soulful than Anything Else on TV," *Chicago Daily News*, January 17–18, 1970.

79. Neil L. Clemons, "Slice of Ghetto Life: New Black Soap Opera Draws Mixed Reviews," *Wall Street Journal*, January 26, 1970.

80. "Soul Drama," *Time* in partnership with CNN, February 23, 1970, accessed January 11, 2013, http://bird.whgbetc.com; "The Media: Soul Opera," *Newsweek*, February 23, 1970, 68.

81. Cross, "Proud Bird."

82. "Cry of the Silent," chapter 7, n.d., script in Durham Papers, box 10, folder 5, p. 25.

83. "The Sermon," n.d., script in Durham Papers, box 7, folder, 23, p. 20.

84. Ibid., 23.

85. "Chapter VI: Speaking of Dreams," n.d., script in Durham Papers, box 7, folder, 18, p. 27.

86. Mark, "Birth of the Bird."

87. "Bird of the Iron Feather: A Report to the Ford Foundation," 2, 24.

88. "Chapter 3: Jonah and the Whales," n.d., script in Durham Papers, box 10, folder 2, p. 27.

89. "Jonah 2:10," *Holy Bible* (Cleveland, Ohio: World, n.d.), 565.

90. Mark Durham interview, 2002.

91. Ted Gregory, "The Black Panther Raid and the Death of Fred Hampton," *Chicago Tribune*, December 4, 1969, accessed March 3, 2013, http://www.chicagotribune.com/news/politics/chi-chicagodays-pantherraid-story,0,3414208.story; Susan Rutberg, "Nothing but a Northern Lynching: The Death of Fred Hampton Revisited," March 18, 2010 (updated May 25, 2011), accessed March 3, 2013, http://www.huffingtonpost.com/susan-rutberg/nothing-but-a-northern-ly_b_355670.html.

92. Gitlin, *Sixties*, 350.

93. Joseph, *Dark Days, Bright Nights*, 135; *A Huey P. Newton Story*, PBS, 2002, accessed March 10, 2013, http://www.pbs.org/hueypnewton/actions/actions_formation.html; Charles E. Jones and Judson L. Jeffries, "Don't Believe the Hype": Debunking the Panther Mythology, in Jones, *Black Panther Party*, 27–29.

94. Ibid. 30.

95. "The Target," n.d., script in Durham Papers, box 10, folder 9.

96. Ibid., 32–33.

97. Renault Robinson interview.

98. Bloom and Martin, *Black against Empire*, 246.

99. Renault Robinson interview.

100. Durham interview with MacDonald, 1980.

101. Statement from the Management of the Chicago Educational Television Association Regarding "Bird of the Iron Feather," March 9, 1970, Rockefeller Archives Center, 5.

102. Clarence Petersen, "Why WTTW's 'Soul Series' Expired," *Chicago Tribune*, March 9, 1970.

103. Frank Santos, "Iron Bird's Wings Clipped," *Chicago Daily Defender*, February 26, 1970, 4.

104. Petersen, "Why WTTW's Soul Series Expired," 16; CETA, Project for New Television Programming, Program Budget Proposal, November 7, 1969, Rockefeller Archives Center, 1.

105. Durham interview with MacDonald, 1975.

106. Renault Robinson interview.

107. Abena Joan Brown interview.

108. Marie Brookter to Edward Morris, Memorandum, March 4, 1970, Rockefeller Archives Center; Santos, "Iron Bird's Wings Clipped," 4.

109. Statement from the Management of the Chicago Educational Television Association Regarding "Bird of the Iron Feather," Rockefeller Archives Center, 4–5.

110. Mark Durham interview.

Chapter 11. Globetrotting with The Greatest

1. Ali with Durham, *The Greatest,* 172, 174.

2. Clarice Durham interview, 1999.

3. Neimark, "Man Who Knows," 24.

4. Ali with Durham, *The Greatest,* 11; Hauser, *Muhammad Ali,* 14.

5. Remnick, *King,* 102.

6. Schaap, "Muhammad Ali Then and Now," in Kimball and Schulian, *At the Fights,* 210.

7. Ali with Durham, *The Greatest,* 106.

8. Ibid., 108–9.

9. Ibid., 12.

10. Ibid., 108.

11. Neimark, "Man Who Knows," 25.

12. Remnick, *King,* 149.

13. Ibid., 113.

14. Remnick, *King,* 180.

15. Hauser, *Muhammad Ali,* 69, 71.

16. Remnick, *King,* 190–94, 198–99.

17. Ibid., 205–8; Hauser, *Muhammad Ali,* 82–83; Ali with Durham, *The Greatest,* 204–5, 212.

18. Ali with Durham, *The Greatest,* 206.

19. Ibid., 202–3; Remnick, *King*, 209–12.

20. Durham interview with MacDonald, 1975; Ali with Durham, *The Greatest*, 12–13.

21. George Plimpton, "Miami Notebook: Cassius Clay and Malcolm X," in Kimball and Schulian, *At the Fights*, 190.

22. Ibid.

23. Neimark, "Man Who Knows," 28.

24. Hauser, *Muhammad Ali*, 172, 179.

25. Ibid., 13.

26. Charles F. Harris interview; Charles F. Harris, "Currents," *Publisher's Weekly*, unpublished, January 19, 1970, 9; History of Random House, accessed June 22, 2013, http://www.fundinguniverse.com/company-histories/random-house-inc-history.

27. Charles F. Harris interview.

28. Ibid.; Harris, "Currents," 10; Neimark, "Man Who Knows," 24.

29. "Ali Has a 'Different' Fight in Germany," *Chicago Defender*, October 13, 1975, 26.

30. Earl Durham interviews, 2002, 2000.

31. Durham interview with MacDonald, 1975.

32. Robert Lipsyte, "'I Don't Have to Be What You Want Me to Be,' Says Muhammad Ali," *New York Times*, March 7, 1971.

33. Neimark, "Man Who Knows," 22.

34. Ibid.

35. Caldwell Durham interview; Clotilde Durham Smith interview.

36. Clarice Durham interview, 2011.

37. Chanie Durham, "Excerpts from the Valedictory Speech of Chanie Durham."

38. Caldwell Durham interview.

39. "Bird of the Iron Feather Press," *Jet*, September 1970, accessed June 26, 2013, http://whgbetc.com/iron/press.html.

40. Chicago Emmy online files, 1969–1970, accessed June 26, 2013, http://chicagoemmyonline.org/files/2013/04/1969–1970.pdf.

41. Robert F. Fuzy to David M. Davis, November 3, 1970, Ford Foundation, Rockefeller Archives Center, 1; John C. Rahmann to Howard R. Dressner, October 19, 1972, Ford Foundation, Rockefeller Archives Center; "Mail Copy TWX Message #731 Memo to All Stations, 8/18/71," Ford Foundation, Rockefeller Archives Center.

42. Clarice Durham interview, 2011; Charles F. Harris interview.

43. "Toni Morrison Receives Presidential Medal of Freedom," accessed December 19, 2014, http://www.princeton.edu/main/news/archive/S33/55/59O8; Toni Morrison Biographical, accessed June 22, 2013, http://www.nobelprize.org/nobel_prizes/literature/laureates/1993/morrison-bio.html.

44. Toni Morrison interview; Morrison, *Bluest Eye*.

45. Toni Morrison interview.

46. Ibid.

47. Neimark, "Man Who Knows," 26.

48. Hauser, *Muhammad Ali*, 208; Ali with Durham, *The Greatest*, 268–74.

49. Ali with Durham, *The Greatest*, 308, 302; Hauser, *Muhammad Ali*, 209.

50. Ali with Durham, *The Greatest*, 314–17.

51. Dave Anderson, "Guess Who Came to Ali's Book Party," *New York Times*, November 13, 1975; Neimark, "Man Who Knows," 26.

52. Neimark, "Man Who Knows," 26.

53. Toni Morrison interview.

54. Ali with Durham, *The Greatest*, 324.

55. Lipsyte, "I Don't Have to Be What You Want Me to Be,' 59.

56. Joe Frazier and Muhammad Ali, audio tape, August 1970, Clarice Durham personal files; Ali with Durham, *The Greatest*, 229–44.

57. Ibid., 245–47.

58. Hauser, *Muhammad Ali*, 219.

59. Ali with Durham, *The Greatest*, 353–55.

60. Ibid., 403–4.

61. Hauser, *Muhammad Ali*, 238–39.

62. Ali with Durham, *The Greatest*, 13.

63. Toni Morrison interview.

64. Neimark, "Man Who Knows," 26; Ali with Durham, *The Greatest*, 183.

65. Ali with Durham, *The Greatest*, 183.

66. Ibid., 200.

67. Toni Morrison interview

68. Biography of Richard Milhous Nixon, Nixon Library, accessed June 26, 2013, http://www.nixonlibrary.gov/thelife/nixonbio.pdf, 4.

69. Durham interview with MacDonald, 1975; Neimark, "Man Who Knows," 26.

70. Neimark, "Man Who Knows," 28.

71. Ibid., 26.

72. Ibid., 28.

73. Ibid., 25.

74. Ali with Durham, *The Greatest*, 18.

75. Ibid.

76. Toni Morrison interview.

77. Bennett Johnson interview, 2002.

78. Richard Durham and Jim Jacobs, audio tape, n.d., Clarice Durham personal files; Bennett Johnson interview, 2002.

79. Hauser, *Muhammad Ali*, 260–63.

80. Mark Durham interview, 2002.

81. Ibid.

82. Hauser, *Muhammad Ali*, 264.

83. Mark Durham interview, 2002.

84. Ibid.

85. Hauser, *Muhammad Ali*, 265.

86. Richard Durham, creative brainstorming in Kinshasa, Zaire, audio tape, n.d., Clarice Durham personal files.

87. Ibid.

88. Mark Durham interview, 2002.

89. Nixon Biography, accessed June 26, 2013, http://www.nixonlibrary.gov/thelife/nixonbio.pdf, 5–6.

90. Hauser, *Muhammad Ali*, 269.

91. Mark Durham interview, 2002.

92. Ibid.

93. Ali with Durham, *The Greatest*, 386.

94. Rose Jennings interview.

95. Hauser, *Muhammad Ali*, 260.

96. Ali with Durham, *The Greatest*, 393.

97. Hauser, *Muhammad Ali*, 271.

98. Ali with Durham, *The Greatest*, 404.

99. Ibid., 406.

100. Hauser, Muhammad Ali, 271.

101. Neimark, "Man Who Knows," 28.

102. Ali with Durham, *The Greatest*, 407.

103. Ibid., 412–13.

104. Ibid., 415.

105. Anderson, "Guess Who Came to Ali's Book Party?" 57.

106. Ismael Reed, "A Palooka He Ain't," *New York Times,* November 30, 1975.

107. Philip E. Borries, "On Dinosaurs, Politics, Money, and Ali's Favorite Subject," *Chicago Tribune,* November 30, 1975.

108. David Shaw, "Ali: Now a Socio-Political Symbol: Two Views of Muhammad Ali," *Los Angeles Times,* December 7, 1975.

109. Ali with Durham, *The Greatest*, 65.

110. Ibid., 69–72.

111. Ibid., 73–76.

112. Remnick, *King,* 89.

113. Ibid., 90.

114. "Ali to Portray Himself in Film," *New York Times,* November 6, 1975; Muhammad Ali to Play Himself in Film," *Chicago Defender,* November 15, 1975.

115. Clarice Durham interview.

116. "Film: Ali's Greatest Isn't," *Harford Courant,* May 27, 1977; Hauser, *Muhammad Ali,* 344; Vincent Canby, "Ali's Latest Victory Is 'The Greatest,'" *New York Times,* May 21, 1977.

117. Neimark, "Man Who Knows," 24.

Chapter 12. Black Political Power

1. Travis, *Harold,* 203–4.

2. Neimark, "Man Who Knows," 28.

3. Clarice Durham interview, 1999; Oscar Brown Jr. interview.

4. Neimark, "Man Who Knows," 28.

5. Durham interview with MacDonald, 1980; Lloyd W. Daley to Mr. [Prichard] Durham, February 8, 1961, in Durham Papers, box 6, folder 6, p. 1.

6. Durham interview with MacDonald, 1975; Neimark, "Man Who Knows," 28.

7. Oscar Brown Jr. interview.

8. Ibid; Clarice Durham interview.

9. "Hannibal Barca," accessed April 25, 2013, http://www.angelfire.com/rebellion/historicalheros/hannibal.html; Robert Fleming, "Hannibal the Hero," *Black Issues Book Review*, January–February 2005, 50–51.

10. Neimark, "Man Who Knows," 29.

11. Charles A. Davis interview.

12. Oscar Brown Jr. interview.

13. Ibid.

14. Durham interview with MacDonald, 1980.

15. Quinn, *The Original Sin*; Bennett Johnson interview; Neimark, "Man Who Knows," 22.

16. Clarice Durham interview, 2011.

17. "Muslim Leader Invests in Fisheries in West Indies Islands," *New York Amsterdam News*, February 7, 1976; Bennett Johnson, "Draft of the Investment Memorandum for the Liberian Gold Project," October 26, 1981, Bennett Johnson Papers, Harsh Research Collection (hereinafter Johnson Papers); Bennett Johnson interview, 2002.

18. Ibid.

19. Ibid.

20. Clarice Durham interview, 2011.

21. Pamela G. Hollie, "Rukmini Sukarno: An Indonesian Christina Onassis?" *New York Times*, December 3, 1977, accessed June 20, 2013, http://query.nytimes.com/mem/archive/pdf?res=F10D17F83D5F127588DDAA0894DA415B878BF1D3.

22. Bennett Johnson interview, 2002.

23. Clarice Durham interview, 2011.

24. Hollie, "Rukmini Sukarno," 29.

25. "Summary of Proposal to Fund the Black Arts Celebration," n.d., Johnson Papers, box Black Arts Celebration, folder BAC Project Draft, p. 1.

26. Levinsohn, *Harold Washington*, 17–18; "Population of the 20 Largest U.S. Cities, 1900–2010," accessed April 29, 2013, http://www.infoplease.com/ipa/A0922422.html.

27. Rivlin, *Fire on the Prairie*, 4, 8.

28. Ibid., 9; Reed, *Depression*, 6.

29. Rivlin, *Fire*, 51; Bennett Johnson interview, 2002; Earl Durham interview, 2002.

30. Conrad Worrill interview; Levinsohn, *Harold Washington*, 91–92; "The Chicago League of Negro Voters," pdf, n.d., accessed June 20, 2013, http://www.google.com/search?client=safari&rls=en&q=Lemuel+E.+Bentley&ie=UTF-8&oe=UTF-8.

31. Conrad Worrill interview; Lenin, *Essential Works*.

32. Conrad Worrill interview.

33. Rivlin, *Fire*, 19.

34. Ibid.; Grimshaw, *Bitter Fruit*, 116; Patricia Sullivan, "Edward V. Hanrahan, 88, Dies: Prosecutor Oversaw Fatal 1969 Raid of Black Panthers in Chicago," *Washington Post*, June 12, 2009, accessed June 5, 2013, http://articles.washingtonpost.com/2009-06-12/news/36827913_1_police-officers-police-tactics-black-panthers.

35. Bennett Johnson interview, 2002.

36. Rivlin, *Fire*, 52.

37. Dickey, PoKempner, and Muwakkil, *Harold!*, 40.

38. Bennett Johnson interview, 2002.

39. Renault Robinson interview; Grimshaw, *Bitter Fruit*, 167; Dickey, PoKempner, and Muwakkil, *Harold!* 51.

40. Renault Robinson interview.

41. Bobby Rush interview; Rivlin, *Fire*, 67.

42. Rivlin, *Fire*, 67.

43. Dickey, PoKempner, and Muwakkil, *Harold!* 51; Rivlin, *Fire*, 58.

44. Clarice Durham interview, 2011.

45. Earl Durham interview, 2000.

46. Clarice Durham interview, 2011

47. Ibid; Renault Robinson interview.

48. Rivlin, *Fire*, 71.

49. Ibid., 75–76; Dickey, PoKempner, and Muwakkil, *Harold!* 55.

50. Ibid., 59.

51. Robert Starks interview, July 2, 2002.

52. Renault Robinson interview.

53. Dickey, PoKempner, and Muwakkil, *Harold!* 64; Renault Robinson interview; Travis, *Harold*, 150–51.

54. Robert Starks interview.

55. Earl Durham interview, 2002.

56. Robert Starks interview; Rivlin, *Fire*, 131–32; Conrad Worrill interview.

57. Renault Robinson interview.

58. Robert Starks interview.

59. Ibid.; Mark Durham interview, 2002.

60. Renault Robinson interview.

61. Rivlin, *Fire*, 54.

62. Rose Jennings interview.

63. James Ralph, "Operation PUSH," *Encyclopedia of Chicago,* 2005, accessed April 25, 2013, http://encyclopedia.chicagohistory.org/pages/934.html; Rainbow PUSH Coalition, "Brief History," accessed April 25, 2013, http://rainbowpush.org/pages/brief_history.

64. Robert Starks interview.

65. Ibid., 140.

66. Robert Starks interview.

67. Ibid.; Rivlin, *Fire*, 140–41.

68. Arthur Daley, "Louis Proves His Own Prediction: Conn Could Run, But Couldn't Hide," *New York Times,* June 20, 1946; "The Brown Bomber's Immortal Words: He Can Run But He Can't Hide," Quote/Counterquote, January 8, 2012, accessed May 10, 2013, http://www.quotecounterquote.com/2012/01/he-can-run-but-he-cant-hide.html.

69. Robert Starks interview.

70. Grimshaw, *Bitter Fruit*, 174.

71. Ibid., 174–76.

72. Ibid.

73. Robert Starks interview.

74. Susan Kubian, "Brezeczek, Here and Now," *Chicago Tribune*, February 21, 1993, accessed December 20, 2014, http://articles.chicagotribune.com/1993-02-21/features/9303183310_1_chicago-police-department-superintendent-position-richard-m-daley.

75. Robert Starks interview.

76. Grimshaw, *Bitter Fruit*, 176.

77. Robert Starks interview; Dickey, PoKempner, and Muwakkil, *Harold!* 90.

78. Ibid., 101; Rivlin, *Fire*, 185.

79. Robert Starks interview.

80. Rivlin, *Fire*, 175; Grimshaw, *Bitter Fruit*, 180.

81. Travis, *Harold*, 191.

82. Dickey, PoKempner, and Muwakkil, *Harold!* 107.

83. Robert Starks interview.

84. Ibid.

85. Dickey, PoKempner, and Muwakkil, *Harold!* 125; Grimshaw 182; Rivlin, *Fire*, 196.

86. Travis, *Harold*, 196.

87. Robert Starks interview; Charles A. Davis interview.

88. Charles A. Davis interview.

89. Ibid; Travis, *Harold*, 203–8.

90. Charles A. Davis interview.

91. Bennett Johnson interview, 2002.

92. Ibid; Clarice Durham interview, 2011.

93. Ibid.

94. Ibid.

95. Ibid.; Mark Durham interview, 2010.

96. Clarice Durham interview, 2011.

97. Ibid.

98. Ibid.; Mark Durham interview, 2010.

99. Mark Durham interview, 2010.

100. Clarice Durham interview, 2011.

101. Ibid.

102. Ibid.

Epilogue

1. Judi Moore Latta interview, January 25, 2013; National Public Radio, "Harriet Tubman," *Destination Freedom*, February 1987, audio CD in Durham Papers, box 19, AV 3.

2. Clarice Durham interview, 1999; MacDonald, *Richard Durham's Destination Freedom*, xiv.

3. Clarice Durham interview, 2011.

4. Donnie L. Betts, "The Poet of Bronzeville: The Story of Gwendolyn Brooks," audio CD featuring Oscar Brown Jr., Fred Pinkard, and Studs Terkel, 2000, *Destination Freedom: Black Radio Days*, accessed March 10, 2013, http://www.blackradiodays.com/praudio3.htm.

5. National Radio Hall of Fame: Richard Durham, 2014, accessed December 19, 2014, http://www.radiohof.org/richard_durham.htm.

6. Museum of Broadcast Communications, National Radio Hall of Fame Induction Ceremony Program, November 3, 2007.

7. "*Destination Freedom*: Free Download and Streaming, Internet Archive," accessed May 2, 2013, http://archive.org/details/DestinationFreedom; CBS Radio Workshop, "The Heart of the Man," and "Sweet Cherries in Charleston," accessed May 2, 2013, http://archive.org/details/OTRR_CBS_Radio_Workshop_Singles; "Richard Durham's Destination Freedom, Additional AV Highlights: *Bird of the Iron Feather*, January 14 and 29, 1970," accessed June 30, 2013, http://www.jfredmacdonald.com/rddf/index.htm.

8. Richard Durham interview with J. Fred MacDonald, 1975, audio CD in Durham Papers, box 19, AV 4; Richard Durham interview with J. Fred MacDonald, 1980, audio CD in Durham Papers, box 19, AV 7; Richard Durham interview by John Dunning, January 16, 1983, audio CD in Durham Papers, box 19, AV 8; "Richard Durham's Destination Freedom, Additional AV Highlights: Richard Durham interviews, 1975 and 1980," accessed July 29, 2013, http://www.jfredmacdonald.com/rddf/index.htm.

9. "Writer Richard Durham: Won Peabody Award," *Chicago Tribune*, May 2, 1984; Earl Calloway, "Set Rites for Richard Durham, Writer," *Chicago Defender*, April 30, 1984, 22; Ali with Durham, *The Greatest*, jacket cover; Neimark, "Man Who Knows," 22; George Foster Peabody Awards, "Who We Are: Message from the Director," 2014, accessed December 19, 2014, http://www.peabodyawards.com/about#originawards.

10. George Foster Peabody Awards, "CBS Radio Institutional Award," 1948, accessed December 19, 2014, http://www.peabodyawards.com/award-profile/cbs-radio-institutional -award-for-outstanding-programming-in-the-promotion.

11. "National Fame, President's Award Mark 'Democracy USA's' First Year," *Chicago Defender*, May 10, 1947, 12.

12. Vernon Jarrett interview; Oscar Brown Jr. interview.

13. Charles A. Davis interview.

14. Martin, *Mind of Frederick Douglass*, 174–75; Quintard Taylor, "The Black Past Remembered and Reclaimed, An Online Reference Guide to African American History," accessed June 23, 2013, http://www.blackpast.org/?q=1857-frederick-douglass-if-there -no-struggle-there-no-progress.

15. Charles A. Davis interview.

16. Ibid.

Bibliography

Ali, Muhammad, with Richard Durham. *The Greatest: My Own Story.* New York: Random House, 1975.

Allen, Ernest, Jr. "Religious Heterodoxy and Nationalist Tradition: The Continuing Evolution of the Nation of Islam." *Black Scholar* 26, no. 34 (1996): 2–34.

Allen, Robert L. *The Port Chicago Mutiny: The Story of the Largest Mass Mutiny Trial in U.S. Naval History.* Berkeley: Heyday, 1993.

American Business Consultants. *Red Channels: The Report of the Communist Influence in Radio and Television.* New York: Counterattack, 1950.

Anderson, James D. *The Education of Blacks in the South, 1960–1935.* Chapel Hill: University of North Carolina Press, 1988.

Badger, Anthony J. *The New Deal: The Depression Years, 1933–1940.* Chicago: Dee, 1989.

Barnouw, Erik. *Radio Drama in Action: Twenty-Five Plays of a Changing World.* New York: Rinehart, 1945.

———. *Tube of Plenty: The Evolution of American Television.* New York: Oxford University Press, 1990.

Bearden, Romare, and Harry Henderson. *A History of African-American Artists: From 1972 to the Present.* New York: Pantheon, 1993.

Belafonte, Harry, with Michael Shnayerson. *My Song: A Memoir.* New York: Knopf, 2011.

Bennett, A. Leroy. *International Organizations.* 2nd ed. Englewood Cliffs, N.J.: Prentice-Hall, 1980.

Best, Wallace. *Passionately Human, No Less Divine: Religion and Culture in Chicago.* Princeton: Princeton University Press, 2013.

Bloom, Joshua, and Waldo E. Martin Jr. *Black against Empire: The History and Politics of the Black Panther Party.* Berkeley: University of California Press, 2013.

Bogle, Donald. *Brown Sugar.* New York: Da Capo, 1980.

———. *Prime Time Blues: African Americans on Network Television.* New York: Farrar, Straus, and Giroux, 2001.

Bone, Robert. "Richard Wright and the Chicago Renaissance," *Callaloo* 28 (Summer 1986): 446–68.

Bone, Robert, and Richard A. Courage. *The Muse in Bronzeville: African American Creative Expression in Chicago, 1932–1950.* New Brunswick, N.J.: Rutgers University Press, 2011.

Bontemps, Arna. "Famous WPA Authors." *Negro Digest,* June 1950, 43–47.

———, ed. *Golden Slippers: An Anthology of Negro Poetry for Young Readers.* New York: Random House, 1941.

Branch, Taylor. *At Canaan's Edge: America in the King Years, 1965–68.* New York: Simon and Schuster, 2006.

———. *Parting the Waters: America in the King Years, 1954–63.* New York: Simon and Schuster, 1988.

Braxton, Joanne M., ed. *The Collected Poetry of Paul Laurence Dunbar.* Charlottesville: University Press of Virginia, 1993.

Brown, Earl. *Why Race Riots? Lessons from Detroit.* Public Affairs Pamphlets 87. New York: Public Affairs Committee, 1944.

Buchanan, A. Russell. *Black Americans in World War II.* Santa Barbara: Clio, 1977.

Bunche, Ralph J. *The Political Status of the Negro in the Age of FDR.* Edited by Dewey W. Grantham. Chicago: University of Chicago Press, 1973.

Bundles, A'lelia. *On Her Own Ground: The Life and Times of Madam C. J. Walker.* New York: Scribner, 2001.

Burns, Ben. *Nitty Gritty: A White Editor in Black Journalism.* Jackson: University Press of Mississippi, 1996.

Chicago Commission on Race Relations. *The Negro in Chicago: A Study of Race Relations and a Race Riot.* Chicago: University of Chicago Press, 1922.

Christmas, Faith. "Television Black Bird is Ready to Fly." *Chicago Daily Defender,* October 22, 1969.

Clark Hine, Darlene, and John McCluskey Jr. *The Black Chicago Renaissance.* Urbana: University of Illinois Press, 2012.

Clayton, Edward T. "Four Chicago Pioneers," *Negro Digest,* September 1950, 90–94.

Clegg, Claude Andrew, III. *An Original Man: The Life and Times of Elijah Muhammad.* New York: St. Martin's, 1997.

Cross, Robert. "Proud Bird with a Black, Blunt Tale." *Chicago Tribune Magazine,* March 1, 1970.

Culver, John C., and John Hyde. *American Dreamer: A Life of Henry A. Wallace.* New York: Norton, 2000.

Denning, Michael. *The Cultural Front: The Laboring of American Culture in the Twentieth Century.* London: Verso, 2010.

Department of the Interior. *Negro Education: A Study of the Private and Higher Schools for Colored People in the United States.* Volume 2, bulletin, 1916, no. 39. Washington, D.C.: GPO, 1917.

Dickey, Antonio, Marc PoKempner, and Salim Muwakkil, *Harold! Photographs from the Harold Washington Years.* Evanston, Ill.: Northwestern University Press, 2007.

Dolinar, Brian, ed. *The Negro in Illinois: The WPA Papers.* Urbana: University of Illinois Press, 2013.

Drake, St. Clair, and Horace Cayton. *Black Metropolis: A Study of Negro Life in a Northern City.* Chicago: University of Chicago Press, 1993.

Du Bois, W. E. B. *Black Reconstruction in America, 1860–1880.* New York: Free Press, 1998.

———. *The Souls of Black Folk.* New York: Penguin, 1989.

Duncan, Otis Dudley, and Beverly Duncan. *The Negro Population of Chicago: A Study of Residential Succession.* Chicago: University of Chicago Press, 1957.

Dunning, John. *On the Air: Encyclopedia of Old Time Radio.* Oxford: Oxford University Press, 1998.

Durham, Caldwell. "My Tour of Duty." Unpublished manuscript, 2005.

Durham, Chanie. "Narrative of the Life of Chanie Durham, Founder of the Wendell Phillips Evening School Alumni, Recorded by Herself, Edited by Claudia M. Durham, Daughter," n.d.

Dyja, Thomas. *The Third Coast: When Chicago Built the American Dream.* New York: Penguin, 2013.

Ehrlich, Matthew C. *Radio Utopia: Postwar Audio Documentary in the Public Interest.* Urbana: University of Illinois Press, 2011.

Evanzz, Karl. *The Messenger: The Rise and Fall of Elijah Muhammad.* New York: Pantheon, 1999.

Federal Writers' Project of the Works Progress Administration. *The WPA Guide to 1930s Illinois.* New York: Pantheon, 1983.

Fleming, Robert. "Hannibal the Hero." *Black Issues Book Review,* January–February 2005.

Forrest, Leon. *The Furious Voice for Freedom: Essays on Life.* Wakefield, R.I.: Asphodel, 1994.

Franklin, John Hope, and Alfred A. Moss Jr. *From Slavery to Freedom: A History of African Americans.* 8th ed. New York: Knopf, 2004

Gellman, Erik S. *Death Blow to Jim Crow: The National Negro Congress and the Rise of Militant Civil Rights.* Chapel Hill: University of North Carolina Press, 2012.

Gilyard, Keith. *John Oliver Killens: A Life of Black Literary Activism.* Athens, Ga.: University of Georgia Press, 2010.

Gitlin, Todd. *The Sixties: Years of Hope, Days of Rage.* New York: Bantam, 1993.

Godfrey, Donald G., and Frederic A. Leigh, eds. *Historical Dictionary of American Radio.* Westport, Conn.: Greenwood, 1998.

Gray, Frances Clayton, and Yanick Rice Lamb. *Born to Win: The Authorized Biography of Althea Gibson.* Hoboken, N.J.: Wiley, 2004.

Green, Adam. *Selling the Race: Culture, Community, and Black Chicago, 1940–1955.* Chicago: University of Chicago Press, 2007.

Grimshaw, William J. *Bitter Fruit: Black Politics and the Chicago Machine, 1931–1991.* Chicago: University of Chicago Press, 1992.

Grossman, James R. *Land of Hope: Chicago, Black Southerners, and the Great Migration.* Chicago: University of Chicago Press, 1989.

Grossman, James R., Ann Durkin Keating, and Janice L. Reiff. *The Museum of Broadcast Communications Encyclopedia of Chicago.* Chicago: University of Chicago Press, 2004.

Halberstam, David. *The Children.* New York: Random House, 1998.

Halpern, Rick. *Down on the Killing Floor: Black and White Workers in Chicago's Packinghouses, 1904–1954.* Urbana: University of Illinois Press, 1997.

Herbst, Alma. *The Negro in the Slaughtering and Meat-Packing Industry in Chicago.* New York: Ayer, 1971.

Hine, Darlene Clark, ed., Elsa Barkely Brown and Rosalyn Terborg-Penn, assoc. eds. *Black Women in America: A Historical Encyclopedia.* Brooklyn, N.Y.: Carlson, 1993.

Hine, Darlene Clark, and John McCluskey Jr. *The Black Chicago Renaissance.* Urbana: University of Illinois Press, 2012.

Homel, Michael W. *Down from Equality: Black Chicagoans and the Public School, 1920–41.* Urbana: University of Illinois Press, 1984.

Hook, Sidney. *Towards the Understanding of Karl Marx: A Revolutionary Interpretation.* Expanded edition. Edited by Ernest B. Hook. Amherst, N.Y.: Prometheus, 2002.

Horowitz, Roger. *Negro and White, Unite and Fight! A Social History of Industrial Unionism in Meatpacking, 1930–90.* Urbana: University of Illinois Press, 1977.

Hughes, Langston. "Simple Solution to Viet Nam War: Draft All Older White Men First."

———. "Simple: Give MLK's Nobel Prize to Brave Selma Woman." *Muhammad Speaks,* April 23, 1965.

———. *Shakespeare in Harlem: A New Volume of Poems.* New York: Knopf, 1942.

Hughes, Langston, and Milton Meltzer. *Black Magic: A Pictorial History of the African American in the Performing Arts.* Englewood Cliffs, N.J.: Da Capo, 1967.

Jablonsky, Thomas J. *Pride in the Jungle: Community and Everyday Life in Back of the Yard Chicago.* Baltimore, Md.: Johns Hopkins University Press, 1993.

Jackson, Lawrence P. *The Indignant Generation: A Narrative History of African American Writers and Critics, 1934–1960.* Princeton, N.J.: Princeton University Press, 2011.

Jones Charles E., ed. *The Black Panther Party Reconsidered.* Baltimore, Md.: Black Classics, 1998.

Joseph, Peniel E. *Dark Days, Bright Nights: From Black Power to Barack Obama.* New York: Basic Civitas, 2010.

Kahn, E. J., Jr. *Jock: The Life and Times of John Hay Whitney.* New York: Doubleday, 1981.

Karnow, Stanley. *Vietnam: A History; The First Complete Account of Vietnam at War.* New York: Viking, 1983.

Kent, George E. *A Life Gwendolyn Brooks.* Lexington: University Press of Kentucky, 1990.

Kimball, George, and John Schulian, eds. *At the Fights: American Writers on Boxing.* New York: Library of America, 2011.

Kingslow, Janice. "I Refuse to Pass." *Negro Digest,* May 1950, 22–31.

Larson, Kate Clifford. *Bound for the Promised Land: Harriet Tubman, Portrait of an American Hero.* New York: One World/Ballantine, 2004.

Lawson, John Howard. *Theory and Technique of Playwriting.* New York: Hill and Wang, 1960.

Leab, Daniel J. *A Union of Individuals: The Formation of the American Newspaper Guild, 1933–1936.* New York: Columbia University Press, 1970.

Lee, Alfred McClung, and Norman D. Humphrey, *Race Riot (Detroit, 1943).* New York: Octagon, 1968.

Lenin, Vladimir Ilyrich. *Essential Works of Lenin: "What Is To Be Done" and Other Writings.* New York: Bantam, 1966.

Lenthall, Bruce. *Radio's America: The Great Depression and the Rise of Modern Mass Culture.* Chicago: University of Chicago Press, 2007.

Levinsohn, Florence Hamlish. *Harold Washington: A Political Biography.* Chicago: Chicago Review Press, 1983.

Lewis, David Levering. *W. E. B. Du Bois: The Fight for Equality and the American Century, 1919–1963.* New York: Holt, 2000.

Lewis, George E. *A Power Stronger than Itself: The AACM and American Experimental Music.* Chicago: University of Chicago Press, 2008.

Lincoln, C. Eric. *The Black Muslims in America.* 3rd ed. Grand Rapids, Mich.: Eerdmans, 1994.

Lipsyte, Robert. "'I Don't Have to Be What You Want Me to Be,' Says Muhammad Ali." *New York Times,* March 7, 1971.

MacDonald, J. Fred. *Blacks and White TV: Afro-Americans in Television since 1948.* Chicago: Nelson-Hall, 1983.

———. *Don't Touch That Dial: Radio Programming in American Life, 1920–1960.* Chicago: Nelson-Hall, 1979.

———. "Radio's Black Heritage: Destination Freedom, 1948–1950." *Phylon* 39, no. 1 (March 1978): 66–73.

———, ed. *Richard Durham's Destination Freedom: Scripts from Radio's Black Legacy, 1948–50.* New York: Praeger, 1989.

MacDougall, Curtis D. *Gideon's Army: Volume 3, The Campaign and the Vote.* New York: Marzani and Munsell, 1965.

Mangione, Jerre. *The Dream and the Deal: The Federal Writers' Project, 1935–1943.* Boston: Little, Brown, 1972

Marable, Manning. *Malcolm X: A Life of Reinvention.* New York: Viking Penguin, 2011.

Mark, Norman. "Bird of the Bird: New Soap Opera Will be Blacker and More Soulful than Anything Else on TV." *Chicago Daily News,* January 17–18, 1970.

Markowitz, Norman D. *The Rise and Fall of the People's Century: Henry Wallace and American Liberalism, 1941–1948.* New York: Free Press, 1973.

Martin, Waldo E. Jr. *The Mind of Frederick Douglass.* Chapel Hill: University of North Carolina Press, 1984.

Mavigliano, George J., and Richard Lawson. *The Federal Art Project in Illinois, 1935–1943.* Carbondale: Southern Illinois University Press, 1990.

McLemore, Richard Aubrey, ed. *A History of Mississippi, Volumes 1 and 2.* Jackson: University and College Press of Mississippi, 1973.

McMillen, Neil R. *Dark Journey: Black Mississippians in the Age of Jim Crow.* Urbana: University of Illinois Press, 1989.

Miller, Randall M., and John David Smith, eds. *Dictionary of Afro-American Slavery.* Westport, Conn.: Greenwood, 1988.

Morrison, Toni. *The Bluest Eye.* New York: Pockets, 1970.

Muhammad, Elijah. "What the Black Muslims Believe." *Negro Digest,* November 1963, 3–6.

Mullen, Bill V. *Popular Fronts: Chicago and African-American Cultural Politics, 1935–46.* Urbana: University of Illinois Press, 1999.

Navasky, Victor S. *Naming Names*. New York: Viking, 1980.

Neimark, Paul. "The Man Who Knows Muhammad Ali Best." *Sepia*, May 1976.

Newman, Mark. "On the Air with Jack L. Cooper: The Beginning of Black Appeal Radio," *Chicago History* 12 (Summer 1983): 51–58.

O'Dell, Cary. *Women Pioneers in Television: Biographies of Fifteen Industry Leaders*. Jefferson, N. C.: McFarland, 1997.

Ohmart, Ben. *Don Ameche: The Kenosha Comeback Kid*. Albany, Ga.: Bear Manor, 2007.

Penkower, Monty Noam. *The Federal Writers' Project: A Study in Government Patronage of the Arts*. Urbana: University of Illinois Press, 1977.

Perkins, Eugene. "Chicago: Crisis in Theater." *Black World*, April 1973, 27–37, 83.

Peterson, Clarence. "TV Today: New Series Is Soap with a Difference," *Chicago Tribune*, January 19, 1970.

Plekhanov, George. *The Role of the Individual in History*. New York: International, 1940.

Powdermaker, Hortense. *After Freedom: A Cultural Study in the Deep South*. New York: Russell and Russell, 1968.

Pride, Armistead S., and Clint C. Wilson II. *A History of the Black Press*. Washington, D.C.: Howard University Press, 1997.

Quinn, Anthony. *The Original Sin*. Boston: Little, Brown, 1972.

Rampersad, Arnold. *The Life of Langston Hughes, Volume 1: 1902–1941; I, Too, Sing America*. New York: Oxford University Press, 2002.

———. *The Life of Langston Hughes, Volume II: 1941–1967; I Dream a World*. New York: Oxford University Press, 2002.

Raushenbush, Esther. *John Hay Whitney Foundation: A Report of the First Twenty-Five Years*. New York: John Hay Whitney Foundation, 1972.

Reagon, Bernice Johnson. *We'll Understand It By and By: Pioneering African American Gospel Composers*. Washington: Smithsonian Institution Press, 1992.

Reed, Christopher Robert. *The Depression Comes to the South Side: Protest and Politics in the Black Metropolis, 1930–1933*. Bloomington: Indiana University Press, 2011.

Remnick, David. *King of the World: Muhammad Ali and the Rise of an American Hero*. New York: Random House, 1998.

Rivlin, Gary. *Fire on the Prairie: Chicago's Harold Washington and the Politics of Race*. New York: Holt, 1992.

Robinson, Cyril. *Marching with Dr. King: Ralph Helstein and the United Packinghouse Workers of America*. Santa Barbara, Calif.: Praeger, 2011.

Rothel, David. *Who Was That Masked Man? The Story of the Lone Ranger*. San Diego: Barnes, 1981.

Rowland, Eron Opha (Moore), *History of Hinds County, Mississippi, 1821–1922*. Jackson: Mississippi Historical Society, 1922.

Rowley, Hazel. *Richard Wright: The Life and Times*. New York: Holt, 2001.

Savage, Barbara Dianne. *Broadcasting Freedom: Radio, War, and the Politics of Race, 1938–1948*. Chapel Hill: University of North Carolina Press, 1999.

Schapsmeier, Edward L., and Frederick H. *Prophet in Politics: Henry A. Wallace and the War Years, 1940–1965*. Ames: Iowa State University Press, 1970.

Schultz, Rima Lunin, and Adele Hast, eds. *Women Building Chicago, 1790–1990*. Bloomington: Indiana University Press, 2001.

Smethurst, James Edward. *The Black Arts Movement: Literary Nationalism in the 1960s and 1970s*. Chapel Hill: University of North Carolina Press, 2005.

Smith, Judith E. *Visions of Belonging: Family Stories, Popular Culture, and Postwar Democracy, 1940–1960*. New York: Columbia University Press, 2004.

Smith, Maureen. "Muhammad Speaks and Muhammad Ali: Intersections of the Nation of Islam and Sport in the 1960s." *International Sports Studies 1999–2000*, 22, no. 1, 54–69.

Solomon, Mark. *The Cry Was Unity: Communists and African Americans, 1917–1936*. Jackson: University Press of Mississippi, 1998.

Sporn, Paul. *Against Itself: The Federal Theater and Writers' Projects in the Midwest*. Detroit, Mich.: Wayne State University Press, 1995.

Stange, Maren. *Bronzeville: Black Chicago in Pictures, 1941–1943*. New York: New Press, 2003.

Sterling, Christopher H., ed. *The Museum of Broadcast Communications Encyclopedia of Radio*. New York: Fitzroy Dearborn, 2004.

Sterling, Christopher H., and John M. Kittross, eds. *Stay Tuned: A Concise History of American Broadcasting*. 2nd ed. Belmont, Calif.: Wadsworth, 1990.

Sterling, Christopher H., and Michael C. Keith, eds. *Encyclopedia of Radio: Volumes 1–3*. New York: Fitzroy Dearborn, 2004.

Stromquist, Shelton, and Marvin Berman, eds. *Unionizing the Jungles: Labor and Community in the Twentieth-Century Meatpacking Industry*. Iowa City: University of Iowa Press, 1997.

Sydnor, Charles Sackett. *Slavery in Mississippi*. Gloucester, Mass.: American Historical Assoc., 1933.

Taylor, David A. *Soul of a People: The WPA Writers' Project Uncovers Depression America*. Hoboken, N.J.: Wiley, 2009.

Terkel, Studs. *Hard Times: An Oral History of the Great Depression*. New York: New Press, 1986.

———. *A Life in Words*. New York: Holt, 1996.

Tracy, Steven C. *Writers of the Black Chicago Renaissance*. Urbana: University of Illinois Press, 2011.

Travis, Dempsey J. *Harold: The People's Mayor, An Authorized Biography of Mayor Harold Washington*. Chicago: Urban Research, 1989.

Trevino, Jesus Salvador. *Eyewitness: A Filmmaker's Memoir of the Chicano Movement*. Houston, Tex.: Arte Publico, 2001.

United States Commission on Civil Rights. *Window Dressing on the Set: Women and Minorities in Television; A Report of the United States Commission on Civil Rights*. Washington, D.C.: University of California Libraries reprint, 1977.

Von Eschen, Penny M. *Race against Empire: Black Americans and Anticolonialism, 1937–1957*. Ithaca, N.Y.: Cornell University Press, 1997.

Walker, Margaret. *Richard Wright: Daemonic Genius; A Portrait of the Man—A Critical Look at His Work*. New York: Amistad, 1988.

Waller, Judith C. *Radio: The Fifth Estate*. Boston: Houghton Mifflin, 1946.

Washington, Mary Helen. *The Other Blacklist: The African American Literary and Cultural Left of the 1950s*. New York: Columbia University Press, 2014.

Waters, Enoch P. *American Diary: A Personal History of the Black Press*. Chicago: Path, 1987.

Watkins, Mel. *On the Real Side: A History of African American Comedy*. Chicago: Chicago Review, 1999.

Watts, Jill. *God, Harlem, U.S.A.: The Father Divine Story*. Berkeley: University of California Press, 1992.

Weems, Robert E., Jr. *Black Business in the Black Metropolis: The Chicago Metropolitan Assurance Company, 1925–1985*. Bloomington: Indiana University Press, 1996.

Wharton, Vernon Lane. *The Negro in Mississippi, 1865–1890*. Westport, Conn.: Greenwood, 1984.

Wilkerson, Isabel. *The Warmth of Other Suns: The Epic Story of America's Great Migration*. New York: Random House, 2010.

Williams, Juan, and Dwayne Ashley. *I'll Find a Way or Make One: A Tribute to Historically Black Colleges and Universities*. New York: Amistad, 2004.

———. *Eyes on the Prize: America's Civil Rights Years, 1954–1965*. New York: Viking, 1987.

Wilson, Charles H., Sr. *Education for Negroes in Mississippi Since 1910*. Boston: Meador, 1947.

Witcover, Jules. *The Year the Dream Died: Revisiting 1968 in America*. New York: Warner, 1997.

Wolseley, Roland E. *The Black Press, U.S.A.: A Detailed and Understanding Report on What the Black Press Is and How It Came to Be*. Ames: Iowa State University Press, 1971.

Woodford, John. "Testing America's Promise of Free Speech: Muhammad Speaks in the 1960s; A Memoir." *Voices of the African Diaspora: The CAAS Research Review* 7 (Fall 1991): 3–16.

Woodruff, Nan Elizabeth. *American Congo: The African American Freedom Struggle in the Delta*. Cambridge, Mass.: Harvard University Press, 2003.

Wright, Richard. *12 Million Black Voices*. New York: Thunder's Mouth, 2002.

———. "Blueprint for Negro Writing." *New Challenge: A Literary Quarterly* 2, no. 11 (Fall 1937): 53–65.

Archives

Archdiocese of Chicago. Archives and Records.

Bontemps, Arna. Papers. Special Collections Research Center. Syracuse University Library.

Divine, Father. Papers. Manuscripts, Archives and Rare Books Library. Emory University.

Durham, Richard. Papers. Vivian G. Harsh Research Collection of Afro-American History and Literature. Chicago Public Library.

Federal Writers Project. Manuscripts Department. Abraham Lincoln Presidential Library.

Ford Foundation. Archives. Rockefeller Archives Center.

Forrest, Leon. Papers. Northwestern University Archives. Northwestern University.

Hall Branch Library Archives. Vivian G. Harsh Research Collection of Afro-American History and Literature, Chicago Public Library.

Hughes, Langston. Papers. James Weldon Johnson Collection. Yale Collection of American Literature. Beinecke Rare Book and Manuscript Library. Yale University.

Illinois Writers Project/The Negro in Illinois. Papers. Manuscripts Department. Abraham Lincoln Presidential Library.

Illinois Writers Project/The Negro in Illinois. Papers. Vivian G. Harsh Research Collection of Afro-American History and Literature. Chicago Public Library.

Johnson, Bennett. Papers. Vivian G. Harsh Research Collection of Afro-American History and Literature. Chicago Public Library.

Killens, John Oliver. Papers. Manuscripts, Archives and Rare Books Library. Emory University.

Lochard, Metz T.P. Papers. Moorland-Spingarn Research Center. Howard University.

MacDougall, Curtis. Papers. Northwestern University Archives. Northwestern University.

Moving Image and Recorded Sound Collection. Schomburg Center for Research in Black Culture. New York Public Library.

National Negro Congress. Papers. Manuscripts Collections, Schomburg Center for Research in Black Culture. New York Public Library.

Palmer, Alice and Edward. Papers. Vivian G. Harsh Research Collection of Afro-American History and Literature. Chicago Public Library.

Phillips, Irna. Papers. Wisconsin Historical Society.

Public Broadcasting Service. Archives.

Sheil, Bernard. Papers. Archdiocese of Chicago. Archives and Records.

United Packinghouse, Food and Allied Workers of America. Papers. Wisconsin Historical Society.

United States Copyright Office. Library of Congress.

United States Work Projects Administration Records. Federal Writers Project. Negro Studies Project. Manuscript Division. Library of Congress.

United States Work Projects Administration Records. Federal Writers Project/Studies Projects. Radio Scripts, Illinois. Manuscript Division. Library of Congress.

Vivian G. Harsh Research Collection of Afro-American History and Literature. Chicago Public Library.

Waller, Judith. Papers. Wisconsin Historical Society.

Washington, Harold. Archives and Collections. Special Collections Department. Chicago Public Library.

Whitney, John Hay. Foundation Records. Manuscripts and Archives. Yale University Library.

Interviews with the author

Barrett, Brenetta Howell. December 14, 2007. Chicago, Illinois.

Black, Timuel Jr. June 27, 2002; July 8, 2009. Chicago, Illinois.

Brown, Abena Joan. March 22, 2002. Chicago, Illinois.

Brown, Oscar Jr. June 7, 2000. Los Angeles. California.

Burroughs, Margaret. July 1, 2002. Chicago, Illinois.

Childs, Charles S. November 10, 2010. Chicago, Illinois.

Cowherd, Darryl. August 20, 2009. Washington, D.C.

Davis, Charles A. June 2, 2001. Chicago, Illinois.

Davis, Marguerite. March 19, 2001. Chicago, Illinois.

Durham, Caldwell. March 16, 2010. Los Angeles, California.

Durham, Clarice. December 27, 1999; March 19, 2001; July 15, 2010; March 12, 2011; December 5, 2011. Chicago, Illinois.

Durham, Earl. December 23, 2000; June 28, 2002. Chicago, Illinois.

Durham, Mark. March 23, 2002; July 15, 2010. Chicago, Illinois.

Harris, Charles F. March 6, 2013. Washington, D.C.

Hodges, Louise. June 28, 2002. Chicago, Illinois.

Kashif, Ghayth Nur. June 17, 2002. Washington, D.C.

Jarrett, Vernon. March 20, 2002. Chicago, Illinois.

Jennings, Rose. May 30, 2001. Chicago, Illinois.

Johns, Meredith. March 22, 2002. Chicago, Illinois.

Johnson, Bennett. December 14, 2000; March 22, 2002; December 12, 2007. Chicago, Illinois.

Johnson, Okoro Harold. June 1, 2001. Chicago, Illinois.

Latta, Judi Moore. January 25, 2013. Washington, D.C.

Madhubuti, Haki. July 3, 2002. Chicago, Illinois.

Morrison, Toni. March 30, 2011. Baltimore, Maryland.

Mosby, Donald. September 30, 2011. Chicago, Illinois.

Muhammad, Askia. October 11, 2011. Chicago, Illinois.

Orear, Leslie F. June 17, 2009. Chicago, Illinois.

Palmer, Edward "Buzz." December 15, 2007. Chicago, Illinois.

Perry, Al. September. February 28, 2013. Chicago, Illinois.

Robinson, Renault. March 12, 2010. Chicago, Illinois.

Rogers, Ira. January 1, 2008. Chicago, Illinois.

Rush, Bobby, June 21, 2012. Washington, D.C.

Rush, Harold Lee Jr., December 19, 2012. Chicago, Illinois.

Saunders, Doris. June 10, 2001. Chicago, Illinois.

Sengstacke, Robert. June 23, 2009. Chicago, Illinois.

Simpson, Rosie. December 16, 2007. Chicago, Illinois.

Smith, Clotilde Durham. February 8, 2000. Washington, D.C.

Starks, Robert. July 2, 2002. Chicago, Illinois.

Terkel, Studs. May 30, 2001. Chicago, Illinois.

Woodford, John. June 14, 2001. Ann Arbor, Michigan.

Worrill, Conrad. March 16, 2010. Chicago, Illinois.

Wyatt, Addie. March 19, 2001. Chicago, Illinois.

Additional Interviews

Brown, Oscar, Jr., with J. Fred MacDonald. February 1975.
Durham, Richard, with J. Fred MacDonald. February 1975.
Durham, Richard, with J. Fred MacDonald. June 13, 1980.
Heck, Homer, with J. Fred MacDonald. June 12, 1980.
Durham, Richard, with John Dunning. January 16, 1983.

Index

Durham, Clarice (nee Davis), *45*, *141*; on
 Ali's autobiography, 147; birth of Mark,
 91; career of, 79, 115; and *Destination
 Freedom*, 76, 77; Durham's death, 177–78;
 education of, 49; and *Here Comes Tomorrow*, 70; housing issues, 107, 138, 140–41;
 marriage, 43–45, 48–49, 115; meeting
 Durham, 3
Durham, (Claudia) Marie, 16, 27, 34, 79;
 photo, *79*
Durham, Curtis George, 10–17, *15*, 24, 29,
 107, 126
Durham, Curtis George, Jr. "C.G.," 16, 27,
 79, 152
Durham, Earl, *45*; on Ali, 151; career of, 79;
 on Durham, 28, 34, 79, 104–5; Durham's
 death, 177; Durham's influence on, 7–8,
 30; on Jarrett, 68; on League of Negro
 Voters, 168–69; on Nation of Islam, 118,
 122; and the Progressive Party, 71; and
 UPWA presidency, 112
Durham, Isadore. *See* Durham, Richard "Dick"
Durham, Mark Adam, *5*; on Ali's biography,
 144; and *Bird of the Iron Feather*, 139; birth
 of, 91; college, 124; Durham's death, 177;
 Durham's funeral, 2, 5–6; student protests,
 129; as writer, 159–60
Durham, Maudeline, 16–17
Durham, Maya, 3
Durham, Napoleon, 12
Durham, Richard "Dick," *45*, *79*, *140–41*,
 156, *159*, *175*; about, 2, 4–5; and American
 Newspaper Guild, 58, 60; birth of Mark,
 91; and boxing, 27–28; childhood, 23–30;
 and the Communist Party, 6, 40, 51, 125;
 death of, 177; Detroit riots, 50; on economics, 39, 94–95, 122, 166–67; as editor,
 125–28; education, 23–24, 34; FBI file,
 60, 121; and funeral, 1–8; heart attack, 170,
 177; and Herbert Muhammad Enterprises,
 166–67; housing issues, 107, 138, 140–41;
 and H. Washington, 164, 167–77; Illinois
 Writers' Project (IWP), 3, 37–41; as Isa-
 dore/Izzy, 4, 10, 12, 16–30, 34; lawsuit
 against NBC/WMAQ, 99–102, 111; and
 League of Negro Voters, 168–69; legacy
 of, 180–81; literary influences on, 30–33;
 marriage, 43–45, 48–49, 115; on MLK,
 129; as *Muhammad Speaks* editor, 117–29,

134, 138; name changes, 26, 28, 33–35;
 and Nation of Islam, 117–29; on organizing of Negroes, 50–51; as Quinn ghostwriter, 166; and racially inclusive universalism, 81; religious views, 143; as reporter,
 52–60; and Richard the Lionheart, 4, 26;
 social activism of, 43, 48, 65, 181; as TV
 ghostwriter, 131; on UN charter, 58; unfinished projects, 115–16, 165–66, 180; and
 United Packinghouse Workers of America,
 2, 102–12; as Vern, 4, 8, 28, 33–34, 181;
 writing philosophy, 31, 45–46, 48, 92, 94–
 95, 116, 157. *See also Destination Freedom*
Durham, Richard "Dick," (articles, brochures
 and essays): *Action against Jim Crow: UP-
 WA's Fight for Equal Rights*, 105; "A Day at
 the Relief Station," 36–37; "Don't Spend
 Your Money Where You Can't Work,"
 39–41; review of Carnegie's *How to Win
 Friends . . .*, 37–38
Durham, Richard "Dick" (books): *The Greatest: My Own Story*, 4, 146–63
Durham, Richard "Dick" (poetry): *City*, 18;
 Cotton Croppers, 9; *Dawn Patrol*, 36; *Death
 in a Kitchenette*, 32–33; *Hell's Kitchen*,
 32–33
Durham, Richard "Dick" (radio or television
 scripts and series): *Art for Our Sake*, 46; *At
 the Foot of Adams Street*, 46; *Bird of the Iron
 Feather*, 130–45, *152–53*, 169, 180; *CBS
 Radio Workshop*, 114–16, 179; *Democracy
 U.S.A.*, 47, 59–65, 67, 71; "Goya: The Disas-
 ters of War," 42–43; Harriet Tubman play,
 97–98; *Here Comes Tomorrow*, 14, 68–70,
 134; *The Lone Ranger*, 47–48; "Prescription
 for Pallbearers," 141; "Speaking of Dreams,"
 143; "Sweet Cherries in Charleston,"
 114–16; "The Heart of the Man," 114; "The
 Sermon," 142; "The Target," 143; "What's
 New," 66. *See also Destination Freedom*
Durham, (Smith) Clotilde, 16–19, 24–25, 27,
 29, 34, 45–46, 79, 116
Durham, Vern. *See* Durham, Richard "Dick"
Durham, Winifred, 16, 27, 79
Du Sable, Jean Baptiste Point, 164, 175
Dyson, Lyn, 179

Ebenezer Baptist Church, 29
economic discrimination, 39–41

SONJA D. WILLIAMS is a professor in the Department of Media, Journalism, and Film at Howard University and the winner of three George Foster Peabody Awards as a radio producer. Her credits include the radio series *Wade in the Water: African American Sacred Music Traditions* and *Black Radio: Telling It Like It Was.*

THE NEW BLACK STUDIES SERIES

The University of Illinois Press
is a founding member of the
Association of American University Presses.

University of Illinois Press
1325 South Oak Street
Champaign, IL 61820-6903
www.press.uillinois.edu